Among the Thugs

Bill Buford is a staff writer for *The New Yorker*, where he was previously the fiction editor for eight years. He was editor-in-chief for *Granta* magazine for sixteen years and was also the publisher of Granta Books. He is the author of *Heat*. He lives in Lyon.

AMONG
THE THUGS
BILL BUFORD

arrow books

5 7 9 10 8 6

Arrow Books
20 Vauxhall Bridge Road
London SW1V 2SA

Arrow Books is part of the Penguin Random House group of companies
whose addresses can be found at global.penguinrandomhouse.com

Penguin
Random House
UK

First published in Great Britain by Martin Secker & Warburg in 1991
First published in paperback by Mandarin paperbacks in 1992

Reissued by Arrow Books in 2001
Reissued by Arrow Books in 2018

Parts of this book have previously appeared in
The Sunday Times and *Esquire*

www.penguin.co.uk

A CIP catalogue record for this book is available from the British Library.

ISBN 9781784759544

Typeset in 11/13 pt Sabon MT by Jouve (UK), Milton Keynes
Printed and bound in Great Britain by Clays Ltd, Elcograf S.p.A.

Penguin Random House is committed to a sustainable future for our
business, our readers and our planet. This book is made from Forest
Stewardship Council® certified paper.

MIX
Paper from
responsible sources
FSC® C018179

For Stephen Booth

CONTENTS

Part One

A Station Outside Cardiff 3

Manchester 15

Turin 27

Sunderland 101

Manchester 105

Part Two

Bury St Edmunds 125

Cambridge 157

Dawes Road, Fulham 173

Part Three

Düsseldorf 207

Sardinia 263

Acknowledgements 317

PART ONE

A STATION OUTSIDE CARDIFF

One of the causes of the downfall of Rome was that people, being fed by the State . . . ceased to have any responsibility for themselves or their children, and consequently became a nation of wasters. They frequented circuses, where paid performers appeared before them in the arena, much as we see the crowds now flocking to look on at paid players playing football . . . Thousands of boys and young men, pale, narrow-chested, hunched-up, miserable specimens, smoking endless cigarettes, numbers of them betting, all of them learning to be hysterical as they groan or cheer in panic unison with their neighbours – the worst sound of all being the hysterical scream of laughter that greets any little trip or fall of a player. One wonders whether this can be the same nation which had gained for itself the reputation of being a stolid, pipe-sucking manhood, unmoved by panic or excitement, and reliable in the tightest of places. Get the lads away from this – teach them to be manly.

R. Baden-Powell
Scouting for Boys (1908)

SOME TIME AGO, I came home from Wales by train. The station was a village station just outside Cardiff, and I arrived early. I bought a cup of tea. It was a cold Saturday evening, and only three or four other passengers were on the platform. A man was reading a newspaper, rocking back and forth on his feet. We waited, and there was an announcement on the loudspeaker about an unscheduled train. A little later, there was another announcement: the unscheduled train was about to appear, and everyone was to stand ten feet from the edge of the platform. It was an unusual instruction, and the man with the newspaper raised an eyebrow. Perhaps, I thought, it was a military train of some kind. A few minutes later, police appeared, emerging from the stairs nearby.

The train was a football special, and it had been taken over by supporters. They were from Liverpool, and there were hundreds of them – I had never seen a train with so many people inside – and they were singing in unison: 'Liverpool, la-la-la, Liverpool, la-la-la.' The words look silly now, but they did not sound silly. A minute before there had been virtual silence: a misty, sleepy Welsh winter evening. And then this song, pounded out with increasing ferocity, echoing off the walls of the station. A guard had been injured, and as the train stopped he was rushed off, holding his face. Someone inside was trying to smash a window with a table leg, but the window wouldn't break. A fat man with a red face stumbled out of one of the carriages, and six policemen rushed up to him, wrestled him to the ground and bent his arm violently behind his back. The police were over-reacting – the train was so packed that the fat man had popped out of an open door – but the police were frightened. For that matter, I was frightened (I remember my arms folded stupidly across my chest), as was everyone else on the platform. It was peculiar: I was at a railway station where everyone around me spoke Welsh; I was there to catch a train: then this sudden display. I thought that it was intended for us, that this violent chant was a way of telling us that they, the supporters, were in the position to do anything they wanted.

The train left. It was silent.

I got home at one-thirty in the morning, and the country seemed to consist of a long cordon of police. At Paddington Station two hundred officers were waiting to escort everyone from the platform to the Underground. I changed trains four times; three were taken over by supporters. One was torn apart: the seats had been ripped out, and the bar, which had been closed beforehand, was broken up, its metal shutter-door split into pieces and drink handed out to anyone who walked past. I did not know what was more surprising, the destructiveness, which was gratuitous and relentless, or that, with so many police, no one seemed able to stop it: it just went on. Hoping to avoid trouble, I sat in a first-class carriage at the very front of one train, opposite a man who had paid for his first-class ticket. He was a slim, elegant man with a thin moustache, wearing a woollen suit and expensive, shiny shoes: a civilized sort of fellow reading a civilized sort of book – a hardback novel with a dust-jacket. A supporter had been staring at him for a long time. The supporter was drunk. Every now and then, he lit a match and threw it at the civilized man's shiny shoes, hoping to set his trousers on fire. The civilized man ignored him, but the supporter, puffy and bloodshot, persisted. It was a telling image: one of the disenfranchised, flouting the codes of civilized conduct, casually setting a member of a more privileged class alight.

It was obvious that the violence was a protest. It made sense that it would be: that football matches were providing an outlet for frustrations of a powerful nature. So many young people were out of work or had never been able to find any. The violence, it followed, was a rebellion of some kind – social rebellion, class rebellion, something. I wanted to know more. I had read about the violence and, to the extent that I thought about it, had assumed that it was an isolated thing or mysterious in the way that crowd violence is meant to be mysterious: unpredictable, spontaneous, the mob. My journey from Wales suggested that it might be more intended, more willed. It offered up a vision of the English Saturday, the shopping day, that was different from the one I had known: that in the towns and cities, you might find hundreds of police, military in their comprehensiveness, out to contain young, male sports fans who, after attending an athletic contest, were determined to break or destroy the things that were in their way. It was hard to believe.

I repeated the story of my journey to friends, but I was surprised by how unsurprised they were. Some acted as if they were disgusted; others were amused; no one thought it was anything extraordinary. It was one of the things you put up with: that every Saturday young males trashed your trains, broke the windows of your pubs, destroyed your cars, wreaked havoc on your town centres. I didn't buy it, but it seemed to be so. In fact the only time I felt that I had said something surprising was when I revealed that, although I had now seen a football crowd, I had never been to an English football match. This, it seemed, was shocking.

And so, I explained: that although I had come to England as a student in 1977 and stayed on, I had attended only one football game and that was years before when I happened to be in Mexico

7

City: the Mexican national team, which was not very good, was playing host to my home team visiting from the United States, which was terrible. There may have been two hundred people in attendance. Mexico won, eight-nil. In the suburbs of Los Angeles where I grew up, the game of 'soccer' (as we called it) was not a young male's pastime.

My friends were unimpressed. *Never* been to a match? They were incredulous. The implication seemed to be that *that* was why I found the behaviour of the supporters so bizarre and difficult to understand.

I do not remember many things about my visit to the Tottenham Hotspur football ground at White Hart Lane, where two friends took me to see my first English football match at the end of the 1983 season. I don't remember if any goals were scored. I don't remember the other team. I do remember that we were late and that it took twenty minutes of pushing, grabbing, squeezing, groaning, inching, striving, wrestling before finally securing our place, a tiny expanse of cold concrete step, crushed between a number of lads – how else to describe them? – ten years younger than me and five stone heavier whose passion for expression seldom went beyond the simple but effectively direct (and often repeated) phrase: 'You fuckin' bastard.' I remember the mirth that accompanied the spectacle of the individual below us who, detecting precipitation along the back of his neck, reached behind him to discover that he was being urinated upon from above. And I remember the unease I felt realizing that the two young men near me were wearing National Front badges – one of my friends was Indian, the other a dark Latin American. The two young men and their friends began a chant – 'Wogs out' – which was repeated with increasing volume until it was interrupted by a fight which was then interrupted by the police, whose progress towards it, pushing, grabbing, squeezing, groaning, inching, striving, wrestling, and clubbing, was inhibited when their helmets were removed and thrown on to the pitch.

8

For my friends it was an ordinary day out – a bit amusing when the policemen lost their helmets, but otherwise nothing special. True, you wouldn't expect someone in, say, the theatre to urinate upon other members of the audience, but lads don't go to the theatre, do they? Lads go to matches on Saturday.

I thought I'd go on my own. I didn't know that it wasn't done, that lads went with lads or that lads went with dads, but there was so much I didn't know – which was the point. I wanted to find out what I didn't know; I wanted to meet one of 'them' and didn't know any other way to go about it.

And so, with the new season, I went to Stamford Bridge. I knew about Chelsea, the reputation of its supporters and of 'the Shed' – the canopied standing-room terraces on the Chelsea side of the ground. I arrived early. On the way, I saw many police – they were at each stop along the District Line – but by the time I reached Fulham Broadway they were wherever I looked. There were dogs at the top of the stairs of the Underground station and, outside, horses bearing police with four-foot truncheons. As I walked towards the ground, I saw men with radios: there was one on almost every corner. A helicopter was circling overhead, and vans were driving slowly past the pubs and down the back streets. And then something occurred that I could never have imagined. I heard the clop-clop sound of horses, and jeering, and broken glass, and shouts of abuse. Coming down the Broadway was an escort consisting of ten horses and a chain of police surrounding a compact but large body of people – maybe a thousand: they were the visitors.

It seems curious that I should have been surprised, having now seen this same procession so many times since, but I was. The procession consisted of ordinary people, dedicated supporters of a team, many of them middle-aged. Along with their sons or wives or friends from work, they had organized a Saturday outing, bought their tickets in advance, booked a coach for the return journey, and yet they were in such danger of being physically attacked that they had to be protected by a battalion of police with dogs and horses, followed overhead by a helicopter.

I entered the ground and was frisked – my comb, because it had long teeth, was confiscated – and emerged from the turnstile to find people everywhere, on the steps, sitting atop fences, on posts, suspended from bits of architecture. There was a narrow human alley, and I joined the mob pushing its way through for a place from which to watch the match.

Except that there was no place. There was a movable crush. It was impossible, once inside, to change my mind – to decide that I didn't want to see the game after all, that I wanted to go home – because I couldn't move left or right, let alone turn around and walk back the way I came. There was only one direction: forward. For some reason, there was an advantage, an advantage worth defending, in being one step ahead of wherever it was that you happened to be. And that was where everybody was trying to go.

There was a range of tactics for achieving this. The most common was the *simple squeeze*: by lifting your crushed arm from between the two bodies that had wedged you in place and slipping it in front and by then twisting yourself in such a way that your body, obeying natural principles, actually followed your arm, you could inch towards that mysterious spot just ahead of you. The simple squeeze was popular – I assumed that most people had learned the technique trying to buy a drink in London pubs – and everybody did it, until interrupted by the *shove*.

The principle of the shove was this: somebody, somewhere behind you, frustrated at not getting to this mysterious spot just one step ahead, would give up and throw his weight into the person in front of him; then, amid cries of 'fuckin' bastard', everybody tumbled forward. Nobody fell if only because each person was pressed so tightly against the one in front who was in turn pressed so tightly against the one in front of him that no one, apparently, was in any *real* danger. But I wondered about the person at the very front and was convinced that somebody must be feeling very frightened at the increasingly likely prospect of being crushed against a wall – for eventually there must be a wall. And it must have been this fear, felt by the panicked, slowly-suffocating one at the front whose ribs were buckling painfully, which contributed to the *counter-shove*, an effort of animal strength, which seemed to occur shortly after you had abandoned the simple squeeze and, being unable to stop yourself from tumbling uncontrollably forwards, had resigned yourself to the authority of the shove, when suddenly, inexplicably, there was the counter-shove and you were travelling uncontrollably backwards.

The movement never ceased.

I had always assumed that a sporting event was a paid-for entertainment, like a night at the cinema; that it was an exchange: you gave up a small part of your earnings and were rewarded by a span (an hour, two hours) of pleasure, frequently characterized by features – edible food, working lavatories, a managed crowd, a place to park your car – that tended to encourage you to return the following week. I thought this was normal. I could see that I was wrong. What principle governed the British sporting event? It appeared that, in exchange for a few pounds, you received one hour and forty-five minutes characterized by the greatest possible exposure to the worst possible weather, the greatest number of people in the smallest possible space and the greatest number of obstacles – unreliable transport, no parking, an intensely dangerous crush at the only exit, a repellent polio pond to pee into, last minute changes of the starting time – to keep you from ever attending a match again.

And yet, here they all were, having their Saturday.

Yes: here they all were, but having met the unspectacular challenge of getting myself to a football match on my own, what was I meant to do next? How was I to go about getting to know one of 'them'? I wanted to meet a football thug, but to my untrained eye everyone around me looked like one. I identified a likely thuggish-looking prospect – in that he was bigger than the others and more energetic, screaming and singing in a way that suggested incipient epilepsy – but the police identified him as well. Before the match began he was ejected for no apparent reason other than that he *looked* like he might do something. What next? Hi, you look ugly and violent, can I buy you a drink? I was uncomfortable, swaying in the crush, trying to make eye contact or strike up a conversation – it wasn't the place for a chat – and, after a while, I became convinced that my manner was starting to make everyone around me uncomfortable as well: that they thought that I was a strange, creepy little moron, and that I should disappear, *and* that I was a deviant homosexual who deserved to be injured badly. 'Stop staring at me like that,' one of them said, and so I gave up and tried to watch the game, but I couldn't find it – there were too many people in the way – and so I simply gave up. And swayed.

I did not judge my first outing on my own to have been a success.

Other matches followed.

I took the Metropolitan Line to the nether regions of East London to watch West Ham, but I remember little about the visit except the sign that I saw on my way out: 'Remember Ibrox, Please Leave Slowly.' 'Ibrox' is Ibrox Park in Glasgow, and so I went to Glasgow as well: it was there, in 1971, that sixty-six people were asphyxiated from the crush trying to get out. I attended a match at the appropriately named 'Plough Lane', the wooden, rickety ground of the Wimbledon football team, an architect's bad memory stewing in the stench of the enveloping pollution and muck. It was the first time in my life as a spectator that I felt I might be overcome by the odours rising out of my seat, so powerfully rotten were the stands on which it had been fixed. I went to Millwall, south of the Thames, famous for its crowd violence. No other ground, I discovered, had been closed more times from the trouble caused by its supporters. But I found no crowd violence. I was grateful to have found the match. The ground is hidden – even the overhead lights seem to be subterranean – at the end of narrow Victorian streets and dark tunnels, amid railway tracks and heaps of bricks and tiles that must date from the Blitz. And then suddenly there it was, the evocatively-named 'Den' on Cold Blow Lane opposite the Isle of Dogs.

There were other excursions – Roker Park in Sunderland; Hampden in Glasgow; the supposedly grand Hillsborough Stadium in Sheffield – and, while I couldn't say that I had developed a rapport with any one of 'them' *yet*, I did find that I was developing a taste for the game. I had figured out how to stand on the terraces and watch the play on the pitch – an achievement of sorts. In fact I was also starting to enjoy the conditions of the terraces themselves. This, I admit, surprised me. This, it would seem, was neither natural nor logical. It was, I see now on reflection, not unlike alcohol or tobacco: disgusting, at first; pleasurable, with effort; addictive, over time. And perhaps, in the end, a little self-destroying.

MANCHESTER

What are we to do with the 'Hooligan'? Who or what is responsible for his growth? Every week some incident shows that certain parts of London are more perilous for the peaceable wayfarer than remote districts of Calabria, Sicily, or Greece, once the classic haunts of brigands. Every day in some police-court are narrated the details of acts of brutality of which the sufferers are unoffending men and women. So long as the 'Hooligan' maltreated only the 'Hooligan' – so long as we heard chiefly of the attacks and counter-attacks of bands, even if armed sometimes with deadly weapons – the matter was far less important than it has become . . . There is no looking calmly, however, on the frequently recurring outbursts of ruffians, the systematic lawlessness of groups of lads and young men who are the terror of the neighbourhood in which they dwell.

Our 'Hooligans' go from bad to worse. They are an ugly growth on the body politic, and the worse circumstance is that they multiply, and that School Boards and prisons, police magistrates and philanthropists, do not seem to ameliorate them. Other great cities may throw off elements more perilous to the State. Nevertheless the 'Hooligan' is a hideous excrescence on our civilization.

The Times, 30 October 1890

IN THE SPRING of 1984, Manchester United reached the semi-finals of the Cup-Winners Cup and was scheduled to play Turin's Juventus. The teams were to play twice: the first leg in Manchester, the second, two weeks later, in Turin. I had been intrigued by Manchester United for some time. Before May 1985, English teams had not been banned from playing on the continent; the supporters of Manchester United, however, had been: by the team itself. I wanted to find out what these supporters were like. It seemed an extraordinary thing for the team's management to ban its own fans.

The first match was on a Wednesday evening, and I got a train to Manchester from London at around three in the afternoon. Inside, it was the familiar sight: people packed into the seats, on the floor, suspended from the luggage racks, playing cards, rolling dice, drinking unimaginable quantities of alcohol, steadily sinking consciousness into a blurry stupor.

I walked from carriage to carriage, looking for one of 'them', and came across someone who was truly spectacular to look at, qualifying for that special category of human being – one of its most repellent specimens. He had a fat, flat bulldog face and was extremely large. His T-shirt had inched its way up his belly and was discoloured by something sticky and dark. The belly itself was a tub of sorts, swirling, I would discover, with litres and litres of lager, partly-chewed chunks of fried potato and moist, undigested balls of over-processed carbohydrate. His arms – puffy, doughy things – were stained with tattoos. On his right bicep was an image of the Red Devils, the logo of the Manchester United team; on his forearm, a Union Jack.

When I came upon him, he had just tossed an empty beer can into the overhead luggage rack – quite a few were there already – and had started in on a bottle of Tesco's vodka.

I introduced myself. I was writing about football supporters. Did he mind if I asked him some questions?

He stared at me. Then he said, 'All Americans are wankers.' And paused. 'All journalists,' he added, showing, perhaps, that his mind did not work along strictly nationalist lines, 'are cunts.'

We had established a rapport.

His name was Mick and, on arriving in Manchester, he rushed me across the street to a nearby pub for three pints of beer, drunk with considerable speed. I accompanied Mick to the match, where he led me to the Stretford End, the standing-room section of Old Trafford, packed, enclosed, so that the chants, showing an impressive command of history and linguistic dexterity – 'Where were you in World War Two?'; *'Va fanculo'* ('Fuck off' in Italian) – were so amplified that it was hours before my ears stopped ringing: as I fell asleep that night I found myself relentlessly repeating the not especially somniferous slogan that 'Mussolini was a wanker.' At half-time, Mick rushed off again for refreshment, which this time included two meat pies, a cheeseburger and a plastic cup of something which Mick insisted was lager but whose temperature and consistency reminded me of vegetable soup. I couldn't touch it, and not losing a minute, Mick – waste not, want not – drank mine as well. At the end of the match, Mick grabbed me by my sleeve, tugged me through the crowd, ushered me down the Warwick Road North – a quick stop for two orders of fish'n'chips, grease pouring through the newspapers, Mick's T-shirt by now a work of art – and then across the street into the pub, where, after three quick rounds at the bar, Mick bought a further two pints before sitting down with me at a table. I was the one who asked that we sit. I was starting to bloat.

In Mick, I felt that I had finally met one of 'them'. At the same time, I felt that perhaps he wasn't the best one of 'them' to have met. There were problems. For a start I could see that he was not going to fit easily into my thesis: he was not unemployed or, it seemed, in any way disenfranchised. Instead he appeared to be a perfectly happy, skilled electrician from Blackpool, recently brought in as part of a team rewiring a block of flats in London. He also had a very large wad of twenty-pound notes stuffed into his trousers: I know this because Mick continued to buy rounds, and the wad never seemed to diminish.

There had to be quite a lot of money if only because Mick had not missed a match in four years. Not one. In fact, Mick said he couldn't imagine how it would be possible to miss one in the future. The future, I pointed out, was quite a long time, and Mick agreed, but, still, it was not a prospect – 'Miss Man United?' – that his mind could accommodate comfortably. I didn't know how he had been permitted to leave his building site earlier in the day to catch the train up to Manchester, but I knew that he intended to be back there first thing in the morning. Some time later in the night, after closing time, he would wander down to Manchester Piccadilly and, with cans of lager stuffed into his coat pockets, make his way to the milk train that would get him to London in time for work. I have, since wondered what it would be like to have your house rewired by Mick and imagined that moment – the children just finishing their breakfast, the rush to get them off to school – when the bell rings and there, with the members of your curious family clustering round the door beside you, is Mick, recently ejected from the milk train, still swaying, a light fixture in hand.

It was my turn to buy a round and when I returned Mick

explained to me how the 'firm' worked. He mentioned some of the characters, whose nicknames were remarkably self-explanatory: Bone Head, Paraffin Pete, Speedie, Barmy Bernie, One-Eyed Billy, Red (the communist) and Daft Donald, a fellow of notoriously limited intelligence who tended to destroy things with chains. At the time, he was in jail. For that matter, at one time or another, just about everyone, if not actually in jail, was at least facing a criminal charge or had recently been tried for one. Mick, who was not of a violent disposition, had been arrested once, although it was, he assured me, an unusual occurrence and one marred by bad timing: the police happened to enter the pub the moment that Mick, standing astride the unfortunate lad whom he had almost rendered unconscious, had raised a bar stool in the air, poised to bring it crashing down with maximum force and maximum damage. 'But I wasn't actually going to do it,' Mick said. There was no chance to argue, because in no time Mick was up again and heading for the bar, saying over his shoulder, 'Same again?'

Same again?

I could not see how I would make it to closing time. I got up to go to the loo – my fifth visit – and, hearing a terrible sloshing sound from within, reached out to a chair for support. Mick's thirst appeared unstoppable, or was at least as unstoppable as his stomach was large, and his stomach was very, very large. By the time I returned from the loo, there he was again, approaching the table, two pint glasses in hand. For a moment, the scene appeared to me in duplicate: a watery second Mick and an endless succession of pint glasses in his many hands. I was in trouble. I exhaled deeply. My stomach rolled. Once again, there was another, completely full pint glass. Once again, the froth on top. It was detestable. I stared at it.

Mick gulped.

Most of the supporters, he went on to explain, alcohol having no visible effect, came from either Manchester or London. 'The

20

ones from London are known as the Cockney Reds. Gurney is a Cockney Red. He doesn't travel anywhere unless he's on the jib.'

Mick was surprised I didn't know what 'being on the jib' meant. I was surprised I was able to pronounce the words.

'Being on the jib,' Mick continued, with only a half-pint now remaining in his glass, 'means never spending money. That's always the challenge. You never want to pay for Underground tickets or train tickets or match tickets. In fact, if you're on the jib when you go abroad, you usually come back in profit.'

'In profit?'

'Yeah. You know. Money.'

Manchester United's firm was known as the ICJ, the Inter-City Jibbers (named after the British Rail commuter service), and Mick proceeded to list the great moments in the ICJ's history – in Valencia and Barcelona during the World Cup when it was in Spain, in France during the qualifying matches for the European championship. Or Luxembourg. That, apparently, was from where Banana Bob returned wearing a fur coat and diamond rings on each of his fingers. Or Germany. That was where he boarded the train back to London with his underpants full of Deutschmarks. Roy Downes was another one. He had just been released from prison in Bulgaria, where he had been caught trying to crack the hotel safe. And there was Sammy. 'Sammy is a professional.'

'A professional hooligan?'

'No, no. A professional thief.'

Sammy, Roy Downes and Banana Bob were all leaders, or at least that's how Mick described them. I had no idea that there were leaders. It sounded like some kind of tribe. Clearly I would have to meet them. They were the ones to get to. I pursued the subject.

What, I asked Mick innocently, made a leader exactly?

'Doing,' Mick said and then paused, clearly refining his thought, 'yes, doing the right thing in the right circumstances at the right time.'

Ah. 'That's not,' I offered gently, 'a particularly helpful definition.'

I asked if there was one principal leader at United, but Mick said, No, there wasn't one leader, which was a problem, but several. 'Sammy, Roy, Banana Bob, Robert the Sneak Thief. They all end up competing with each other. And each has his own firm, his own following – with as many as thirty or forty people. Most of the followers are little fifteen- and sixteen-year-olds who are out to prove they can be a "bob" and will do anything. They're the most dangerous. They're the ones who start most of the fights. They're like sub-lieutenants and they answer only to their own leader. Sammy probably has the most loyal following.'

And then Mick stopped, suddenly.

I thought that my questions were making him uncomfortable – leaders? sub-lieutenants? little armies? – but, no, Mick was looking at my beer, noticing that, while he had finished his pint, my glass was still full, although I had repeatedly brought it to my lips. 'You're not much of a drinker, are you?'

It was eleven o'clock at last, and someone was calling 'Time' (beautifully, I thought), and I calculated that in addition to an order of fish'n'chips and a thoroughly indigestible cheeseburger I had had two cans of lager and eight pints of bitter. That was a lot, I thought. I had done rather well. But now Mick was telling me that I wasn't much of a drinker. Mick certainly was. He was not keeping track of what he consumed, but I was so impressed that I was. In addition to a newspaper full of fish'n'chips, his *two* cheeseburgers, his *two* meat pies, his *four* bags of bacon-flavoured crisps *and* the Indian take-away he was about to purchase on his way to the station, Mick had had the following: four cans of Harp lager, a large part of a bottle of Tesco's vodka and *eighteen* pints of bitter. As the pub closed, Mick bought a further four cans of lager for the train-ride home.

It was an expensive business being a football supporter, and I could see that it was important that Mick not miss work in the morning. For although Mick might have talked about being on the jib as if it were the most natural thing in the world, I noticed that he had a return ticket to London and had had a ticket for the match. All in all, he had spent about sixty pounds that evening. He mentioned that, the previous Saturday, he had spent about the same. He also said that he had spent £155 the day before on a package tour to Turin for the second match with Juventus. That is, between Saturday and Wednesday, Mick had spent £275 on football. In all likelihood he would spend another fifty or sixty pounds the following Saturday – £335 in a week, an exceptional week perhaps, but, even so, more than most members of the British population were spending on their monthly mortgages.

The package to Turin was interesting for another reason. As I knew, Manchester United's supporters were banned from matches played in Europe – the ban, according to Mick, was because there was a riot every time the team played abroad – but it appeared to be enforced in a rather casual way: the club's management had simply refused to take up the standard allocation of tickets for the visiting team. But what was to stop the supporters from going over on their own and buying from touts? Or what was to stop some enterprising entrepreneur from buying a lot directly from Italy and selling them expensively here in England?

Mick explained the package, which included air fare, hotel, and match tickets – seats, not standing. That was a big feature: they would be good tickets. He pulled out a tiny newspaper clipping, two centimetres of a column, taken from the *Manchester Evening News*. It was all being handled by a travel agent whom, for reasons that will eventually become apparent, I cannot refer to by his real name. I will call him Bobby Boss. And his agency? The Bobby Boss Travel Agency.

Mick disappeared into the Manchester night – the streets around Old Trafford were now deserted – and started off on the two-mile walk to the station, eating a second Indian take-away on the way, his weighted coat pockets swinging with his stride. He was, it must be said, not fun to look at, but, finally, not a bad sort. For all his stories of violence and mayhem, he himself seemed to play by the rules. It was just a good time out; it was a club. He was excited to have the chance to talk about it, and the more he talked about it the more excited he got. He was open and generous and trusting. That was the thing: he trusted me.

I FOUND BOBBY Boss in Soho, up stairs that smelled vividly of the people who had slept there the night before and in a very big room shared with several other businesses, each divided by an elaborate but flimsy network of highly portable plywood partitions. In fact, I did not find Bobby Boss himself, but only his business, represented by a perfectly agreeable receptionist named Jackie or Nicky or Tracy, something light and cheerful, someone, in any event, who seemed not to share my anxiety about embarking on a clandestine trip that had been banned by the management of Manchester United, the supporters' club, the Football Association and the UEFA executive. Business was business; I gave her £155 and she gave me a piece of paper. It said 'Received with thanks.' Match tickets, I was assured, would come later.

The journey began the following week, many hours before the sun came up, just outside the Cumberland Hotel by Marble Arch. For some reason, the airport had been changed the night before and a minibus had been hired to drive us all to Manchester. Nobody in the group found this particularly remarkable. On the other hand, there was nothing particularly remarkable about the group. There was a boy in glasses, with a clogged-up nose, who kept saying, 'There'll be no trouble. We are here for the football.' There was a lawyer. And there was a bunch of kids. Why was I doing this? I knew nobody. Mick, although meant to be working in London, wasn't there. I resolved never again to make travel plans after drinking eight pints of beer.

As it turned out I did happen to sit among three people who

knew each other, Steve – an electrician, who was married and lived in St Ives, the sleepy, suburban town forty miles north of London – and an improbably named pair, Ricky and Micky, good-looking boyish fellows in jeans and jackets. I asked them what they did, and they were guarded and suspicious – just what was an American doing on this minibus, anyway? 'This and that,' Ricky said, and turned to his paper, the *Sun*, which everybody else was reading as well. I couldn't be bothered. It was five o'clock in the morning. I couldn't imagine that Ricky and Micky – who, with their floppy dark hair and innocent round faces, looked like teenage pop stars from the early sixties – could possibly be relevant to what I was doing. But I had much to learn.

We arrived at Manchester Airport around nine o'clock. Mick was there after all, looking grey and bleary-eyed – obviously the morning after a night spent with a real drinker. He had grown more and more enthusiastic about the prospect of seeing his name in print, and, hoping that I might be accompanied by a photographer, had dressed for the occasion: a T-shirt – 'I don't have a drinking problem unless I can't find a drink' – and, regrettably, a pair of very tight-fitting shorts. He had sun-glasses and an instamatic camera and was in a great hurry to get to the duty-free shop. I asked him if he could identify any of the people he had mentioned to me before – Sammy, Banana Bob, Roy Downes, Robert the Sneak Thief – but they were not to be on the flight. Foot-soldiers, that's what I would learn we were called. Those on the flight were just the troops. The generals, as would be expected of them, made separate travel arrangements.

Until I came to live in England I had always assumed that the ugly tourist – with his money, his broad accent, his ignorance – was an American. But the American tourist – intimidated by the size of the world and always surprised at just how old it is – is a quiet, deferential one, even if a little goofy to look at sometimes. He's not ugly. I had not been to the Costa del Sol yet. I had not met a lager lout. I had not met tourist trash. Tourist trash, who travels only on package holidays, has an ever-present little camera, a peculiar way of dressing which usually exposes great expanses of flesh best left covered and an irrepressible appetite for cheap wine, two-litre bottles of lager and, regardless of the country or the language, vast, greasy, *Mail-on-Sunday*-newspaper quantities of fish'n'chips. Tourist trash is conspicuous when it travels. But football supporters are different; they're worse. Much, much worse.

Two hundred fifty-seven Manchester United supporters arrived on Wednesday morning, courtesy of Bobby Boss, to travel by air to Turin to a match from which they had been banned. Most of the supporters on the plane knew each other: this was a club outing. Nobody knew where we'd be staying; nobody had a match ticket. But everyone was in a holiday mood; everyone was proud to be a member of tourist trash. There were so many pictures to take. There was the picture of checking in for the flight. The picture of entering the duty-free shop and the one of leaving the duty-free shop. There was the one of opening the bottle bought from the duty-free shop and the one, taken once we had acquired our cruising altitude, of the duty-free shop bottle half-empty. And while I admit it seemed a little peculiar to find so many people half-way through litre bottles of vodka at ten o'clock in the morning, our flight to Turin was largely uneventful – noisy, spirited, but finally no different from what I supposed any other English package holiday must be like. The group seemed harmless on the whole, and fun, and I found that all of it – the strain of my early rising, the discomfort of riding from London to Manchester with a boy who could not afford a handkerchief, the sudden exposure to so many peculiar people – was starting to drop away. Frankly, I was enjoying myself. The fact, however, was this: tourist trash was on its way to devastate the country it was visiting.

For then it arrived in Turin.

TURIN

A *mob* is a strange phenomenon. It is a gathering of heterogeneous elements, unknown to one another (except on some essential points such as nationality, religion, social class); but as soon as a spark of passion, having flashed out from one of these elements, electrifies this confused mass, there takes place a sort of sudden organization, a spontaneous generation. This incoherence becomes cohesion, this noise becomes a voice, and these thousands of men crowded together soon form but a single animal, a wild beast without a name, which marches to its goal with an irresistible finality. The majority of these men would have assembled out of pure curiosity, but the fever of some of them soon reaches the minds of all, and in all of them there arises a delirium. The very man who came running to oppose the murder of an innocent person is the first to be seized with the homicidal contagion, and moreover, it does not occur to him to be astonished at this.

Gabriel Tarde
The Penal Philosophy (1912)

THE FIRST PERSON to greet the group in Turin, there at the foot of the ramp, was a man named Michael Wicks. Mr Wicks was the Acting British Consul. He was about fifty – a tweed jacket, a Foreign Office accent, educated – and relentlessly friendly. Mr Wicks was almost always smiling, and he continued smiling even when he met the first one off the plane, an extremely fat boy called Clayton.

Clayton had a number of troubles but his greatest one was his trousers. In all likelihood Clayton will have trouble with his trousers for the rest of his life. His stomach was so soft and large – no adjective seems big enough to describe its girth – that his trousers, of impressive dimensions to begin with, were not quite large enough to be pulled up high enough to prevent them from slipping down again. Clayton emerged from the airplane and waddled down the ramp, clasping his belt buckle, wrestling with it, trying to wiggle it over his considerable bulk. He was singing, 'We're so proud to be British.' His eyes were closed, and his face was red, and he repeated his refrain over and over again, although nobody else was singing with him.

Mick was not far behind. He had finished his bottle of vodka and was drinking a can of Carlsberg Special Brew that he had snapped up from the drinks trolley as he bumped past it on his way out. On reaching the end of the ramp, Mick was greeted by

Mr Wicks. Mick was confused. Mr Wicks did not look Italian. Mick paused, started to utter something, in the puffy, considered way that characterizes the speech of a man who has consumed a litre of spirits in the span of ninety minutes. And then Mick belched. It was a spectacular belch, long and terrible, a brutal, slow bursting of innumerable noxious gastric bubbles. It was a belch that invited speculation: about the beverages, the foods and the possible quantities that had contributed to a spray so powerful that it seemed to rise endlessly from deep within Mick's tortured torso. But Mr Wicks was unflappable. He was happy to view Mick as no different from any other tourist who had found the excitement of air travel a bit much to contain comfortably. Clearly a diplomat through and through, Mr Wicks was not offended. I don't think it was possible to offend Mr Wicks. He just smiled.

The others followed. They were also singing – on their own or arm in arm with friends – and their songs, like Clayton's, were all about being English and what a fine thing that was. Something had happened to the group shortly after landing; there had been a definitive change. As the plane approached the terminal, someone had spotted the army: it was waiting for them, standing in formation.

The army!

This was not going to be an ordinary passage through passport control: the plane was about to be surrounded, not by the police – you could see them clustered near the loading ramp – but by a troop of Italian soldiers. The soldiers were funny-looking, according to Mick, who was sitting next to me. Actually the phrase he used was 'fuckin' poofters'. They wore strange uniforms and brightly-coloured berets; the soldiers were not English – that was the point; the soldiers were *foreign*.

The effect was immediate: these were no longer supporters of Manchester United; they were now defenders of the English nation. They had ceased to be Mancunians; in an instant, their origins had, blotter-like, spread from one dot on the map of the country to the entire map itself. They were now English: English *and*, apparently, dangerous. People stood up, while the plane was taxi-ing, amid protests from a stewardess to sit down again, and, as if on cue, began changing their clothes, switching their urban, weekday dress for a costume whose principal design was the Union Jack. All at once, heads and limbs began poking through Union Jack T-shirts and Union Jack swimming suits and one pair (worn unusually around the forehead) of Union Jack boxer shorts. The moment seemed curiously prepared for, as if it had been rehearsed. Meanwhile, everyone had started singing 'Rule Britannia' – sharp, loud, spontaneous – and they sung it again, louder and louder, until finally, as the terminal grew near, it was not being sung but shouted:

> *Rule, Britannia! Britannia, rule the waves!*
> *Britons never, never, never shall be slaves.*
> *When Britain first, at Heaven's command,*
> *Arose from out the azure main,*
> *When Britain first arose from out the azure main,*
> *This was the charter, the charter of the land,*
> *And heavenly angels sung the strain:*
> *Rule, Britannia! Britannia, rule the waves!*
> *Britons never, never, never shall be slaves!*
> *Rule, Britannia! Britannia, rule the waves!*
> *Britons never, never, never shall be slaves!*

The Italians, too, had changed their identity. They had ceased to be Italians: they were now 'Eyeties' and 'wops'.

This was what Mr Wicks greeted, a man whose friendly relationship with reality I found to be intriguing. After all, here he was, having decided to meet an airplane full of supporters who, having been banned from the match that they were about to attend, were about to wreak crime and mayhem upon the city of Turin. What could he have done? It is easy to say after the event: he should have informed the civil aviation authorities that this particular charter flight must not be allowed to land and that everyone on it should be returned to Britain. *That* was what he should have done. But on what pretext could he have done such a thing? Mr Wicks's alternative – the only one – was to declare his faith in the humanity of what came out of the airplane, even though such a declaration meant overlooking so many things – like Clayton or Mick or the Union Jack boxer shorts worn as a tribal head-dress or the expression of unequivocal terror on the eight flight attendants' faces or the fact that by eleven-thirty in the morning 257 litres of eighty-proof spirits that had been purchased an hour and a half beforehand had already been consumed. 'Everybody,' Mr Wicks said, still smiling, as everybody came zig-zagging down the loading ramp, 'everybody is here to have a good time.'

Everybody *was* here to have a good time, and everybody agreed. But where was the man in charge? Mr Wicks asked after Mr Robert Boss of the Bobby Boss Travel Agency, but no one could help. No one knew his whereabouts. For that matter, no one knew where we'd be staying or where we might find our tickets for the match. In fact, most people, including myself, were so grateful to have found a plane waiting for us at Manchester airport and so surprised that it had conveyed us to Italy that we weren't in a great rush to ask more questions, fearing that by looking too closely at what we had it might all fall apart. It was better – and, after so much drink drunk so fast, easier – to believe that somehow it would all work out.

Then from the back of the plane emerged an attractive, chirpy woman with the bouncy cheerfulness of an American cheerleader. She introduced herself – 'Hi, I'm Jackie' – and announced that she was in charge and that everything was going to be fine. Jackie turned out to be a police cadet who had abandoned her training because she decided that she wanted to

32

travel and see the world instead. She had met Bobby Boss at a party. He offered her the world – and this job. This trip to Turin, in the company of 257 football supporters, was her first time abroad. Jackie was twenty-two years old.

Mr Wicks was concerned.

What do you do, I wondered, when your instinct is telling you to arrest everyone, and your sense of justice is telling you that you can't, and your mind, thoroughly confused, is telling you to smile a lot, and then you discover that in place of the person responsible for your predicament you have instead a twenty-two-year-old police drop-out surrounded by 257 drunken boys on her first time abroad?

What would you do?

What Mr Wicks did was this: still smiling, he confiscated everyone's passport (the appearance of an American one, I would learn, raising the momentary fear that the CIA was involved). Mr Wicks appeared to be thinking that he might want to control who was allowed to leave. He wouldn't – Mr Wicks would simply want everyone to leave – but that was later. At the time, Mr Wicks was trying to limit the consequences of what, in his heart of hearts, he must have known he could not prevent. He had prepared an information sheet of useful phone numbers arranged with an ominous sense of priorities. The number of the British Consulate was first, followed by the numbers of the police, the hospital, the ambulance service and, finally, the airport. Another sheet was filled with a number of damage-limiting phrases in Italian ('Will you get a doctor quickly, please?'), and it closed with the wishful imperative that, now in a foreign country, each member of the group was to conduct himself as an ambassador for Britain, not something that the Claytons and the Micks or anyone else needed to be encouraged to do: their sense of Britishness, irrevocably intact, was verging on imperial. Mr Wicks led everyone in a schoolmasterly manner through passport control and then gathered them together for an old fashioned locker-room pep talk – they were all to be on their best behaviour – concluding with the disclosure that he had arranged a police escort. It consisted of four motorcycles and two squad cars for each of the four buses that were waiting outside. All this intelligent and careful work revealed a man of great forethought. Yet you could see in Mr Wicks's eyes – as he stood in the shade of the terminal awning, all that tweed and education waving to us, as one by one each bus pulled out for the noisy drive into the city – that he had failed. Something very terrible was about to happen, and it would somehow be his fault. There was the realization – his face seemed to convey the pain and the regret of it – that he had just granted freedom to a body of unusual beings, beings who should be treated in a humane fashion (fed, viewed, appreciated with affection) but who should never have been allowed to enter the city of Turin. Never. Not even on a leash. Or in a cage. And yet, optimist to the end, Mr Wicks was still smiling.

A police escort is an exhilarating thing. I felt it to be exhilarating. I didn't particularly like the idea that I did, but I couldn't deny that I was sharing something of the experience of those around me, who, their shouting momentarily muted by the deafening sound, now felt themselves to be special people. After all, who is given a police escort? Prime ministers, presidents, the Pope – *and* English football supporters. By the time the buses reached the city – although there was little traffic, the sirens had been turned on the moment we left the parking lot – the status of their occupants had been enlarged immeasurably. Each intersection we passed was blocked with cars and onlookers. People had gathered on every street, wondering what all the fuss was about, wanting to get a look, and several blocks ahead you could see more people, bigger crowds, more congestion. The sound of twenty sirens is hard to miss. Who in the city of Turin could not have known that the English had arrived?

The English themselves, moved by the effect they were having, started to sing, which they managed to do more loudly than the brain-penetrating sirens that heralded their entrance into the city. To sing so powerfully was no small achievement, although to describe the noise that emerged from the bus as singing is to misrepresent it. One song was 'England'. This was repeated over and over again. There were no more words. Another, more sophisticated, was based on the tune of 'The Battle Hymn of the Republic'. Its words were:

> *Glory, glory, Man United*
> *Glory, glory, Man United*
> *Glory, glory, Man United*
> *Yours troops are marching on! on! on!*

Each 'on' was grunted a bit more emphatically than the one before, accompanied by a gesture involving the familiar upturned two fingers. There was an especially simple tune, 'Fuck the Pope' – simple because the words consisted exclusively of the following: *Fuck the Pope*. 'Fuck the Pope' was particularly popular, and, despite the sirens and speed, at least two buses (the one I was in and the one behind us) succeeded in chanting 'Fuck the Pope' in some kind of unison.

I noticed Clayton. He was several rows in front. Somehow Clayton, like an unwieldy lorry, had reversed himself into a position in which the opened window by his seat was filled by his suddenly exposed and very large buttocks – his trousers, this time, deliberately gathered round his knees, the cheeks of his suddenly exposed and very large buttocks clasped firmly in each hand and spread apart. Just behind him was a fellow who was urinating through his window. People were standing on the seats, jerking their fists up and down, while screaming profanities at pedestrians, police, children – any and all Italians.

Then someone lobbed a bottle.

It was bound to happen. There were bottles rolling around on the floor or being passed from person to person, and it was inevitable that, having tried everything else – obscene chants, abuse, peeing – someone would go that much further and pick up one of the empty bottles and hurl it at an Italian. Even so, the use of missiles of any kind was a significant escalation, and there was the sense, initially at least, that bottle-throwing was 'out of order'.

'What the fuck did you do that for?' someone shouted, angry, but not without a sense of humour. 'What are you, some kind of hooligan?'

A meaningful threshold had been crossed. Moments later there was the sound of another bottle breaking. And a second, and a third, and then bottles started flying out of most windows – of each of the four buses.

I wondered: if I had been a citizen of Turin, what would I have made of all this?

After all, here I'd be, at the foot of the Alps, in one of the most northern regions of Italy, surrounded by an exquisite, historic brick architecture, a city of churches and squares and arcades and cafés, a civilized city, an intellectual city, the heart of the Communist Party, the home of Primo Levi and other writers and painters, and, during my lunch hour, when perhaps I, a Juventus supporter like everyone else, had gone out to pick up my ticket for the match that evening, I heard this powerful sound, the undulating whines of multiple sirens. Were they ambulances? Had there been a disaster? All around me people would have stopped and would be craning their necks, shielding their eyes from the sun, until finally, in the distance we would have spotted the oscillating blue and white lights of the approaching police. And when they passed – one, two, three, four buses – would my response be nothing more than one of fascination, as in the window of each bus, I would see faces of such terrible aggression – remarkable aggression, intense, inexplicably vicious? Perhaps my face would be splattered by the spray of someone's urine. Perhaps I would have to jump out of the way of a bottle being hurled at my head. And perhaps, finally, I would have responded in the manner chosen by one Italian lad, who, suddenly the target of an unforeseen missile, simply answered in kind: he hurled a stone back.

The effect on those inside the buses was immediate. To be, suddenly, the target came as a terrible shock. The incredulity was immense: 'Those bastards,' one of the supporters, exclaimed, 'are throwing stones at the windows,' and the look on his face conveyed such urgent dismay that you could only agree that a stone-throwing Italian was a very bad person indeed. The presumption – after all a window could get broken and someone might get hurt – was deeply offensive, and everyone became very, very angry. Looking around me, I realized that I was no longer surrounded by raving, hysterically nationalistic social deviants; I was now surrounded by raving, hysterically nationalistic social deviants *in a frenzy*. They were wild, and anything that came to hand – bottles, jars of peanuts, fruit, cartons of juice, anything – was summarily hurled through the windows. 'Those bastards,' the lad next to me said, teeth clenched, lobbing an unopened beer can at a cluster of elderly men in dark jackets. 'Those bastards.'

Everyone was now very excited. But no one was more excited than our bus driver. Amid all this, few people had noticed that our bus driver had been rendered insane.

I had been nervous about the bus driver for some time. Since entering the city, he had been trying to bring everyone to order. He could see what was going on in the large rear-view mirror above his head. He tried dealing with his passengers diplomatically: he had no reason to believe that they were, in any fundamental sense, different from others he had driven before. But his request for order was ignored. And so he remonstrated. He appealed with his hands, his face, his whole body, as if to say,

'Please, there are laws and we must obey them.' This time, he was not ignored, but the response was not the desired one. The entire bus, which had been singing something about the Falklands or Britannia or the Queen, started chanting in unison that the driver should fuck himself. They then changed languages and said the same, more or less, in Italian.

I did not think this was a good idea. I cannot begin to convey the strength of my feeling. After all, the driver was just trying to do his job. Our lives were in his hands. In fact, our lives were *literally* in his hands. And it was with those hands that he expressed his unhappiness.

What he wanted, I suspect, was to stop the bus and order everyone off. He'd had enough. But he couldn't stop because he had three other coaches hurtling at top speed behind him. Nor could he go any faster because he had two motorcycle policemen in front. Unable to go forwards or backwards, he expressed his rage by going sideways: by swinging the steering-wheel violently to the left, to the right and then back again. Those lads perched atop the seats found that they were not perched atop anything at all. Very few of us were: so violent were the driver's movements that most of the slippery vinyl seats were emptied. Jackie, our twenty-two-year-old caretaker, had stood up and turned, with school-matronly authority, to reprimand her unruly following, but when she opened her mouth a strange, incomprehensible gurgling came out and then she, like everyone else, was catapulted off her feet. The interesting thing about the driver's rage was that the act of venting it seemed to increase it, as if expressing his anger showed him how really angry he was. His face started changing colour – it was now a very deep red – when he swung the steering-wheel again, and we lurched to the left, and then again swung it to the right, and back we tumbled. I feared, watching the terrible chromatic display across his features, that something was about to burst. I feared that his heart would seize up and, mid-way through another lurching swing of the steering-wheel, he would clutch his chest, leaving the bus to spin into the oncoming traffic.

And then: a rainbow. The streets, which had been getting tighter and tighter, opened, at last, on to a square: Piazza San Carlo. Light, air, the sky, and the bus slowly, undeniably, coming to rest. We had arrived.

More to the point: we were not dead, or, rather, *I* was not dead. We had survived the drive from the airport. As we were disembarking, the supporter ahead of me turned, just before stepping off the bus, and shouted at the driver: that had been completely out of order. And then, drawing deep from within his sinuses, he spat into the driver's face, and missed, leaving a drooping wet, elastic ball dripping from his shoulder.

And so four coaches of supporters arrived to attend the match that they had been banned from attending only to discover that many people had got there before them. Where had they come from? The square was packed. As we pulled in, someone waved to us, one hand wild above his head, the other clinging to his penis, urinating into a fountain. There could be no doubt about his nationality, or, for that matter, any of the others', familiar bloated examples of an island race who, sweltering under the warm Italian sun, had taken off their shirts, a great, fatty manifestation of the history of pub opening hours, of gallons and gallons of lager and incalculable quantities of bacon-flavoured crisps. They were singing: 'Manchester, la-la-la, Manchester, la-la-la.' They had the appearance of people who had been at the square, singing and drinking and urinating into the fountain, for many days. The pavement was covered with large empty bottles.

There was some confusion about where we were meant to be staying. Four hotels had been booked, and, while Jackie was trying to sort out who was meant to be where, flipping through the correspondence on her clipboard, she was interrupted by a terrible howl.

A woman dressed in black rushed out into the street and started wailing. Nobody could understand what she was saying, except the police – the police were everywhere – and five of them followed the woman back into one of the hotels. You could still hear her howling as she ascended the stairs inside. Jackie had stopped flipping through her correspondence and her face had assumed an uncertain shape. It was flattened as though she had been punched. It was a face – experiencing some kind of pre-verbal dread – that was trying to figure out how to express itself. You could tell that, although she didn't know what would happen next, she should have a response prepared beforehand.

I don't know how it had been done so quickly, but, shortly after arriving, several supporters had broken into the rooms on the hotel's second floor. Within minutes, they had gone through eight rooms, popping open the doors, dumping drawers on the floor, turning out the closets, looking for cash, traveller's cheques, airline tickets, jewellery. Only one supporter was caught – unable to resist lingering to make a long-distance phone call – and as the police reappeared, culprit in hand, Jackie marched up to him. Before her was a young man, ostensibly her responsibility, whose arms had been twisted behind his back by two policemen. Next to him was the woman in black. She was the manager of the hotel. She was no longer howling; she was also no longer honouring Jackie's booking. Then there was Jackie's clipboard, thick with correspondence, which, while all this was going on, continued in its failure to reveal where everyone was meant to be staying, even if the woman in black would accept them. And finally, diminishing the importance of her clipboard and the answers that it may or may not have yielded up, there was virtually no one else in sight. Room or no room, most supporters, having grown restless watching the party on the square, had vanished.

I spotted Mick who, ever vigilant, had discovered the place to buy cheap beer very cheaply, and who, ever generous, appeared with three two-litre bottles of lager, including one for me. Then Mick made for the middle of the throng, shouting 'C'mon, you Reds' – red for the red of Manchester United's Red Devils – and he, too, vanished, only his upturned two-litre bottle remaining visible above everyone's heads.

The throng itself was something to behold. The flesh exposed was your standard, assembly-line, grey-weather English flesh – bright pink, therefore, and burning rapidly – except in this one respect: everybody had a tattoo. And not just *a* tattoo, but many tattoos. They had tattoos in the places where you expect to find them – on the forearms, say, or the biceps – and everywhere else as well: on their foreheads, or behind their ears, or on the backs of their hands. Some had tattoos up and down the full length of their backs. These were not ordinary tattoos; these were murals on the flesh. There was one fellow who was a billboard for Manchester United Football Club. Looking at him, you could only conclude that this was what he had decided his function in life would be; it was his career. Every centimetre of his back had been given over to variations on the satanic theme suggested by the team name. On the lower part of his back were two red devils. They were drawn in great detail, with tails, fangs, forked tongues and pitchforks. Above the pitchforks, climbing up the spine and fanning across it, was an abundance of flames. Above the flames, around the upper shoulders, were famous players from other teams: you could see that they were meant to be tumbling from the sky (the clouds climbed into the neck) on their way to the hell below. It was narrative art of a sort, and hard not to admire the commitment.

It was also hard not to wonder about the person who would do this to his body. Getting a tattoo is a painful experience, a hot needle poking its way across the surface of the skin, filling up the cells underneath with ink. The pain, however – the blood that comes bubbling up, the rawness – goes away; the result, until it fades in late middle age or is eradicated by surgery, lasts for ever.

All around I saw metres and metres of skin that had been stained with these totemic pledges of permanence. In addition to the cinematic display on this one fellow's back, there was a tattooed neck, encircled with the neatly proportioned letters, M-A-N-C-H-E-S-T-E-R U-N-I-T-E-D. There was a pair of tattooed nipples – they served as the eyes for the head of an especially ornate red devil (spreading across the chest and stomach). And there was a tattooed forehead imprinted with the name 'Bryan Robson', in honour of the Manchester United midfield player (and in the hope, perhaps, that Robson would neither be traded to another football club nor ever die).

I wandered round the square. I was not uncomfortable, mainly because I had decided that I wasn't going to allow myself to be uncomfortable. If I had allowed myself to be uncomfortable then it would follow that I would start to feel ridiculous and ask myself questions like: why am I here? Now that the journey to Turin was properly completed, I had, I realized, done little more than gawk and drink. Mick had disappeared, although I thought I could pick out his bellowing amid the noise around me. Apart from him, however, I knew nobody. Here I was, my little black notebook hidden away in my back trouser pocket, hoping to come up with a way of ingratiating myself into a group that, from what I could see, was not looking for new members. For a moment I had the unpleasant experience of seeing myself as I must have appeared: as an American who had made a long journey to Italy that he shouldn't have known about so that he could stand alone in the middle of what was by now several hundred Manchester United supporters who all knew each other, had probably known each other for years, were accustomed to travelling many miles to meet every week and who spoke with the same thick accent, drank the same thick beer and wore many of the same preposterous, vaguely designed, Top Man clothes.

What was worse, word had got round that I was in Turin to

write about the supporters – a piece of news that few had found particularly attractive. Two people came up and told me that they never read the *Express* (the *Express*?) and that when they did they found only rubbish in it. When I tried to explain that I wasn't writing for the *Express,* I could see that they didn't believe me or – a more unpleasant prospect – thought that, therefore, I must be writing for the *Sun*. Another, speaking *sotto voce*, tried to sell me his story ('The *Star*'s already offered me a thousand quid'). In its way this was a positive development, except that someone else appeared and started jabbing me vigorously in the chest: You don't look like a reporter. Where was my notebook? Where was my camera? What's an American doing here anyway?

There had been other journalists. In Valencia, a Spanish television crew had offered ten pounds to any supporter who was prepared to throw stones, while jumping up and down and shouting dirty words. At Portsmouth, someone had appeared from the *Daily Mail,* working 'undercover', wearing a bomber jacket and Doc Marten boots, but, he was chased away by the supporters: it was pointed out that no one had worn a bomber jacket and a pair of Doc Marten boots for about ten years, except for an isolated number of confused Chelsea fans. And last year, in Barcelona there was a journalist from the *Star*. His was the story that I found most compelling. He had been accepted by most members of the group, but had then kept asking them about the violence. This, I was told, just wasn't done. When is it going to go off? he would ask. Is it going to go off now? Will it go off tonight? No doubt he had a deadline and a features editor waiting for his copy. When the violence did occur, he ran, which was not unreasonable: he could get hurt. In the supporters' eyes, however, he had done something very bad: he had – in their inimitable phrasing – 'shitted himself'. When he returned to complete his story, he was set upon. But they didn't stab him. He wasn't disfigured in any lasting way.

The story about the *Star* journalist was not particularly

reassuring – so great, they didn't stab him; lucky reporter – and I made a mental note not to shit myself under any circumstances. Even so, the story revealed an important piece of information.

Until then, everyone I had spoken to went out of his way to establish that, while he might *look* like a hooligan, he was not one in fact. He was a football supporter. True: if someone was going to pick a fight, he wasn't going to run – he was English, wasn't he? – but he wouldn't go looking for trouble. Everyone was there for the laugh and the trip abroad and the drink and the football.

I did not want to hear this. And when I heard it, I refused to believe it. I had to. The fact was that I had come to Italy to see trouble. It was expensive and time-consuming, and that was why I was there. I didn't encourage it – I wasn't in the position to do so – and I wasn't admitting my purpose to anyone I met. I may not have been admitting it to myself. But *that* was why I was there, prepared to stand on my own with five hundred people staring at me wondering what I was doing. I was waiting for them to be bad. I wanted to see violence. And the fact that the *Star* journalist had witnessed some, that it had finally 'gone off', suggested I might be in the right spot after all.

Violence or no violence, mine was not an attractive moral position. It was, however, an easy one, and it consisted in this: not thinking. As I entered this experience, I made a point of removing moral judgement, like a coat. With all the drink and the luxurious Italian sun, I wouldn't need it. Once or twice, facing the spectacle of the square, the thought occurred to me that I should be appalled. If I had been British I might have been. I *might* have felt the burden of that peculiar nationalist liability that assumes you are responsible for everyone from your own country ('I was ashamed to be British' – or French or German or American). But I'm not British. Mick and his friends and I were not of the same kind. And although I might have felt that I should be appalled, the fact was: I wasn't. I was fascinated.

And I wasn't alone.

A group of Italians had gathered near the square. I walked over to them. There were about a hundred, who, afraid of getting too close, had huddled together, staring and pointing. Their faces all had the same look of incredulity. They had never seen people act in this way. It was inconceivable that an Italian, visiting a foreign city, would spend hours in one of its principal squares, drinking and barking and peeing and shouting and sweating and slapping his belly. Could you imagine a busload from Milan parading round Trafalgar Square showing off their tattoos? 'Why do you English behave like this?' one Italian asked me, believing that I was of the same nationality. 'Is it something to do with being an island race? Is it because you don't feel European?' He looked confused; he looked like he wanted to help. 'Is it because you lost the Empire?'

I didn't know what to say. Why *were* these people behaving in this way? And who were they doing it for? It would make sense to think that they were performing for the benefit of the Italians looking on – the war dance of the invading barbarians from the north and all that – but it seemed to me that they were performing solely for themselves. Over the last hour or so, I could see that the afternoon was turning into a highly patterned thing.

It looked something like this: once a supporter arrived, he wandered round, usually with a friend, periodically bellowing or bumping into things or joining in on a song. Then a mate would be spotted and they would greet each other. The greeting was achieved through an exchange of loud, incomprehensible noises. A little later they would spot another mate (more noise) and another (more noise), until finally there were enough people – five, six, sometimes ten – to form a circle. Then, as though responding to a toast, they would all drink from a very large bottle of very cheap lager or a very large bottle of very cheap red wine. This was done at an exceptional speed, and the drink spilled down their faces and on to their necks and down their chests, which, already quite sticky and beading with perspiration, glistened in the sun. A song followed. From time to time, during a particularly important refrain, each member of the circle squatted slightly, clenching his fists at his sides, as if, poised so, he was able to sing the particular refrain with the extra *oomph* that it required. The posture was not unlike shitting in public. And then the very large bottle with its very cheap contents was drunk again.

The circle broke up and the cycle was repeated. It was repeated again. And again. All around the square, little clusters of fat, sticky men were bellowing at each other.

Near me was a Mick look-alike, a walrus of a fellow with a Wild Bill Hickock moustache. In the middle of his great billboard chest was suspended a tiny black object, like a piece of punctuation. It was a camera. He was wobbling slightly and, thus, with some difficulty, taking a picture. He was concentrating very hard. I couldn't tell what he was photographing. It appeared to be his feet. I tried to make conversation of a sort.

I asked him why he was taking photographs. I was trying to work out why these people had to come all this way, at such expense, to do the things I saw them doing. Drinking large quantities of cheap beer. Endlessly singing English football songs. Photographing their feet. Couldn't this sort of thing be done at home? After all, the match that evening would be on television.

He said that he was taking pictures so that he would have something to remember the trip by.

It's a holiday, innit? he said.

I asked him if he could tell me where we were.

Italy, he said. We're in Italy; and then adding, as though for clarification: Fuckin' Eyeties.

I said, of course, of course, I knew we were in Italy. But did he know where in Italy?

Juventus, he said after a pause, suspecting a trick question.

And then he added, again, as though to reinforce the authority of the statement: Fuckin' Eyeties.

The city of Juventus? I asked.

Fuckin' right, he said. Pause. Fuckin' Eyeties.

I pointed out that Juventus was not the name of a city; it was the name of a football club – Juventus of Torino – but perhaps I failed to convey my point clearly enough. In any event, he was not representative: most people I met knew where they were. But he was typical in that, like him, everyone had a camera. People may have thought a change of clothing or a toothbrush was unnecessary, but no one came without a camera. The trip to Turin was about much more than football; it was a journey, an adventure, a once-in-a-lifetime thing: an excursion so special that everyone had to have snaps to commemorate it. I thought: this is a parody of the holiday abroad. Except that it wasn't a parody. This *was* the holiday abroad. Their dads, they kept telling me, never had a chance to see the world like this.

And yet what was this world? Earlier, on the plane, I had watched a cluster of supporters looking at the photographs from the last trip. It seemed to be a routine, *en route* to the next stop on the European tour, to review the pictures from the last one. The pictures might have been from Luxembourg. On the other hand, they could have been taken in Barcelona. Or Budapest. Or Valencia. Or Paris or Madrid or even Rio or any one of the many foreign cities visited by the banned Manchester United supporters in the last couple of years. The point was: it didn't matter. Each photograph, if not of a duty-free shop, depicted the same pose in one of three possible stages: three or four lads (frequently the same three or four lads) having (*one*) just avoided falling, or (*two*) on the verge of falling, or (*three*) having just fallen, flat on their faces.

Mick reappeared and pointed to the far end of the square, where a silver Mercedes was moving slowly through a street crowded with supporters, Italian onlookers and police. The driver, in a shiny purple track suit, was a black man with a round fleshy face and a succession of double chins. In the back seat were two others, both black. One, I would learn, was named Tony Roberts. The other was Roy Downes.

Roy had arrived at last.

No one had mentioned Tony to me before, but he was impossible to forget once you saw him. He was thin and tall – he towered above everyone else – and had an elaborate, highly styled haircut. The fact was Tony looked exactly like Michael Jackson. Even the colour of his skin was Michael Jackson's. For a brief electric instant – the silver Mercedes, the driver, the ceremony of the arrival – I thought Tony *was* Michael Jackson. What a discovery: to learn that Michael Jackson, that little red devil, was actually a fan of Manchester United. But, then, alas, yes, I could see that: no, Tony was not Michael Jackson. Tony was only someone who had spent a lot of time and money trying to look like Michael Jackson.

There was Tony's wardrobe. This is what I saw of it during his stay in Turin (approximately thirty hours):

One: a pale yellow jump suit, light and casual and worn for comfort during the long hours in the Mercedes.

Two: a pastel-blue T-shirt (was there silk in the mix?), a straw hat and cotton trousers, his 'early summer' costume, worn when he briefly appeared on the square around four o'clock.

Three: his leather look (lots of studs), chosen for the match.

Four: a light woollen jacket (chartreuse) with complementary olive-green trousers for later in the evening, when everyone gathered at a bar.

Five: and finally, another travel outfit for the return trip (a pink cotton track suit with pink trainers).

Later, during the leather phase, I asked Tony what he did for a living, and he said only that he sometimes 'played the ticket game': large-scale touting, buying up blocks of seats for pop concerts or the sporting events at Wimbledon and Wembley and selling them on at inflated prices. I heard also that he was, from time to time, a driver for Hurricane Higgins, the snooker star; that he was a jazz-dancer; that he had 'acted' in some porn films. His profession, I suspect, was the same as that of so many of the others, a highly lucrative career of doing 'this and that', and it wasn't worth looking too deeply into what constituted either the 'this' or the 'that'.

Roy Downes was different. Ever since Mick had mentioned Roy, I had been trying to find out as much about him as I could. I had learned that he had just finished a two-year prison sentence in Bulgaria, where he had been arrested before the match between Manchester United and Leviski Spartak (having just cracked the hotel safe) and that, ever since, people said he wasn't the same: that Roy had become serious, that he never laughed, that he rarely spoke. I had heard that Roy always had money – rolls and rolls of twenty- and fifty-pound notes. That he had a flat in London, overlooking the river. That he saw his matches from the seats and never stood in the terraces with the other supporters, and that he got his tickets free from the players. That he was a lounge lizard: the best place to leave messages for Roy was Stringfellows, a basement bar and night-club on Upper St Martin's Lane in London, with Bob Hoskins bouncers in dinner-jackets, and lots of chrome and mirrors and a small dance floor filled, on the wintry Tuesday night when I later went there (perhaps an off night), with sagging men who had had too much to drink and young secretaries in tight black skirts. (I was let in, stepping past the bouncers and into a bad black-and-white movie, having said – with a straight face – that Roy sent me.)

I couldn't get anybody to tell me what Roy did. Maybe they didn't know or didn't need to know. Or maybe they all knew and didn't want to say. After all, how many of your friends can pick a safe?

Actually I did know one other thing about Roy, but at the time I didn't know that I knew it. I had told a friend about getting caught up in a football train in Wales, and he mentioned an incident he had witnessed that same month. He had been travelling from Manchester, in a train already filled with supporters. When it stopped at Stoke-on-Trent, more fans rushed into his carriage. They were from West Ham and, shouting, 'Kill the nigger cunts,' they set upon two blacks who were sitting nearby. My friend could see only the backs of the West Ham supporters, their arms rising in the air and then crashing down again, the two blacks somewhere in the middle, when he heard: 'They've got a stick, kill the bastards' — the stick evidently referring to a table leg that one of the blacks had managed to break off to defend himself. By the time my friend ran off to find a member of the Transport Police, there was blood on the floor and the seats and some was splattered across the windows. One of the blacks had had his face cut up. But it was the other one they were after. He was stabbed repeatedly — once in the lower chest, a few inches below his heart. A finger was broken, his forehead badly slashed and several of his ribs were fractured. The list of injuries is taken from the 'Statement of Witness' that my friend prepared, and on it are the victims' names, meaningful to me only when I returned from Italy. They were Anthony Roberts and Roy Downes. Roy had been the one they were after, the one who had been repeatedly stabbed.

Roy's car drove round the square, with him waving from the window like a politician, and disappeared. When I spotted him again, about an hour later, Roy was standing on one of the balconies, arms apart, leaning on the rail, surveying the supporters below. He was small but muscular — wiry, lean — and good looking, with strong features and very black skin. He looked, as I had been led to expect, grim and serious. What he saw on the square below him seemed to make him especially grim and serious. In fact he was so grim and serious that I thought it might have been just a little overdone. He looked like he had chosen to be grim and serious in the way that you might pick out a particular article of clothing in the morning; it was what he had decided on instead of wearing red.

It was not an opportunity to miss, and I bounced up the stairs and introduced myself. I was writing a book; I would love to chat. I babbled away – friendly, Californian, with a cheerful, gosh-isn't-the-world-a-wonderful-place kind of attitude, until finally Roy, who did not look up from the square, asked me to Shut up, please. There was, please, no need to talk so much: he already knew all about me.

No one had told me to shut up before. How did he know whatever it was he knew? I suppose I was impressed. This was a person for whom style was no small thing.

Roy, at any rate, wasn't having a lot to do with me, despite my good efforts. These efforts, painful to recall, went something like this.

After expressing my surprise that I was a person worth knowing anything about, I, bubbling and gurgling away, suggested that Roy and I get a drink.

Roy, still surveying the square, pointed out that he didn't drink.

That was fine, I said, carrying on, cheerful to the end: Then perhaps, after his long journey, he might be interested in joining me for a bite to eat.

No.

Right, I said, a little tic I had developed for responding to a situation that was not right but manifestly wrong. I pulled out a pack of cigarettes – I wanted badly to smoke – while taking in the scene below us: there was Mick, standing by himself, a large bottle of something in one hand and a large bottle of something else in the other, singing 'C'mon, you, Reds,' bellowing it, unaccompanied, his face deeply coloured, walking round and round in a circle.

I offered Roy a cigarette.

Roy didn't smoke.

Right, I said, scrutinizing the scene below us with more attention, pointing out how everyone was having such a jolly good time, to which Roy, of course, did not reply. In fact the scene below us was starting to look like a satanic Mardi Gras. There must have been about eight hundred people, and the noise they were making – the English with their songs; the Italians with their cars, horns blaring – was very loud. In normal circumstances, the noise was so loud it would have made conversation difficult. In my current circumstances, nothing could have made conversation any worse.

I carried on. Whatever came into my head found itself leaving my mouth, with or without an exclamatory *Right!*: I talked about football, Bryan Robson, the Continental style – in fact about many things I knew little about – until finally, after a brief aside about something completely inconsequential, I tried to talk to Roy about Roy. I don't recall what I said next; actually I fear I do, which is worse, because I think it was something about Roy's being both black and short and what a fine thing that was to be. And then I paused. The pause I remember precisely because at the end of it Roy looked at me for the first time. I thought he was going to spit. But he didn't. What he did was this: he walked away.

With a slight swagger, hands in his pockets, Clint Eastwood had just strolled off and disappeared down the stairs and walked out of my story.

I wasn't cut out to be a journalist.

I looked to Mick for reassurance, but I wasn't reassured. Mick was an unfortunate sight. He had stopped walking in circles, folded up and fallen asleep. Everyone was singing and shouting around him, but he slept on, undisturbed and blissfully imperturbable, head resting on his forearm, his mouth open and loose. There was no point in waking him, even if it had been possible to do so.

It was time I met more people. I hadn't got through to Roy. Maybe I would later. Maybe it didn't matter. I had had so many I-am-not-going-to-think-about-why-I-am-here lagers that I didn't care if people were going to talk to me. The choices were not complicated: either I would find myself in conversation; or I would find myself not in conversation.

I found myself neither in conversation nor not in conversation but looking into a particularly ugly mouth. I can't recall how I arrived before this mouth – zig-zagging across the square – but once in its presence I couldn't take my eyes off it.

In it, there were many gaps, the raw rim of the gums showing where once there must have been teeth. Of the teeth still intact, many were chipped or split; none was straight: they appeared to have grown up at odd, unconventional angles or (more likely) been redirected by a powerful physical influence at some point in their career. All of them were highly coloured – deep brown or caked with yellow or, like a pea soup, mushy-green and vegetable-soft with decay. This was a mouth that had suffered many slings and arrows along with the occasional thrashing and several hundredweight of tobacco and Cadbury's milk chocolate. This was a mouth through which a great deal of life had passed at, it would appear, an uncompromising speed.

The mouth belonged to Gurney. Mick had told me about Gurney. What he hadn't told me about was the power of Gurney's unmitigated ugliness. It was ugliness on a scale that elicited concern: I kept wanting to offer him things – the telephone number of my dentist or a blanket to cover his head. It was hard not to stare at Gurney. Gurney was one of the older supporters and was well into his thirties. He was looked up to, I discovered, by the younger lads. I never understood why they looked up to him or what they hoped to find when they did. He was balding and unshaven and, having taken off his shirt, you could follow the rivulets of perspiration down his torso. He had been travelling for several days and was covered by a dark film that clogged up and discoloured the pores in his skin.

Gurney was another leader. How many leaders could there be? This was turning into a ruling party committee, but Gurney was different from the other putative generals in that his following was geographically specific. It was called the Cockney Reds – the 'London branch' of the Manchester United supporters. Like Roy, Gurney didn't trust me, at least initially, but I was getting used to not being trusted. In Gurney's case, I was grateful: more trusting and he might have proposed something unsavoury, like shaking my hand. His cockney followers were less suspicious. When I came upon them, they were in the middle of singing one of those songs (squatting slightly). They were in good spirits and, straightaway, started questioning me.

No, I wasn't from the *Express* – I had never read the *Express*.

Yes, I was here to write about football supporters.

Yes, I know you are not hooligans.

What was I doing here, then? Well, that was obvious, wasn't it? I was here to get very, very pissed.

And, with that, I had become one of them, or enough of one of them for them to feel comfortable telling me stories. They wanted me to understand how they were organized: it was the 'structure' that was important to understand.

There were, it was explained, different kinds of Manchester United supporters, and it was best to think of each kind as belonging to one of a series of concentric circles. The largest circle was very large: in it you would find *all* the supporters of Manchester United, which, as everyone kept telling me, was one of the best-supported teams in English football, with crowds regularly in excess of 40,000.

Within that large circle, however, there were smaller ones. In the first were the members of the *official* Manchester United

Supporters' Club – at its peak more than 20,000. The official Manchester United Supporters Club, started in the seventies, hired trains from British Rail – 'football specials' – for conveying fans to the matches, produced a regular magazine, required annual dues and in general kept the 'good' supporters informed of developments in the club and tried to keep the 'bad' supporters from ever learning about them.

In the second circle was the unofficial supporters' club, the 'bad' supporters: the 'firm'.

The firm was divided between those who lived in Manchester and those who did not. Those who did not came from just about everywhere in the British Isles – Newcastle, Bolton, Glasgow, Southampton, Sunderland: these people were the Inter-City Jibbers. Mick had mentioned them: they got their name from taking only the Inter-City fast commuter trains and never the football specials hired by the official supporters' club.

The Inter-City Jibbers themselves were also divided, between those who were not from London and those who were: the Cockney Reds.

I remembered Mick's account of being on the jib. I had much to learn, and most of it I would learn the next day on my return to England. But initially I was sceptical. How was it possible that so many people could travel on the jib? From what I understood about travelling on the jib, it meant not only not paying but actually making money as well.

Roars of laughter followed. Being on the jib was very simple, I was told, and involved no more than defeating the Hector. The Hector was the British Rail ticket-collector, and at the mention of the Hector, everyone started singing the Hector song:

> *Ha ha ha*
> *He he he*
> *The Hector's coming*
> *But he can't catch me.*

On the racks
Under the seats
Into the bogs
The Hector's coming
But he can't catch me.
Ha ha ha
He he he
The ICJ is on the jib again
Having a really g-o-o-o-o-o-o-o-o-o-o-d time.

There were tricks: passing one good ticket between members of a group, making the sound of endless vomiting while hiding in the loo, pretending not to understand English. It was Gurney's ploy to engage the ticket-collector in a battle of wills, giving him everything but a ticket: a sandwich, a cigarette, the ash tray, his shoe, a sock, then his other sock, bits of dirt scraped from beneath his toe-nails, his shirt, the darkly coloured lint from his navel, his belt until – the final destination getting closer the longer the exchange went on – the ticket-collector, fed up, got on with the rest of his job. The ICJ had learned two principles about human nature – especially human nature as it had evolved in Britain.

The first was that no public functionary, and certainly not one employed by British Rail or London Transport, wants a difficult confrontation – there is little pride in a job that the functionary believes to be underpaid and knows to be unrewarding and that he wants to finish so that he can go home.

The second principle was the more important: everyone – including the police – is powerless against a large number of people who have decided not to obey *any* rules. Or put another way: with numbers there are no laws.

It is easy to imagine the situation. You're there, working by yourself at the ticket booth of an Underground station, and two hundred supporters walk past you without paying. What do you do? Or you're working the cash register in a small food shop – one room, two refrigerators, three aisles – and you look up and see that, out of nowhere, hundreds of lads are crowding through your door, pushing and shoving and shouting, until there is no room to move, and that each one is filling his pockets with crisps, meat pies, beer, biscuits, nuts, dried fruit, eggs (for throwing), milk, sausage rolls, litre-bottles of Coke, red wine, butter (for throwing), white wine, Scotch eggs, bottles of retsina, apples, yoghurt (for throwing), oranges, chocolates, bottles of cider, sliced ham, mayonnaise (for throwing) until there is very little remaining on your shelves. What do you do? Tell them to stop? Stand in the doorway? You call the police but as the supporters pour out through the door – eggs, butter, yoghurt and mayonnaise already flying through the air, splattering against your front window, the pavement outside, the cars in the parking lot, amid chants of 'Food fight! Food fight!' – they split up, some going to the left, others to the right, everybody disappearing. (Later, I would travel to Brussels where a café-owner, confronted with the arrogance of numbers – in this case, a group from Tottenham who, after eating the café-owner's food, drinking his beer and breaking his furniture, walked out without paying – responded in kind. He answered irrationality with irrationality, rule-breaking with rule-breaking, pulled out a shotgun hidden underneath the counter and shot a supporter dead – the wrong supporter, as it turned out; one who had paid his bill.)

Gurney and his crew had arrived in Turin by a large minibus that they had hired in London. The bus was called 'Eddie'; the group was called Eddie and the Forty Thieves.

Forty Thieves?

They explained. Their adventures began in Calais. At the first bar they entered, the cashier was on a lunch break, and they popped open a cash register with an umbrella and came away with 4,000 francs. They carried on, travelling south and then along the French coast, robbing a succession of small shops on the way, never paying for petrol or food, entering and leaving restaurants *en masse*, always on the look-out 'for a profit'. I noticed that each member of the Eddie-and-the-Forty-Thieves team was wearing sun-glasses – filched, I was told, from a French petrol station that had a sideline in tourist goods that, it would appear, also included brightly-coloured Marilyn Monroe T-shirts. All of them were wearing Rolex watches.

Most of the supporters on the square had not been on the plane. How had they got here?

They went through a list.

Daft Donald hadn't made it. He had been arrested in Nice (stealing from a clothing shop), and, proving his nickname, was found to be in possession of one can of mace, eighteen Stanley knives (they fell out when he was searched) and a machete.

Robert the Sneak Thief had been delayed – his ferry had been turned back following a fight with Nottingham Forest fans – but he had got a flight to Nice and would be coming by taxi.

A taxi from Nice to Turin?

Robert, I was told, always had money (if you see what I mean), and, although I didn't entirely (see what he meant), I didn't have the chance to find out more because they were well down their list.

Sammy? ('Not here but he won't miss Juventus.' 'Sammy? Impossible.')

Mad Harry? ('Getting too old.')

Teapot? ('Been here since Friday.')

Berlin Red? ('Anybody seen Berlin Red?')

Scotty? ('Arrested last night.')

Barmy Bernie? ('Inside.' 'Barmy Bernie is inside again?') Whereupon there followed the long, moving story of Barmy Bernie, who, with twenty-seven convictions, had such a bad record that he got six months for loitering. Everyone shook his head in commiseration for the sad, sad fate of Barmy Bernie.

Someone from another group appeared, showing me a map, with an inky blue line tracing its route to Turin. It began in Manchester, then continued through London, Stockholm, Hamburg, Frankfurt, Lyon, Marseilles and finally stopped here. A great adventure, not unlike, I reflected, the Grand Tour that young men had made in the eighteenth and nineteenth centuries, and it had cost them – all eleven of them – a total of seven pounds.

Seven pounds, I exclaimed, understanding the principle. What went wrong?

They assured me they would be in profit on the return.

Another lad showed me his rail ticket to Dunkirk. The ticket had been forged and had then, once in Dunkirk, been altered to include Turin and validated with a stolen British Rail stamp (obvious jibbing equipment). This was getting interesting: I had become the audience for a kind of show and tell. When the next one appeared – as though in a queue – he told me how he and his mates had got here by hitch-hiking to Belgium and then hopping on a train. Everything had gone well, until they realized they were on the wrong train (always a little tricky confirming the destination with the Hector). They ended up finally in Switzerland – acceptable, as it was on the way to Turin – but it was one-thirty in the morning, there were no more trains, it was early April in the Alps, there was no place to stay and no money if there had been, and so they slept, huddled together for warmth, in a phone booth.

The circle of supporters who now surrounded me had grown to a considerable size, with one or two regularly disappearing and returning with cans of lager. I had ceased to be the CIA. I was no longer the hack from the *Express*. I appeared to have ended my tenure as an undercover officer of the British Special

Branch. And I was starting to be accepted. I would learn later that I had earned a new status; I had become a 'good geezer'. Yes, that's what I was: a good geezer. What a thing.

I was also someone to whom people needed to tell their stories. There was an implicit responsibility emerging. I was being asked to set the record straight. I was the 'repoyta'. I was given instructions, imperatives, admonitions. I was told:

That they weren't hooligans.

That it was a disgrace that there were so many obstacles keeping them from supporting their team properly.

That they weren't hooligans.

That the management of Manchester United was a disgrace.

That they weren't hooligans.

Until finally I was telling them, yes, yes, I know, I know, I know: you're just here for the drink and the laugh and the football, and, for the first time, despite myself, I wanted to believe it. I was starting to like them, if only because they were starting to like me (the irrational mechanism of the group at work, and I was feeling grateful just to be accepted by it). And it *was* true that no one had been violent. People had been loud, grotesque, disgusting, rude, uncivilized, unpleasant to look at and, in some instances, explicitly repellent – but not violent. And it was possible that they wouldn't be. I had met thieves, villains and drunkards, but I had also met people with real jobs with real responsibilities: an engineer for British Telecom, for instance; a trainee accountant; a bank clerk. Their stories were not about crowd violence but about football: how no one missed a match and about the unrelenting tedium of the weekdays (no football) and the terrible depression that sets in during the summer (no football). It didn't suit my purposes that everyone here should be nothing more than a fanatical fan of the game, but it was conceivable that there really would be no violence, that this was simply how normal English males behaved. It was a terrifying notion, but not an impossible one. After all, the domain of the male spectator has always been characterized by its brutish masculine excesses. Maybe these people were just a bit more excessive than what I was used to.

I was hungry and followed one of the lads across the square to a bar under the arcades. A table had been placed before the entrance to deal with the English supporters, and three or four older women, dressed in black in the Italian way, were running back and forth to the rear of the bar to fetch drink. There must have been about a hundred supporters, pressing against the table, shouting for service. Only English was spoken – the notion that they might have spoken Italian now seems ludicrous – and the English was highly abusive. People were pushing and grabbing, and every now and then someone went off without paying. One supporter had unzipped his shorts and was urinating through the doors of the neighbouring café, splashing the floor, as uncomprehending Italians jumped out of their seats to avoid getting wet. Police were standing nearby, watching, but were uncertain and hesitant.

I returned to the square. I spotted Roy, who appeared to be 'working' the crowd. Things had become louder and uglier, and you could tell that the Italians had become less indulgent and were no longer so amused by their English visitors. They did not look so friendly, and more of their cars were circling the square than before. Roy appeared to be acting as a moderator, regulating everyone's conduct. It was not the role I would have expected of him, but there he was: helping the police, directing traffic or pushing away supporters who were blocking the streets and reprimanding those who had broken bottles or were behaving in a disorderly fashion.

The light was changing and the match would begin soon, but there was no suggestion that it was time to leave. I didn't know how to find the stadium and would, in any event, take my cue from the others, but they seemed to have forgotten about the game. The faces around me had changed their shapes. They had become drunken faces, red and bloated, as if their cheeks had been puffed full with air. Somebody standing next to me – a tall badly sunburnt man wearing very little clothing – was trying to tell me something but I couldn't make it out. He repeated it. Something had engaged his passions, and he was trying to make his point by poking me in the chest with his finger. His aim, though, was unreliable and he missed and was slow to recover and almost fell. His mate, who was also very tall, was swaying, shuffling his feet every now and then to keep his balance and looking fixedly at my left knee, as if for stability. He said nothing. He responded to nothing. He looked only at my knee. I was amused by the idea that if I turned and walked away he would fall. I stood there, my knee happy to keep him upright.

A young, brave Italian had walked to the centre of the square. Most Italians kept their distance and watched from across the street, but this one, a boy of fifteen or sixteen, had approached the group, intrigued by it, wanting to practise his English. He had three hesitant friends who remained about ten feet behind, while he tried to engage one of the supporters in his schoolbook conversation. He asked him if he was 'Anglish'.

He wasn't noticed, but then no one was noticing much of anything, until one lad turned and took him by the shoulder, not without affection. I couldn't hear what was said – it was muttered softly but intensely, with the Italian boy's face registering unease but not fear – when the supporter drew back his leg and slammed the Italian squarely in the crotch with his knee. The Italian boy buckled, swung round and curled up and was rescued by his friends who took him away, while looking back over their shoulders at the English supporter.

It was the first violence I had seen.

Somebody said that Robert had arrived and that his taxi had cost £250, and someone else asked if I knew anyone in England who was planning to record the match – Mick had just been arrested and was going to miss it. I couldn't imagine Mick doing anything to get himself arrested – was it against the law to sleep on the pavement? – but I lost sight of my informant when I had to jump out of the way of a slap of brown liquid suddenly coming in my direction: the supporter who had been staring so fixedly at my knee had vomited.

The English songs were dying down – the supporters were strewn amid the cafés and bars and arcades – but the noise itself seemed to have increased. Most of it was now coming from the Italians. It might have been for no other reason than that the working day was over, and Juventus supporters – car horns blaring, their own chants beginning – felt compelled to drop by and see what the English looked like. And, by now, what they discovered was a sorry sight. Many supporters were still upright but wobbly and, like Mick when he was conscious (and before he was arrested), were singing to themselves. Many were also asleep, sprawled like some aged dead herd animal wherever they happen to fall. Several were bent double, in the familiar tortured posture – faces deep red, the muscles strongly delineated from the strain – of regurgitation. The water in the fountain was foully discoloured.

Someone walked by and casually mentioned that the buses would be leaving in a few minutes. So: there would be a football match after all. I wandered off in their direction, when I saw, standing alone in the arcade, the now very familiar figure of Mr Wicks, Acting British Consul. He was surveying the square, arms folded in front of his chest. Mr Wicks was no longer smiling. Mr Wicks seemed to have lost his sense of tolerance.

'Has anybody,' he said, angry, tense, 'seen Mr Robert Boss?'

THE THING ABOUT reporting is that it is meant to be objective. It is meant to record and relay the truth of things, as if truth were out there, hanging around, waiting for the reporter to show up. Such is the premise of objective journalism. What this premise excludes, as any student of modern literature will tell you, is that slippery relative fact of the person doing the reporting, the modern notion that there is no such thing as the perceived without someone to do the perceiving, and that to exclude the circumstances surrounding the story is to tell an untruth. These circumstances might include the fact that you've rushed to an airplane, had too much to drink on it, arrived, realized that you are dressed for the tropics when in fact it is about to snow, that you have forgotten your socks, that you have only one contact lens, that you're not going to get the interview anyway, and then, at four-thirty, that you've got to file your story, having had to make most of it up. It could be argued that the circumstances have more than a casual bearing on the truth reported.

I do not want to tell an untruth and feel compelled therefore to note that at this moment, shortly after coming across the very disappointed figure of Mr Wicks, the reporter was aware that the circumstances surrounding his story had become intrusive and significant and that, if unacknowledged, his account of the events that follow would be grossly incomplete. And his circumstances were these: the reporter was very, very drunk.

He could not, therefore, recall much about the bus ride apart from a dim, watery belief that there were fewer people in the bus this time and that, astonishingly, he had got the *same* bus driver. The other thing he remembers is that he arrived.

When the coaches of United supporters pulled up into the cool evening shadow cast by the Stadio Comunale, a large crowd was already there. The fact of the crowd – that it would be waiting for the English – was hard to take in at first.

It was especially hard for Harry. Harry was the supporter I found myself sitting next to. But then, Harry was having difficulty taking in much – of anything. Like so many others, Harry had enjoyed the long hot afternoon, and all about him there was that gamey smell that comes from perspiring without interruption for a very long, though interdeterminate, period of time. Harry had been drinking since five that morning and had, by his own estimate, five imperial gallons of lager in his stomach, which, every time he turned, rolled of their own accord. Harry had been busy. He had been one of those who had abused the bus driver on the ride into the city, and he had abused the bus driver on the ride to the ground. He had urinated on to a café table that had, in his inimitable phrasing, a number of 'Eyetie cows' sitting round it, and he had then proceeded to abuse the waiters. In fact he had spent most of the day abusing waiters – many, many waiters. Who could know how many? They all looked so much alike that they blurred into one indiscriminate shape (round and short). He had abused the Acting British Consul, the police, hotel managers, food vendors of every description and any onlooker who didn't speak English – *especially* anybody who didn't speak English. All in all, Harry had had a good day out, and then, in the full, bloated arrogance of the moment, he saw the following: thousands of Italian supporters converging on Harry's coach. They had surrounded it and were pounding on its sides – jeering, ugly and angry. What right had they to be angry?

Do you see what they're doing? Harry said to the bloke behind me, full of indignation. And then if there's trouble, Harry said, they'll blame the English, won't they?

The fellow behind him agreed, but before he could say, 'Fuckin' Eyeties,' the bus started to rock from side to side. The Italians were trying to push the bus, our bus – the bus that had *me* inside it – on to its side.

I had not appreciated the importance of the match that evening, the semi-finals for the Cup-Winners Cup. It had sold out the day the tickets – seventy thousand of them – had gone on sale, and at that moment all seventy thousand ticket-holders seemed to be in view. In my ignorance, I had also not expected to see the English supporters, who were meant to be the hooligans, confronted by Italians who, to my untutored eye, looked like hooligans: their conduct – rushing towards the coaches, brandishing flags – was so exaggerated that it was like a caricature of a nineteenth-century mob. Was this how they normally greeted the supporters of visiting teams?

We remained sitting inside the buses. The drivers weren't opening their doors until more police arrived, and you could see the members of the *carabinieri*, just beyond the mob, pushing the Italian supporters out of the way until all four buses were encircled. They formed a cordon leading to the gate, and only then were we let out, escorted and then frisked by four different very young and very nervous policemen. All around us Italians were fighting to break through the cordon, shouting and gesticulating, their fingers forming the familiar upturned 'V'. This was turning into a very peculiar experience.

It took a long time for the buses to empty and fill the area set aside for us, enclosed by a chain-link fence. All along the fence were more Italians, their jeering insistent. One tried to go over the top and the police ran up to him, pulling him down by his trousers. As the last English supporter made his way into the enclosure, we were told something that I found hard to believe: that, inside, there were no seats.

I realized that I had never been given my match ticket and now I understood why: it didn't exist. Was it possible that a package tour had been arranged without tickets in the confidence that the authorities, afraid of English supporters on the streets, would somehow find a way of getting them into the ground? Bobby Boss, true to character, was not to be found.

And so we remained: standing, surrounded by a police guard and angry Italians, while somebody looked for a place to put the visiting English. At least I hoped somebody was doing that. At some point, during this long wait, the Italian supporters at the very top of the stadium – the top row that could overlook the grounds outside – realized that there was a gaggle of English below them. It must have been an exciting discovery: unlike their compatriots, they were not circumvented by a police cordon; they could – within the laws of gravity – do whatever they wanted. And they did. I remember the moment, looking up into the evening's pink sky, and watching the long, long slow arc of an object hurled from far above as it came closer and closer, gaining speed as it approached, until finally, in those milliseconds before it disclosed its target, I could actually make out what it was – a beer bottle – and then, *crash:* it shattered within three feet of one of the supporters.

Distant muted laughter from up high.

I feared what would follow. An English supporter went down, his forehead cut open. A policeman looked on. He was at a loss about what to do, even though his choices seemed fairly obvious: he could help the injured supporter (an ethical impossibility, since the supporter was a violent criminal); he could send police into the ground to stop the miscreants above us (an ethical contradiction, since *they* were the ones needing protection); he could move the English supporters into a more sheltered position, which must not have occurred to the policeman because what he did was this: nothing. He continued staring blankly as more things rained down upon us. Eventually he became a target as well. Eventually we all became targets, helpless underneath a barrage that consisted principally of beer bottles and oranges. There were so many bottles and so many oranges that the pavement, covered with juice and pulp and skins, was sticky to look at and sparkled from the shattered glass.

Mr Wicks appeared, having arrived in an embassy car. He looked frantic and pale. As he hurried past, I heard him mutter, perhaps as a muted greeting, 'Fucking Boss.'

Alas, Mr Wicks. He may have lost his friendliness but he retained his democratic principles to the end. He must have known that this was his last chance to prevent what he now knew was certain to happen. Was there any possible doubt? He had the police at his disposal; he had the perfect excuse – no seats! Wasn't this the time to gather everyone together and bundle them back to England? But, no, Mr Wicks, the democrat, did this: alternating between English and Italian, he shouted first for the beleaguered Jackie, whom he found hiding behind a policeman – the missiles, despite Mr Wicks's intervention, continued to fall from above – and demanded to know why there were no seats. He then shouted at the police officer in charge, dramatically pointing (the gestures, I thought, were impressively Mediterranean) to the ground around them with its array of objects recently shattered or smashed or squashed from impact. And then he shouted at one of the stadium stewards, who began shouting instructions to the other stadium officials, with the result that in very little time we were told that a space inside had been cleared to accommodate the English supporters.

When finally we were ushered through a tunnel that led to the ground, police in front and police behind, it became apparent that, while the English supporters may have been accommodated, their accommodation wasn't in the most salubrious part of the stadium. We were heading for the bottom steps of the terraces, directly beneath the very people who had been hurling missiles at us while we waited outside.

I did not like the look of this.

I kept thinking of the journalist from the *Daily Star*, the one who ran off when things got violent. He emerged in my mind now as an unequivocally sympathetic figure. He had, the supporters said, shit himself, and it was worth noting that this phrase had now entered my vocabulary.

I was not, I found myself muttering, going to shit myself.

One by one, we walked from out of the darkness of the tunnel into the blinding light of the ground – the sun, though setting, was at an angle and still shining bright – and it was hard to make out the figures around us. There were not many police – I could see that – and it appeared that Italians had spilled on to the pitch in front of the terraces where we were meant to stand, separated only by a chain-link perimeter fence. Once again things were coming at us from the air: not just bottles and pieces of fruit but also long sticks – the staffs of Juventus flags – firecrackers and smoke bombs. The first one out of the tunnel, drunk and arrogant and singing about his English pride, was hit on the back of the head by an eight-foot flag-pole and he dropped to the concrete terrace. Out of the corner of my eye I saw a Union Jack had been set alight, its flames fanned as it was swirled in the air. I saw this only out of the corner of my eye because I was determined not to look up at the Italians above me who were hurling things down, or down to the Italians below who were hurling things up. I had the suspicion that if I happened to make eye-contact with anybody I would be rewarded with a knock on the head. Also I didn't want to lose my concentration. Looking straight ahead, I was concentrating very hard on chanting my new refrain.

I will not shit myself, I will not shit myself.

As we arrived at the patch of concrete allocated for us, television cameramen appeared along the edges of the pitch. They looked Italian (thin, not beer-drinking) and were squatting between the missile-throwing Juventus fans. There was also a number of newspaper photographers. They looked English (fat, clearly beer-drinking). The curious thing about both the television and newspaper men was this: they were only a couple of feet away from the masked, missile-throwing Juventus fans. They could see that the English supporters were being felled – several people were on their knees holding their heads. I couldn't help thinking: it wouldn't take much effort to grab someone's arm, just as it was pulled back to hurl another pole or flare or smoke bomb or beer bottle; it would take even less effort to give one of them a little nudge; it would take virtually no effort at all to say a word or two urging these masked terrorists of the terraces to stop behaving in this way. Nobody did a thing. And while there is the old argument that to have done so would have been considered interventionist – participating in the event that they were meant to be reporting – for me, as one of the targets, such an argument was not very persuasive. They were not worried about getting in the way of the event. They were trying to create it: not only were they not stopping the masked, missile-throwing Juventus fans, but they were also not photographing them. It was images of the English they wanted.

They wanted the English tattoos; their sweaty torsos, stripped to the waist; their two fingers jabbing the air; the vicious expressions on their faces as they hurled back the objects that had been thrown at them. Italians behaving like hooligans? Unheard of. English behaving like English? *That* was interesting! I remember thinking: if the day becomes more violent, who do you blame? The English, whose behaviour on the square could be said to have been so provocative that they deserved whatever they got? The Italians, whose welcome consisted in inflicting injuries upon their visitors? Or can you place some of the blame on these men with their television equipment and their cameras, whose misrepresentative images served only to reinforce what everyone had come to expect.

Somehow the match started, was played, ended. And, while it could be said that there was no single serious incident, it could also be said that there was no moment without one. Several people were hurt, and one supporter was taken away to hospital. During the half-time break, when yet another Manchester lad was felled by a beer bottle, the English supporters, with a sudden roar, rushed to the top of the terraces, trying to climb the wall that separated them from the Italians. The wall was too high to scale, and the supporters ended up jumping up and down, trying to grab the Italians by their shoes until the police arrived to pull them away.

Police kept pouring through the tunnel, now wearing riot gear – moon helmets and blue uniforms instead of green – with obvious instructions to place themselves between each English supporter and everybody else. It was evident that the police continued to regard the English supporters as the problem, and they probably were simply by the fact that they were there. But they were not the only problem, which the police discovered after surrounding every English supporter and ignoring the Italians above them, who, in that uninhibited way that has come to characterize the Mediterranean temperament, continued to express their strong feelings: by the end it appeared to me that the police were being struck down more frequently than the English.

It was a peculiar setting for watching a sporting event, although, oddly, it didn't seem so at the time. The day had consisted of such a strange succession of events that, by this point in the evening, it was the most natural thing in the world to be watching a football game surrounded by policemen: there was one on my left, another on my right, two directly behind me and five in front. It didn't bother me; it certainly didn't bother the supporters, who, despite the distractions, were watching the match with complete attentiveness. And when Manchester United equalized, the goal was witnessed, as it unfolded, by everyone there (except me; I was looking over my shoulder for missiles), and jubilation shot through them, their cheers and songs suddenly tinny and small in that great cavity of the Juventus football ground, its seventy thousand Italians now comprehensively silent. The United supporters jumped up and down, fell over each other, embraced.

But the euphoria was brief. In the final two minutes Juventus scored again. The exhilaration felt but minutes before by that small band of United supporters was now felt – magnified many times – by the seventy thousand Italian fans who, previously humiliated, directed their powerful glee into our corner. The roar was deafening, invading the senses like a bomb.

And with that explosive roar, the mood changed.

What happened next is confusing to recall. Everything started moving at great speed. Everything would continue to move at great speed for many hours. I remember that riot police started kicking one of the supporters who had fallen down. I remember hearing that Sammy had arrived and then coming upon him. He was big, well-dressed, with heavy horn-rimmed glasses that made him look like a physics student, standing underneath the bleachers, his back to the match, an expensive leather bag and camera (Nikon) hanging over his shoulder, having just come from France by taxi. I remember watching Ricky and Micky, the improbable pair I had met on my early-morning minibus in London, scooting underneath the stands, exploiting the moment in which the Italians were embracing, crushed together in their celebrations, to come away with a handful of wallets, three purses and a watch, got by reaching up from below the seats. And I remember some screaming: there had been a stabbing (I didn't see it) and, with the screaming, everyone bolted – animal speed, instinct speed – and pushed past the police and rushed for the exit. But the gate into the tunnel was locked, and the United supporters slammed into it.

It was impossible to get out.

Throughout this last period of the match, I had been hearing a new phrase: 'It's going to go off.'

It's going to go off, someone said, and his eyes were glassy, as though he had taken a drug.

If this keeps up, I heard another say, then it's going to go off. And the phrase recurred – it's going to go off, it's going to go off – spoken softly, but each time it was repeated it gained authority.

Everyone was pressed against the locked gate, and the police arrived moments later. The police pulled and pushed in one direction, and the supporters pushed in another, wanting to get out. It was shove and counter-shove. It was crushing, uncomfortable. The supporters were humourless and determined.

It's going to go off.

People were whispering.

I heard: 'Watch out for knives. Zip up your coat.'

I heard: 'Fill up your pockets.'

I heard: 'It's going to go off. Stay together. It's going to go off.'

I was growing nervous and slipped my notebook into my shirt, up against my chest, and buttoned up my jacket. A chant had started: 'United. United. United.' The chant was clipped and sure. 'United. United. United.' The word was repeated, *United*, and, through the repetition, its meaning started changing, pertaining less to a sporting event or a football club and sounding instead like a chant of unity – something political. It had become the chant of a mob.

'United. United. United. United. United. United . . .'

And then it stopped.

There was a terrible screaming, a loud screaming, loud enough to have risen above the chant. The sound was out of place; it was a woman's screaming.

Someone said that it was the mother of the stabbed boy.

Someone said that it was no such thing, just a 'fucking Eyetie'.

The screaming went on. It appeared that a woman had been caught by the rush to get away and swept along by it. I spotted her: she was hemmed in and thrashing about, trying to find some space, some air. She couldn't move towards the exit and couldn't move away from it, and she wasn't going to be able to: the crush was too great, and it wouldn't stay still, surging back and forth by its own volition, beyond the control of anyone in it. She was very frightened. Her scream, piercing and high-pitched, wouldn't stop. She started hyperventilating, taking in giant gulps of air, and her screams undulated with the relentless rhythm of her over-breathing: it was as if she were drowning in her own high-pitched oxygen, swinging her head from side to side, her eyes wild. I thought: Why hasn't she passed out? I was waiting for her to lose consciousness, for her muscles to give up, but she didn't pass out. The scream went on. Nobody around me was saying a word. I could tell that they were thinking what I was thinking, that she was going to have a fit, that she was going to die, there, now, pressed up against them. It went on, desperate and unintelligible and urgent.

And then someone had the sense to lift her up and raise her above his shoulders – it was so obvious – and he passed her to the person in front of him. And he passed her to the person in front of him. And in this way, she was passed, hand to hand, above everyone's heads, still screaming, still flailing, slowly making her way to the exit, and then, once there, the gate was opened to let her out.

And it was all that was needed. Once the gate had been opened, the English supporters surged forwards, pushing her heavily to one side.

I was familiar with the practice of keeping visiting supporters locked inside at the end of a match until everyone had left, and of using long lines of police, with horses and dogs, to direct the visitors to their coaches. The plan in Turin had been the same, and the police were there, outside the gate, in full riot regalia, waiting for the United supporters. But they weren't ready for what came charging out of the tunnel.

For a start, owing to the trapped woman, the supporters came out earlier than expected – the streets were filled with Juventus supporters – and when they emerged, they came out very fast, with police trailing behind, trying to keep up. They came as a mob, with everyone pressed together, hands on the shoulders of the person in front, moving quickly, almost at a sprint, racing down the line of police, helmets and shields and truncheons a peripheral blur. The line of police led to the coaches, but just before the coach door someone in the front veered sharply and the mob followed. The police had anticipated this and were waiting. The group turned again, veering in another direction, and rushed out into the space between two of the coaches. It came to a sudden stop, and I slammed into the person in front of me, and people slammed into me from behind: the police had been there as well. Everyone turned round. I don't know who was in front – I was trying only to keep up – and nothing was being said. There were about two hundred people crushed together, but they seemed able to move in unison, like some giant, strangely co-ordinated insect. A third direction was tried. The police were not there. I looked behind: the police were not there. I looked to the left and the right: there was no police anywhere.

What was the duration of what followed? It might have been twenty minutes; it seemed longer. It was windy and dark, and the trees, blowing back and forth in front of the street lamps, cast long, moving shadows. I was never able to see clearly.

I knew to follow Sammy. The moment the group broke free, he had handed his bag and camera to someone, telling him to give them back later at the hotel. Sammy then turned and started running backwards. He appeared to be measuring the group, taking in its size.

The energy, he said, still running backwards, speaking to no one in particular, the energy is very high. He was alert, vital, moving constantly, looking in all directions. He was holding out his hands, with his fingers outstretched.

Feel the energy, he said.

There were six or seven younger supporters jogging beside him, and it would be some time before I realized that there were always six or seven younger supporters jogging beside him. When he turned in one direction, they turned with him. When he ran backwards, they ran backwards. No doubt if Sammy had suddenly become airborne there would have been the sight of six or seven younger supporters desperately flapping their arms trying to do the same. The younger supporters were in fact very young. At first I put their age at around sixteen, but they might have been younger. They might have been fourteen. They might have been nine: I take pleasure, even now, in thinking of them as nothing more than overgrown nine-year-olds. They were nasty little nine-year-olds who, in some kind of pre-pubescent confusion, regarded Sammy as their dad. The one nearest me had a raw, skinny face with a greasy texture that suggested an order of fish'n'chips. He was the one who turned on me.

Who the fuck are you?

I said nothing, and Fish'n'chips repeated his question – Who the fuck are you? – and then Sammy said something, and Fish'n'chips forgot about me. But it was a warning: the nine-year-old didn't like me.

Sammy had stopped running backwards and had developed a kind of walk-run, which involved moving as quickly as possible without breaking into an outright sprint. Everybody else did the same: the idea, it seemed, was to be inconspicuous – not to be seen to be actually running, thus attracting the attention of the police – but nevertheless to jet along as fast as you could. The effect was ridiculous: two hundred English supporters, tattooed torsos tilted slightly forwards, arms straight, hurtling stiffly down the pavement, believing that nobody was noticing them.

Everyone crossed the street, decisively, without a word spoken. A chant broke out – 'United, United, United' – and Sammy waved his hands up and down, as if trying to bat down the flames of a fire, urging people to be quiet. A little later there was another one-word chant: this time it was 'England'. They couldn't help themselves. They wanted so badly to act like normal football supporters – they wanted to sing and behave drunkenly and carry on doing the same rude things that they had been doing all day long – and they had to be reminded that they couldn't. Why this pretence of being invisible? There was Sammy again, whispering, insistent: no singing, no singing, waving his hands up and down. The nine-year-olds made a shushing sound to enforce the message.

Sammy said to cross the street again – he had seen something –

and his greasy little companions went off in different directions, fanning out, as if to hold the group in place, and then returned to their positions beside him. It was only then that I appreciated fully what I was witnessing: Sammy had taken charge of the group – moment by moment giving it specific instructions – and was using his obsequious little lads to ensure that his commands were being carried out.

I remembered, on my first night with Mick, hearing that leaders had their little lieutenants and sergeants. I had heard this and I had noted it, but I hadn't thought much of it: it sounded too much like toyland, like a war game played by schoolboys. But here, now, I could see that everything Sammy said was being enforced by his entourage of little supporters. Fish'n'chips and the other nine-year-olds made sure that no one ran, that no one sang, that no one strayed far from the group, that everyone stayed together. At one moment, a cluster of police came rushing towards us, and Sammy, having spotted them, whispered a new command, hissing that we were to disperse, and the members of the group split up – some crossing the street, some carrying on down the centre of it, some falling behind – until they had got past the policemen, whereupon Sammy turned round, running backwards again, and ordered everyone to regroup: and the little ones, like trained dogs, herded the members of the group back together.

I trotted along. Everyone was moving at such a speed that, to ensure I didn't miss anything, I concentrated on keeping up with Sammy. I could see that this was starting to irritate him. He kept having to notice me.

What are you doing here? he asked me, after he had turned round again, running backwards, doing a quick head-count after everyone had regrouped.

He knew precisely what I was doing there, and he had made a point of asking his question loudly enough that the others had to hear it as well.

Just the thing, I thought.

Fuck off, one of his runts said suddenly, peering into my face. He had a knife.

Didja hear what he said, mate? Fish'n'chips had joined the interrogation. He said fuck off. What the fuck are you doing here anyway, eh? Fuck off.

It was not the time or the occasion to explain to Fish'n'chips why I was there, and, having got this far, I wasn't about to turn around now.

I dropped back a bit, just outside of striking range. I looked about me. I didn't recognize anyone. I was surrounded by people I hadn't met; worse, I was surrounded by people I hadn't met who kept telling me to fuck off. I felt I had understood the drunkenness I had seen earlier in the day. But this was different. If anyone here was drunk, he was not acting as if he was. Everyone was purposeful and precise, and there was a strong quality of aggression about them, like some kind of animal scent. Nobody was saying a word. There was a muted grunting and the sound of their feet on the pavement; every now and then, Sammy would whisper one of his commands. In fact the loudest sound had been Sammy's asking me what I was doing there, and the words of the exchange rang round in my head.

What the fuck are you doing here anyway, eh? Fuck off.
What the fuck are you doing here anyway, eh? Fuck off.

I remember thinking in the clearest possible terms: I don't want to get beaten up.

I had no idea where we were, but, thinking about it now, I see that Sammy must have been leading his group around the stadium, hoping to find Italian supporters along the way. When he turned to run backwards, he must have been watching the effect his group of two hundred walk-running Frankensteins was having on the Italian lads, who spotted the English rushing by and started following them, curious, attracted by the prospect of a fight or simply by the charisma of the group itself, unable to resist tagging along to see what might happen.

And then Sammy, having judged the moment to be right, suddenly stopped, and, abandoning all pretence of invisibility, shouted: 'Stop.'

Everyone stopped.

'Turn.'

Everyone turned. They knew what to expect. I didn't. It was only then that I saw the Italians who had been following us. In the half-light, street-light darkness I couldn't tell how many there were, but there were enough for me to realize – holy shit! – that I was now unexpectedly in the middle of a very big fight: having dropped back to get out of the reach of Sammy and his lieutenants I was in the rear, which, as the group turned, had suddenly become the front.

Adrenalin is one of the body's more powerful chemicals. Seeing the English on one side of me and the Italians on the other, I remember seeming quickly to take on the properties of a small helicopter, rising several feet in the air and moving out of everybody's way. There was a roar, everybody roaring, and the English supporters charged into the Italians.

In the next second I went down. A dark blur and then smack: I got hit on the side of the head by a beer can – a full one – thrown powerfully enough to knock me over. As I got up, two policemen, the only two I saw, came rushing past, and one of them clubbed me on the back of the head. Back down I went. I got up again, and most of the Italians had already run off, scattering in all directions. But many had been tripped up before they got away.

Directly in front of me – so close I could almost reach out to touch his face – a young Italian, a boy really, had been knocked down. As he was getting up, an English supporter pushed the boy down again, ramming his flat hand against the boy's face. He fell back and his head hit the pavement, the back of it bouncing slightly.

Two other Manchester United supporters appeared. One kicked the boy in the ribs. It was a soft sound, which surprised me. You could hear the impact of the shoe on the fabric of the boy's clothing. He was kicked again – this time very hard – and the sound was still soft, muted. The boy reached down to protect himself, to guard his ribs, and the other English supporter then kicked him in the face. This was a soft sound as well, but it was different: you could tell that it was his face that had been kicked and not his body and not something protected by clothing. It sounded gritty. The boy tried to get up and he was pushed back down – sloppily, without much force. Another Manchester United supporter appeared and another and then a third. There were now six, and they all started kicking the boy on the ground. The boy covered his face. I was surprised that I could tell, from the sound, when someone's shoe missed or when it struck the fingers and not the forehead or the nose.

I was transfixed. I suppose, thinking about this incident now, I was close enough to have stopped the kicking. Everyone there was off-balance – with one leg swinging back and forth – and it wouldn't have taken much to have saved the boy. But I didn't. I don't think the thought occurred to me. It was as if time had dramatically slowed down, and each second had a distinct beginning and end, like a sequence of images on a roll of film, and I was mesmerized by each image I saw. Two more Manchester United supporters appeared – there must have been eight by now. It was getting crowded and difficult to get at the boy: they were bumping into each other, tussling slightly. It was hard for me to get a clear view or to say where exactly the boy was now being kicked, but it looked like there were three people kicking him in the head, and the others were kicking him in the body – mainly the ribs but I couldn't be sure. I am astonished by the detail I can recall. For instance, there was no speech, only that soft, yielding sound – although sometimes it was a gravelly, scraping one – of the blows, one after another. The moments between the kicks seemed to increase in duration, to stretch elastically, as each person's leg was retracted and then released for another blow.

The thought of it: eight people kicking the boy at once. At what point is the job completed?

It went on.

The boy continued to try to cushion the blows, moving his hands around to cover the spot were he had just been struck, but he was being hit in too many places to be able to protect himself. His face was now covered with blood, which came from his nose and his mouth, and his hair was matted and wet. Blood was all over his clothing. The kicking went on. On and on and on, that terrible soft sound, with the boy saying nothing, only wriggling on the ground.

A policeman appeared, but only one. Where were the other police? There had been so many before. The policeman came running hard and knocked over two of the supporters, and the others fled, and then time accelerated, no longer slow-motion time, but time moving very fast.

We ran off. I don't know what happened to the boy. I then noticed that all around me there were others like him, others who had been tripped up and had their faces kicked; I had to side-step a body on the ground to avoid running on top of it.

In the vernacular of the supporters, it had now 'gone off'. With that first violent exchange, some kind of threshold had been crossed, some notional boundary: on one side of that boundary had been a sense of limits, an ordinary understanding – even among this lot – of what you didn't do; we were now someplace where there would be few limits, where the sense that there were things you didn't do had ceased to exist. It became very violent.

A boy came rushing towards me, holding his head, bleeding badly from somewhere on his face, watching the ground, not knowing where he was going, and looked up just before he would have run into me. The fact of me frightened him. He thought I was English. He thought I was going to hit him. He screamed, pleading, and spun round backwards to get away and ran off in another direction.

I caught up with Sammy. Sammy was transported. He was snapping his fingers and jogging in place, his legs pumping up and down, and he was repeating the phrase, It's going off, it's going off. Everyone around him was excited. It was an excitement that verged on being something greater, an emotion more transcendent – joy at the very least, but more like ecstasy. There was an intense energy about it; it was impossible not to feel some of the thrill. Somebody near me said that he was happy. He said that he was very, very happy, that he could not remember ever being so happy, and I looked hard at him, wanting to memorize his face so that I might find him later and ask him what it was that made for this happiness, what it was like. It was a strange thought: here was someone who believed that, at this precise moment, following a street scuffle, he had succeeded in capturing one of life's most elusive qualities. But then he, dazed, babbling away about his happiness, disappeared into the crowd and the darkness.

There was more going on than I could assimilate: there were violent noises constantly – something breaking or crashing – and I could never tell where they were coming from. In every direction something was happening. I have no sense of sequence.

I remember the man with his family. Everyone had regrouped, brought together by the little lieutenants, and was jogging along in that peculiar walk-run, and I noticed that in front of us was a man with his family, a wife and two sons. He was shooing them along, trying to make them hurry, while looking repeatedly over his shoulder at us. He was anxious, but no one seemed to notice him: everyone just carried on, trotting at the same speed, following him not because they wanted to follow him but only because he happened to be running in front of us. When the man reached his car, a little off to the side of the path we were following, he threw open the door and shoved the members of his family inside, panicking slightly and badly bumping the head of one of his sons. And then, just as he was about to get inside himself, he looked back over his shoulder – just as the group was catching up to him – and he was struck flatly across the face with a heavy metal bar. He was struck with such force that he was lifted into the air and carried over his car door on to the ground on the other side. Why him, I thought? What had he done except make himself conspicuous by trying to get his family out of the way? I turned, as we jogged past him, and the supporters behind me had rammed into the open car door, bending it backwards on its hinges. The others followed, running on top of the man on the ground, sometimes slowing down to kick him – the head, the spine, the ass, the ribs, anywhere. I couldn't see his wife and children, but knew they were inside, watching from the back seat.

There was an Italian boy, eleven or twelve years old, alone, who had got confused and ran straight into the middle of the group and past me. I looked behind me and saw that the boy was already on the ground. I couldn't tell who had knocked him down, because by the time I looked back six or seven English supporters had already set upon him, swarming over his body, frenzied.

There was a row of tables where programmes were sold, along with flags, T-shirts, souvenirs, and as the group went by each table was lifted up and overturned. There were scuffles. Two English supporters grabbed an Italian and smashed his face into one of the tables. They grabbed him by the hair on the back of his head and slammed his face into the table again. They lifted his head up a third time, pulling it higher, holding it there – his face was messy and crushed – and slammed it into the table again. Once again the terrible slow motion of it all, the time, not clock-time, that elapsed between one moment of violence and the next one, as they lifted his head up – were they really going to do it again? – and smashed it into the table. The English supporters were methodical and serious; no one spoke.

An ambulance drove past. Its siren made me realize that there was still no police.

The group crossed a street, a major intersection. It had long abandoned the pretence of invisibility and had reverted to the arrogant identity of the violent crowd, walking, without hesitation, straight into the congested traffic, across the bonnets of the cars, knowing that they would stop. At the head of the traffic was a bus, and one of the supporters stepped up to the front of it, and from about six feet, hurled something with great force – it wasn't a stone; it was big and made of a metal, like the manifold of a car engine – straight into the driver's windscreen. I was just behind the one who threw this thing. I don't know where he got it from, because it was too heavy to have been carried for any distance, but no one had helped him with it; he had stepped out of the flow of the group and in those moments between throwing his heavy object and turning back to his mates he had a peculiar look on his face. He knew he had done something that no one else had done yet, that it had escalated the violence, that the act had crossed another boundary of what was permissible. He had thrown a missile that was certain to cause serious physical injury. He had done something bad – extremely bad – and his face, while acknowledging the badness of it, was actually saying something more complex. It was saying that what he had done wasn't all that bad, really; in the context of the day, it wasn't that extreme, was it? What his face expressed, I realized – his eyes seemed to twinkle – was no more than this: I have just been naughty.

He had been naughty and he knew it and was pleased about it. He was happy. Another happy one. He was a runt, I thought. He was a little shit, I thought. I wanted to hurt him.

The sound of the shattering windscreen – I realize now – was a powerful stimulant, physical and intrusive, and it had been the range of sounds, of things breaking and crashing, coming from somewhere in the darkness, unidentifiable, that was increasing steadily the strength of feeling of everyone around me. It was also what was making me so uneasy. The evening had been a series of stimulants, assaults on the senses, that succeeded, each time, in raising the pitch of excitement. And now, crossing this intersection, traffic coming from four directions, supporters trotting on top of cars, the sound of this thing going through the windscreen, the crash following its impact, had the effect of increasing the heat of the feeling: I can't describe it any other way; it was almost literally a matter of temperature. There was another moment of disorientation – the milliseconds between the sensation of the sound and knowing what accounted for it, an adrenalin moment, a chemical moment – and then there was the roar again, and someone came rushing at the bus with a pole (taken from one of the souvenir tables?) and smashed a passenger's window. A second crashing sound. Others came running over and started throwing stones and bottles with great ferocity. They were, again, in a frenzy. The stones bounced off the glass with a shuddering thud, but then a window shattered, and another shattered, and there was screaming from inside. The bus was full, and the passengers were not lads like the ones attacking them but ordinary family supporters, dads and sons and wives heading home after the match, on their way to the suburbs or a village outside the city. Everyone inside must have been covered with glass. They were shielding their faces, ducking in their seats. There were glass splinters everywhere: they would cut across your vision suddenly. All around me people were throwing stones and bottles, and I felt afraid for my own eyes.

We moved on.

I felt weightless. I felt nothing would happen to me. I felt that anything might happen to me. I was looking straight ahead, running, trying to keep up, and things were occurring along the dark peripheries of my vision: there would be a bright light and then darkness again and the sound, constantly, of something else breaking, and of movement, of objects being thrown and of people falling.

A group of Italians appeared, suddenly stepping forward into the glare of a street lamp. They were different from the others, clearly intending to fight, full of pride and affronted dignity. They wanted confrontation and stood there waiting for it. Someone came towards us swinging a pool cue or a flag-pole, and then, confounding all sense, it was actually grabbed from out his hands – it was Roy; Roy had appeared out of nowhere and had taken the pole out of the Italian's hands – and broken it over his head. It was flamboyantly timed, and the next moment the other English supporters followed, that roar again, quickly overcoming the Italians, who ran off in different directions. Several, again, were tripped up. There was the sight, again, of Italians on the ground, wriggling helplessly while English supporters rushed up to them, clustering around their heads, kicking them over and over again.

Is it possible that there was simply no police?

Again we moved on. A bin was thrown through a car showroom window, and there was another loud crashing sound. A shop: its door was smashed. A clothing shop: its window was smashed, and one or two English supporters lingered to loot from the display.

I looked behind me and I saw that a large vehicle had been overturned, and that further down the street flames were issuing from a building. I hadn't seen any of that happen: I realized that there had been more than I had been able to take in. There was now the sound of sirens, many sirens, different kinds, coming from several directions.

The city is ours, Sammy said, and he repeated the possessive, each time with greater intensity: It is *ours, ours, ours*.

A police car appeared, its siren on – the first police car I had seen – and it stopped in front of the group, trying to cut it off. There was only one car. The officer threw open his door, but by the time he had got out the group had crossed the street. The officer shouted after us, helpless and angry, and then dropped back inside his car and chased us down, again cutting us off. Once again, the group, in the most civilized manner possible, crossed the street: well-behaved football supporters on their way back to their hotel, flames receding behind us. The officer returned to his car and drove after us, this time accelerating dangerously, once again cutting off the group, trying, it seemed to me, to knock down one of the supporters, who had to jump out of the way and who was then grabbed by the police officer and hurled against the bonnet, held there by his throat. The officer was very frustrated. He knew that this group was responsible for the damage he had seen; he knew, beyond all reasonable doubt, that the very lad whose throat was now in his grip had been personally responsible for mayhem of some categorically illegal kind; but the officer had not personally seen him do anything. He hadn't personally seen the group do anything. He had not seen anyone commit a crime. He saw only the results. He kept the supporter pinned there, holding him by the throat, and then in disgust he let him go.

A fire engine passed, an ambulance and finally the police – many police. They came from two directions. And once they started arriving, it seemed that they would never stop. There were vans and cars and motorcycles and paddy wagons. And still they came. The buildings were illuminated by their flashing blue lights. But the group of supporters from Manchester, governed by Sammy's whispered commands, simply kept moving, slipping past the cars, dispersing when needing to disperse and then regrouping, turning this way, that way, crossing the street again, regrouping, reversing, with Sammy's greasy little lieutenants bringing up the rear, keeping everyone together. They were well-behaved fans of the sport of football. They were once again the law-abiding supporters they had always insisted to me that they were. And, thus, they snaked through the streets of the ancient city of Turin, making their orderly way back to their hotels, the police following behind, trying to keep up.

'We did it,' Sammy declared, as the group reached the railway station. 'We took the city.'

BETWEEN THE HOURS of one and two in the morning, the square was once again the interesting place to be. Many people were there.

There were the Italians. Twelve hours before, these same Italians had been generous and accommodating: they had been confronted by a body of unkempt drunken foreigners who littered the streets, urinated into their fountains and stole from the tills of their cafés and shops, and yet they would not be offended. They laughed; they were amused. These were the antics of an island race; the English, as everybody knows, are a mad people.

By the early hours of Thursday morning, the Italians had ceased being amused. I heard them as they approached the square, marching down the side-streets, chanting, or in their cars, holding down their horns, driving round the square, shouting angrily from their windows. The most frightening were the ones who were already here. I could see them but I couldn't hear them. They stood, awesomely silent, in the centre of the square itself. I watched them from the entrance to my hotel – the supporters were inside at the bar – and I could make out their menacing silhouettes in the darkness. I was told that they had knives and bottles broken off at the neck and heavy sticks. They were waiting: at some point, the English would have to go home. The Italians were stretched from one end of the square to the other, row upon row. They didn't move; no one among them was talking.

There were others on the square as well. There was the army. I didn't know when the troops had been called in.

They had not been there earlier, when Sammy led us past the

railway station – the police still trailing behind – and then into the hotel bar, which, I was surprised to discover, was already crowded with supporters. It was packed, and was humid and steamy and marked by a strong barnyard smell. I spotted Mick, sober now, who had spent several hours in jail, having inadvertently broken someone's leg (in two places) during a disagreement, and was eager to learn of everything he had missed. I spotted Roy, who – such was the evening's achievement – was talking not only like a normal human being but also in an animated and extrovert fashion: he was describing the run through the city to those who had not joined in. There was Tony – dressed elegantly for the evening – and Gurney, as repellent as ever. I was back among friends, and there was some comfort in that. The nine-year-olds must have gone to bed.

There was little talk of the match and no evident regret that the team would not be playing in the final – the fortunes of Manchester United Football Club had been obscured by the larger concerns of the evening and how the Italians had 'shat themselves'. There was a sense of closure to the evening, an end-of-a-good-day's-work atmosphere.

I got a beer and sat in a corner. The supporters were sprawled on the floor and propped against the walls, tending wounds, which, mainly to the hands, were bleeding and wrapped in T-shirts. Despite the exhaustion – the effort of wreaking mayhem on a major city was considerable – the gathering was alive, noisy with grunts and profanities. Their rudeness was their vitality, and these people were very rude; they were committed to rudeness, as though it were their moral banner. There were only two waitresses amid the four hundred or so supporters, and the women could not have had a worse working day. As one was delivering a tray of bottled lager – answering to the imperative of, 'Oi, bitch, give us some beer' – a supporter pulled out his penis and wagged it in her face. Another one, paying, threw his money at her feet.

The supporters did not have a developed aptitude for meeting new people. They did not like people, apart from themselves. In fact, they didn't like anything — much. I reflected on the values at the heart of their community. I composed a list.

Likes:
Lager in pint glasses.
Lager in two-litre bottles.
The Queen.
The Falkland Islands.
Manchester United Football Club.
Margaret Thatcher.
Goals.
Rolex watches.
War movies.
The Catholic Church.
Expensive jumpers.
Being abroad.
Sausages.
Lots of money.
Themselves.

That was the most important item: they liked themselves; them and their mates.

The list of dislikes, I decided, was straightforward. It was (over and above Tottenham Hotspur) the following: the rest of the world.

The rest of the world is a big place, and its essential inhabitant is the stranger. The supporters did not like the stranger. The stranger — shopkeepers, employees of the London Underground or British Rail, old men in your way on the escalator, people asking for directions, someone trying to get your vote, bus-conductors, waitresses, members of the Labour Party, people in the seat next to you, simply people *in the way* — was detestable.

And there was no stranger more strange, and therefore no stranger more detestable, than the foreigner. The foreigner was the one they really hated (it was not admissible that they, being from England and now in Italy, might have been foreigners). The problem with foreigners was this: they were incomplete. For some reason, foreigners had never quite climbed all the way up the evolutionary ladder; there was a little *less* of the foreigner – especially foreigners of a dark complexion, not to mention foreigners of a dark complexion who were also trying to sell you something. They were the worst.

And then something calamitous occurred: the hotel ran out of beer.

It was the middle of the night, and the hotel had been emptied of its stocks of alcohol. No beer? The news was greeted with an incredulity that exceeded anything expressed so far. No hotel, no match tickets, no match: these were nothing compared to the announcement that there was no beer. With the news, everyone – the maimed, the drunk, the comatose – rose to his feet and charged the bar. This looked bad. The hotel manager appeared, conciliatory, offering orange juice. This made things worse.

As they surged forward, I dropped back. It would be safer, I thought, outside. And that was when I realized that the troops had been called in.

I had no choice but to notice the troops because the moment I stepped out one of them blocked my way with an automatic rifle, turned me round and marched me to the wall. The troops must have been gathering for some time. The *carabinieri* had failed; the riot police had failed; now it was the army's turn. I suspect there were only about a hundred troops, but they represented an altogether different order of control: suddenly we were in a NATO exercise. The soldiers were wearing camouflage-green infantry uniforms and big heavy black shiny boots and carrying very authoritative-looking guns. They also had fifteen armoured personnel carriers and a tank. The tank was on the other side of the square, pointing in our direction. This was not a comfortable idea. I have had a gun barrel pointed at me, and I didn't like it. I had never been at the end of a barrel of a tank, although it was probably because the barrel of the tank was pointed in our direction that the Italians on the square remained on the square.

I thought I would stay put for a while – the wall where I had been placed offered a reasonable vantage point from which to view events – and so I missed the expressions on the faces of the four hundred or so supporters as they turned from the counter of the bar they had been pounding and faced an army colonel flanked by eager soldiers with automatic weapons. The colonel ordered that the bar be vacated, and more soldiers rushed in – they were incapable of walking – and pushed everyone into a single file line.

Mr Wicks arrived.

I had expected him. He had been chasing around the city to bring us a little surprise – he left it in the back seat of his car – but knew everything that had taken place in the meanwhile. He knew what had happened after the match, about the angry Italians waiting in the dark, that the army had been called in, and even what the Italian newspapers were going to say in the morning – he had seen them.

Mr Wicks: I had grown fond of him and his faith in humanity. He had such high hopes for what had come out of the airplane in the morning. And now: he wasn't angry or upset; he was resigned.

'You lot,' Mr Wicks said, shaking his head. 'You lot really did it this time.'

The first armoured personnel carrier pulled up. It was a peculiar-looking contraption – something between a farm tractor and a World War Two tank, camouflaged for the tropical rain forest. A hatch opened, a small thing in the front, and out popped a soldier. He, too, was one of the eager ones and, on gaining his feet, he sprinted to the colonel standing by the hotel entrance. It was only then that I understood why these strange combat vehicles were needed. Only a few English supporters were staying at this particular hotel. Most were elsewhere – somewhere on the other side of the square; somewhere, that is, on the other side of the Italians waiting in the dark. One of the evening's ironies had revealed itself: the Italian authorities were about to provide an armed escort to ensure that the United supporters got to their hotels without being maimed by angry locals out for revenge. The Italian army had been called out to convey the English to their beds, in groups of five, huddled inside an armoured personnel carrier.

There was one problem: few English supporters knew where they were staying.

In her way, Jackie had been trying to tell the supporters where they were staying since we arrived in Turin. The colonel by her side reassured her that this time none of them would slip away. Jackie, satisfied, gathered together the papers on her clipboard and proceeded to call out the names – loudly, clearly, imperiously – one by one. On hearing his name, each supporter was instructed to step forward and was then rushed away by two soldiers to a waiting armoured personnel carrier. The first vehicle was filled and drove off. And then the second. By the third vehicle, the supporters were well into one of their chants, urging the Pope to get fucked, but Jackie was not to be deterred. Jackie was in control at last.

Mr Wicks, meanwhile, had returned from his car, having fetched his surprise. It was Mr Robert Boss.

I was disappointed. I had got used to the idea that Bobby Boss didn't exist; that he had been invented by the supporters, an elaborate laundering operation that allowed them to buy tickets, book hotels, even hire guides like Jackie so that they could then go about the business of doing what that they had been banned from doing.

But there he was: a fact, the man himself.

He was short, dumpy and balding, and wearing a white linen suit that would have flattered a man many times thinner.

Although the evening had grown cool, Bobby Boss was perspiring heavily, and his suit, which was tight behind the arms, was sticking heavily to his back. His forehead was damp and clammy, and his skin had the quality of wet synthetic underpants.

Mr Wicks turned out to be something of a detective and had tracked down Bobby Boss in Turin's most expensive restaurant – it was, Mr Wicks had concluded, Mr Robert Boss's business to know where to find quality – and pulled him away before he could finish his meal. This was, I was told, the first time that Bobby Boss had seen the people on one of his package tours. It had not been Bobby Boss's intention ever to see them; it was only his affection for pasta that had compelled him at the last minute to join the trip. The decision was being regretted; Bobby Boss did not look happy.

Everybody there wanted to ask him questions. They were trying to make him accountable for the damage and the injuries and the embarrassment. I wanted to ask him questions as well and decided that I would phone him when I returned. In my eyes, Bobby Boss was nothing less than evil, a wide-boy of working-class sport, a cowboy on the make, one of the little men who sells you more seats than he has to offer, wants more cash than there are receipts to show for it, an expert in securing a bit of this, a bit of that. Why had he told people there would be seats when there weren't even tickets? I wanted to ask. Why, when the United supporters were banned, had he sold them a package to Turin? But when I phoned, I got the steady tone of a disconnected line. I tried Directory Enquiries. There was no Bobby Boss Travel Agency. I looked in the phone book for Bobby Boss, B. Boss, Robert Boss, R. Boss and tried each one. Bobby Boss, I concluded, had packed up and was into something else.

Jackie was reaching the end of her list, and the last armoured vehicle had rolled up to the front of the hotel. The Italians across the square had grown impatient: they would be heading home soon. The colonel had ordered his soldiers into formation. And

Bobby Boss – his trousers clinging to the skin along the back of his thighs – was engaged in an intense conversation with Mr Wicks. I don't know how he had done it but Bobby Boss had shifted the scrutiny away from himself. He was selling again; he was offering Mr Wicks a discount on a package tour to the next World Cup. He was prepared to throw in the hotel at no extra cost. Bobby Boss was trying very hard to get Mr Wicks to like him. But Mr Wicks was not buying.

The next morning, Mick was first to show up at the square. It was safe now – no soldiers or avenging mobs of Italians – and the atmosphere was distinctly subdued: the morning after the night before. By the time I arrived, Mick was well into an eight-litre bottle of red wine. I have since seen eight-litre bottles of wine – they are called Methuselahs – but I hadn't seen one at the time. It was gigantic and unwieldy but, according to Mick, extremely good value. You had to admire his strength; his stomach must have been made of bricks.

I spotted Clayton. He had not brought a change of clothing and was wrestling with the same pair of trousers, now colourfully stained. I hadn't seen him the night before: having passed out early in the afternoon, he had missed the match and had woken up this morning inside a cardboard box.

By eleven o'clock, most of the supporters had surfaced, and it was evident that, although our flight back was early in the afternoon, the day was not going to be very different from the one before. This was a prospect that was difficult to contemplate, but the fact was everyone had had a head start. The quantity of alcohol already in the bloodstream *before* anyone started drinking again was considerable: a few hours' sleep wasn't about to undo yesterday's good work. And by the time the supporters reached the airport, they were spectacularly drunk – again. They came crashing out of the coaches, tripping over each other, singing loudly, zig-zagging as they roared into the terminal.

I was tired. I had seen enough. But I didn't have a choice: I was going to see more.

When we finally got outside the terminal, one of the supporters passed out. He had just about reached the bus that was to take us to the plane when he dropped to his knees and fell on to his face, unconscious. The temptation must have been to leave him there. It didn't seem sensible that, in his state, he should be allowed to fly: he was bound to get sick; he might have been very ill. None of this was as dangerous as allowing him to remain behind. Four soldiers lifted him up and heaved him on to the bus.

Meanwhile, Mick had started to act up. I don't know what had happened to his eight-litre bottle of red wine. I fear that he had drunk it. He was on to lager now, ordinary can size.

Once outside, Mick had thought it would be amusing if he made a dash for the runway. He sprinted – a sight in itself – into the open territory of the landing-strip, and the airport was thrown into a panic. Someone started shouting in Italian, and ten or twelve soldiers bolted across the tarmac in pursuit of one very large English supporter in a state of dangerous intoxication. Mick stopped just short of the runway and waited for the soldiers, giggling and hooting and pointing his finger. He thought it would be more amusing if, once the soldiers had caught up with him, he then ran off in another direction. More panic, more urgent shouting, as Mick – from our vantage place by the terminal, a large dot in the distance – ran round in circles frantically chased by smaller dots in uniforms. When I returned to England, Mick was to send me a package of photographs that someone had taken after he had been apprehended by the soldiers. 'I don't remember,' Mick wrote, 'any of it happening. Isn't that funny?'

On reflection, I can see now that there had been more people there than expected. I had recognized some of the nine-year-olds from the night before, and I did not think that they had been on the plane from London. I had spotted Roy, who I knew had not been on the plane. But I didn't think much of it. I had other concerns.

My first one had been retrieving my passport. One of the younger supporters had been staring at it uncomprehendingly when it, along with his own British passport, was inexplicably delivered into his hands. The reason why it was in his possession and not mine was because of the perplexing pandemonium at passport control.

Once the supporters had passed into the terminal from the buses outside, they all made straight for the immigration desks. They were weaving and bobbing and swaying from side to side from the drink, but were nevertheless so purposeful that it made me think that the flight was about to leave. But this was not likely: we were early, and, besides, the flight was a charter: what was the hurry? There were cries for order, but they were ignored. I heard the voice of Mr Wicks, rising above the clamour, begging us to form a queue. Two officials were in charge of immigration and passports, and the normal procedure was to pass one by one between their desks. The supporters passed through them, but it wasn't one by one: it was in packs of twenty. Turin is not a busy airport, and the two men would have never been confronted by such a crowd. There was a terrible crush, with people squeezing through sideways and pressed on top of each other. I saw younger supporters crawling on the floor on their hands and knees. One slipped through by going underneath one of the desks.

Once on the other side of passport control, the surge continued: the pack headed straight for the gate. The attendants collecting tickets for Monarch Airways were less protected than the immigration officers, who had desks to hide behind.

The stewardess standing in the door of the plane was next.

It was only when I found my place – suspecting that I was one of the few passengers sober enough to discover the correspondence between the number printed on his boarding pass and the one displayed above his seat – that I understood what had happened. It wasn't simply the case that, once again, English supporters were behaving in a drunk and disorderly way. They were drunk and disorderly for a reason: I had just seen what it was to be on the jib.

I reached down to put my bag away and noticed that there was no room for it: there were two feet. I bent down and confirmed what I felt: there were indeed two feet. The two feet were attached to two legs, which were, as I bent down a little further, attached to an ordinary human body at the far end of which was a human face, a familiar one, that; with his forefinger brought to his lips, was telling me not to say anything.

I looked around the plane, which had grown exceptionally quiet: not, I then appreciated, because it was about take off but because it was about to take off filled with stowaways: they were all crushed underneath the window seats. I didn't know how many there were. I started counting them – I got up to ten – when I realized who was in the seat next to me.

It was Roy, elegantly dressed in a light-blue cotton suit, a white waistcoat, Italian canvas shoes and a diamond ear-ring. I thought afterwards that I should have asked him how he got on the airplane – had he managed to get the Mercedes on board as well? – but I was so taken aback by the fact that he was sitting next to me that I couldn't think of anything to say. For the duration of the flight I couldn't think of anything to say. My luck, it seemed, had changed, and Roy, who couldn't bear to look at me before, had also concluded, I learned later, that I wasn't such a bad sort after all. Roy, too, had decided that I was a good geezer.

Matters on the flight, meanwhile, had become strange. The stewardesses were not supplying anyone with food or drink because they were refusing to walk down the aisle: the last one who tried was still shaken up following a wrestling match she had with Mick, who was now on to vodka, drinking it from a large two-litre, duty-free bottle. The wrestling match had ended up with the stewardess suddenly disappearing behind one of the seats, with her feet, rising above the head-rest, kicking in the air.

Matters had also become confused because there were so many people. Now that the plane had become airborne, the feet I found underneath my seat were no longer there, and the young man to whom they were attached was looking around for a place to sit. He was joined in this by many others. He explained to me that, with no way of getting back to England, he and his friends had decided to join us on our return flight. Although they didn't have a ticket or a boarding pass, they had succeeded in sneaking on board, but then realized that as the flight was fully booked they would have to hide underneath the seats. It seemed fairly ingenious, but it raised doubts in my mind about the measures taken to stop hijackers. I was unable to express these doubts because by this time Roy was creating a bit of a stir. He had emptied one of his trouser pockets. In it there were three things: a large roll of twenty-pound notes; a key-ring, with a small silver knife attached to it (was the Mercedes on board after all?); and a brown envelope containing a large quantity of white powder that Roy proceeded to chop up. Many people had gathered around, with whom Roy, being a generous fellow, was sharing his white powder, now disappearing rapidly up one of the tightly-rolled twenty-pound notes.

When our plane was about to land, there was another problem. No one, from that wayward group of ten, really wanted to climb back underneath the seats, and thus, with a cavalier disregard for international flight regulations, many people were wandering up and down the aisle unable to find a place to sit as the plane descended. One person who was not wandering up and down the aisle was Mick. And that was because he was lying in the middle of it. Mick had abandoned his duty-free bottle of vodka, because Mick had become copiously ill.

Mick's stomach was not made of bricks after all.

I got back to London at about eight o'clock that night, feeling tired and mean and nasty. I was gritty and hungover, and my mind was full of images from the night before. I was in a hurry to get home.

The escalator at the Marble Arch Underground station was not working. My train left in minutes. I bolted down the steps of the station; the stairs were long and steep. There was an old man and woman in front of me. The old woman was helping the man, but they were having trouble negotiating the stairs, taking one gentle step at a time. Both had canes. But together they were also taking up the width of the staircase. I was in a hurry. I started muttering underneath my breath: 'Get on with it.' And still they proceeded, step by step, frail and careful. I said it again: 'Get on with it.' And then something snapped and I shoved them forcefully aside, pushing them sideways with the flat part of my hand. I shot past and then looked back up at them.

'Fuck off,' I said. 'Fuck off, you old cunts.'

Juventus went on to win the final of the Cup-Winners Cup, beating the Porto Football Club two-one at the stadium in Basle in Switzerland. The next season, Juventus was in the European Cup. In the first round, it played the Finnish team Ilves-Kissat and won six-nil. It won the second round, and in the quarter-finals played Sparta Prague: again a victory for Juventus. The semi-final was against Bordeaux. It wasn't until the final that Juventus played an English team again, the first time since Manchester United visited Turin. The team was Liverpool; the stadium was Heysel in Brussels. Juventus won one-nil; the goal was a penalty kick. Before the match began, thirty-nine people died; six hundred were injured.

SUNDERLAND

The mob gathering round Lord Mansfield's house had called on those within to open the door, and receiving no reply . . . forced an entrance . . . they then began to demolish the house with great fury . . . while they were howling and exulting . . . a troop of soldiers, with a magistrate among them, came up, and being too late (for the mischief was by that time done), began to disperse the crowd. The Riot Act being read, and the crowd still resisting, the soldiers received orders to fire, and levelling their muskets, shot dead at the first discharge six men and a woman, and wounded many persons; . . . daunted by the shrieks and tumult, the crowd began to disperse, and the soldiers went away, leaving the killed and wounded on the ground – which they had no sooner done than the rioters came back again, and taking up the dead bodies, and the wounded people, formed into a rude procession, having the bodies in the front . . . in this order they paraded off with a horrible merriment; fixing weapons in the dead men's hands to make them look as if alive . . .

Charles Dickens
Barnaby Rudge (1840)

SUPERINTENDENT R. McALLISTER of the Wearside Police Station in Sunderland was perfectly happy to speak to me about crowd trouble – it was a routine part of his job – but, on seeing that I was American, he was more interested in learning about crowd behaviour at football games in the United States.

'Am I mistaken, Mr Buford,' he asked, 'or is it the case that there is seating for everyone at *every* American football match?' He had heard this was so.

I assured him that it was the case.

'I see,' Superintendent R. McAllister said, and thought.

'Everyone?' he asked again.

'Everyone,' I said.

'I see,' he said, and thought. You could see that he was trying to picture thousands of versions of Roker Park, Sunderland's football stadium – all with seats.

Another question occurred to him.

'Am I mistaken, Mr Buford, or is it the case in American football that, although the play lasts for only sixty minutes, the matches themselves can last for two or even three hours?'

I assured him that such was the case.

'I see,' he said, and thought. Superintendent R. McAllister was a slow man, but a careful one. He wanted to make sure he got things right.

'And am I mistaken, Mr Buford,' he continued, 'or is it the case that, even though the matches might last two or even three hours there is no crowd trouble?'

Crowd trouble, I assured him, was a very rare thing.

He shook his head, uncomprehending. It was all a bit much: thousands of seats, a violent game that lasts for several hours and *no* crowd trouble.

'Am I mistaken, Mr Buford,' the Superintendent continued, 'or is it the case that there are also very few policemen in the grounds of these American football matches?'

Very few, I assured him.

'And yet,' Superintendent McAllister continued, 'there is no trouble?'

'None.'

'None?' he repeated, not disbelieving me exactly, but wanting some kind of proof – some statistics perhaps.

'None,' I said.

Superintendent McAllister shook his head. He said nothing for a very long time. He was thinking.

MANCHESTER

The Stretford End ... is a kind of academy of violence, where promising young fans can study the arts of intimidation. This season the club installed a metal barrier between the fans and the ground. It resembles the sort of cage, formidable and expensive, that is put up by a zoo to contain the animals it needs but slightly fears. Its effect has been to make the Stretford terraces even more exclusive and to turn the occupants into an elite.

Observer, 1 December 1974

THE WEEKEND AFTER my visit to Turin, I took the train to Manchester. Manchester United was at home to West Ham, the East London team, and I had been told to come up for the match. I had been accepted. I had been accepted for the simple reason that I had travelled with the supporters to Italy and had been with them when it had 'gone off'. I had witnessed an experience of great intensity and – like the other supporters returning to tell stories to the friends who had remained behind – I was among the privileged who could say that he had been there.

I was told to show up around mid-morning at the Brunswick, a pub near Manchester's Piccadilly station, but if I was late then I was to go on to Yates's Wine Lodge on the High Street. By one, everyone would be at Yates's.

I arrived just before noon and got to the Brunswick in time to meet some of the people I had heard about. There was Teapot and Berlin Red and One-Eyed Billy and Daft Donald. Daft Donald was the one who had tried to reach Turin but never got past Nice. Daft Donald showed me a canister of CS gas. He said that he always travelled with a canister of CS gas. It stuns them, he said, so that you can then take out their teeth without any resistance.

I spotted a lad named Richard, whom I recognized from Turin. He was flicking through an envelope of photographs that he had picked up that morning from Boots, surrounded by four or five of his friends. They had stayed home; Richard had gone, although he told me later that, because he had gone without first getting permission from his boss, he had probably lost his job – assembly line work at a machine factory. The reason he could say only that he had 'probably' lost his job was because, three days later, he still hadn't showed up for it. But for the moment it didn't matter; he was a celebrity: he had been in Italy when it had 'gone off'.

For Richard, being one of the lads was the best thing a person could be. He became serious and a little sentimental when he spoke about it. The shape of his face changed; it seemed to soften and round out, and his eyebrows knitted up with feeling. 'We look forward to Saturdays,' he said, 'all week long. It's the most meaningful thing in our lives. It's a religion, really. That's how important it is to us. Saturday is our day of worship.'

Richard wanted to explain to me what it meant to be a supporter of Manchester United. I didn't know why at first – whether it was because I was an American and was thus ignorant about these things, or because I was the journalist who might put the record straight, or because I was the most recent member to be admitted into the group – but Richard wasn't the only one. Other people went out of their way to do the same: they wanted me to understand. All day long people stopped me to illustrate, to define, to comment upon the condition of being one of the lads. I cannot remember meeting people so self-conscious about their status and so interested in how it was seen by others. They were members of something exclusive – a club, cult, firm, cultural phenomenon, whatever it might be called – and they valued its exclusivity. They were used to the fact that the world was interested in them and were accustomed to dealing with television and newspaper journalists in a way that few people, however educated in media matters, could hope to be. It was a perverse notion, but they believed that they were involved in an historical moment, that they were making history. And now that they didn't have to hide from me that their thing was violence – now that the pretence of being a good supporter could be abandoned – they all wanted to talk about it.

This put me in an awkward position. What was I meant to do with what people were telling me? I was uncomfortable with the idea of writing in my notebook in front of everybody. I knew that I couldn't pull out a tape-recorder, that something so blatant would destroy the trust. So what did that make me? Was I the reporter or had I been genuinely admitted to the group? And if I had been admitted, should I be explicit about the fact I would be writing about the very people who were befriending me? In retrospect, my confusion, that I was suddenly unsure of my role, was a symptom of the way a group of this sort works – the way it takes you in, proffers support and expects loyalty – and I resolved the matter in a simple way: I avoided it. I ended up excusing myself constantly to get into one of the stalls in the lavatory, where I then sat down and, secure in my privacy, scrawled down everything I had been told. I was being told so much that day that I was having to disappear with considerable regularity – there is only so much you can hold in your head – and I finally had to own up to having stomach problems.

I re-emerged from one lavatory visit to discover a lad who looked exactly like Keith Richards. The likeness was uncanny. What's more, it wasn't Keith Richards at just any time of his life; it was Keith Richards during the worst time. The lad had the same long, leathery, lined face; the druggy offhand manner; the endless cigarettes; the dazed and exhausted appearance of sustained personal abuse. He, too, had been in Italy, but I didn't remember seeing him there. That, he said, was because, through the whole match, he had sat at the bottom of the stairs with his head between his legs vomiting upon his feet. He showed me his boots, still caked with the dried splatterings of the horrors that, at one time, had been contained in his stomach.

It would be, I offered, such a waste to clean them.

The Keith Richards lookalike was disconcertingly self-aware. He knew what a journalist was hoping to find in him and that he provided it. He worked in a factory, making soap powder. 'The perfect profile of a hooligan, isn't it?' he said. 'He works all week at a boring job and can't wait to get out on a Saturday afternoon.'

I nodded and grinned rather stupidly. He was right: the disenfranchised and all that.

He sneered. It was a wonderful sneer – arrogant, composed, full of venom. 'So what do you think makes us tick?' he asked. 'If *we*,' he said, not waiting for my answer, 'did not do it here at football matches then we'd simply end up doing it somewhere else. We'd end up doing it on Saturday night at the pub. It's what's in us, innit?' He had an intense, but rather practised, look of contempt.

What's that? I asked. What is it that's in us?

'The violence,' he said. 'We've all got it in us. It just needs a cause. It needs an acceptable way of coming out. And it doesn't matter what it is. But something. It's almost an excuse. But it's got to come out. Everyone's got it in them.'

Keith Richards was interrupted by Robert. Robert was the one who arrived in Turin by an expensive taxi from Nice. He was also the one who had been telling people in Italy that I worked for the CIA – such was the threat to international stability that the supporters of Manchester United represented. Robert had concluded, even if only tentatively, that I probably wasn't CIA – he was not entirely certain – and that, regardless, I was a good geezer.

Robert was tall and Irish and good-looking and could not take too many things too seriously for too long. He had been listening to Keith Richards's account of the violence and thought it sounded a little too earnest. 'All that's true,' he said, 'but you've got to see the humour. You can't have violence without a sense of humour.'

The time was called out – it was one o'clock – and it was agreed that we should all be moving on to Yates's. Once the move was announced, the pub, although packed, emptied in seconds.

I fell in with Mark, the British Telecom engineer whom I had also met in Italy. Mark was of a philosophic disposition. 'I've been going to matches for years,' he said, 'and I still can't put a finger on it.' Mark was trying to describe the essence of the thing.

'For most lads,' Mark was saying, 'this is all they've got.' He nodded, as we were walking out of the door, towards a cluster of supporters whose common feature was, I must admit, a look of incredible and possibly even unique stupidity.

'During the week,' Mark continued, 'they're nobody, aren't they? But then, when they come to the match, that all changes. They feel like Mr Big.' The implication was that Mark – skilled job, career prospects, pension-fund, wife, future family – was different, that he was somebody. Somebody or nobody, the experience wasn't any less intense for Mark. 'Every now and then,' he said, 'even for me, there is something spectacular, something that makes you feel different afterwards. The Juventus match was like that. That was a once-in-a-lifetime experience.'

He described Italy. 'You remember the moment we entered the ground? Everybody started throwing things at us – bottles, cans, stones, everything. I've got a scar on my forehead from where some Italian jabbed me with a flag-pole. There were only two hundred of us. It was us against them, and we had no idea what was going to happen. There was so many different feelings. Fear, anger, excitement. I've never felt anything like it. We all felt it and every one of us now knows that we have been through something important – something solid. After an experience like that, we're not going to split up. We'll never split up. We'll be mates for life.

'I will never forget these blokes. I will never forget Sammy. For as long as I live, I will be grateful that I could say I knew him. He is amazing. He's got this sixth sense that keeps him from getting caught, and he knows, somehow, when something really big is about to go off, and that's when you find him there at the front. If there was a war, Sammy would be the bloke who'd return with all the medals. He'd be the hero. It's funny, isn't it? Sammy could be put away for years if they knew even half of what he's done, but if he did the same things in a war you'd see his picture in the papers.'

Yates's Wine Bar was a pub and café. As we entered it, a supporter was standing on a table, singing, 'Manchester, la-la-la, Manchester, la-la-la.' Nobody was joining him; despite his antics, the mood was subdued.

Mark was still explaining. 'You see, what it does is this: it gives violence a purpose. It makes us somebody. Because we're not doing it for ourselves. We're doing it for something greater – for us. The violence is for the lads.'

Mark bought me a pint, but we didn't end up staying at Yates's long and I hadn't finished my beer before I noticed that people were starting to drift out of the door.

I was greeted by Steve. Mark may have been right, that football provided meaning for supporters whose lives were otherwise empty, but many supporters had their lives remarkably well sorted out – at least financially: they had money and prospects of getting more. Steve was one. At the age of twenty-two he had a colour television, an expensive camera, a video player, a car, a van, CD and stereo equipment. He was married – his wife was a hairdresser – and was about to secure a mortgage for the purchase of his first home. He lived in one of the southern commuter-belt garden cities not far from London. Like Mick, Steve was an electrician, but, unlike him, Steve was self-employed and running his own business, was already fully informed about the rhythms of cash flow, tax fiddles and the tactics needed to deal with the VAT man. He had opinions about most things and a gentle way of expressing them.

Steve had been on that early-morning coach that took me up

to Manchester airport. I had spent quite a bit of time with him already. I would spend more. In fact, for a while, I went out of my way to spend time with Steve, if only because, being articulate and intelligent, he was good company and because I always believed that he would be able to reveal something about why he, of all people, was attracted to violence of this kind. If the *Daily Mail* had been asked to create a twenty-two-year-old working-class lad with his life sorted out, it could have presented Steve.

There was the language he used. I mentioned Sammy, and Steve would say: 'Ah, yes, Sammy. Me and Sammy go way back.' I mentioned Roy, and Steve would say, 'Ah, Roy. I've known Roy for years.' Steve was only twenty-two. These phrases were an old man's; they sounded like his father's. And when he talked about the violence, he could have been assessing a small business's marketing problems. 'We've got one of the best firms in the country – as you carry on with your research you'll find that very few clubs get the support that Manchester United gets every Saturday – and the last time we played West Ham in London our boys filled three tube trains. There must have been two thousand people. Two thousand people had come to London from all over the country with the sole purpose of routing West Ham. Those are very big numbers. But then nothing happened.'

Extensive preparations had gone into Manchester United's last meeting with West Ham – coaches had been hired, with complex routes into the city to evade the police, the arrival times staggered so that everyone did not appear *en masse*. 'Our trouble,' he said, 'is one of leadership. We have too many leaders, with the result that we have no leaders at all. We're always getting dispersed or split up. West Ham has Bill Gardiner – I've known Bill since I can remember – and you will see him later today. He is always the first man out, flanked on either side by his lieutenants, with everyone else behind. And what he says, goes. He is the general. He doesn't fight much himself any more – when it goes off, he tends to step back and disappear into the crowd – because he can't afford to get arrested.'

Problems of leadership, organization, 'big numbers', a hierarchical command structure: the technocrat phrasing did not obscure that what Steve was describing was a civil disturbance involving several thousand people. Every now and then, I would butt in with a '*why*?' or a '*how*?', but Steve would simply say something like, 'It's human nature, I guess,' or 'I don't know, I never really thought about it,' and then he would be off describing one of the current tactical problems. And in this, he had very developed views.

His essential complaint was that football violence emerged out of such a coherently structured organization that the authorities should just leave it alone. The members of each firm knew those from all the other firms – without a moment's hesitation, Steve could also run through the leaders of Chelsea, Tottenham, Arsenal, Millwall and Nottingham Forest – and, in their ideal world, they should be allowed to get on with fighting each other without unnecessary impediments: 'We know who they are; they know who we are. We know they want it and so do we.' It was a matter of freedom and responsibility: the freedom for them to inflict as much injury on each other as they were prepared to withstand and the responsibility to ensure that others were not involved: with some pride Steve mentioned watching a fight on the terraces that was interrupted to allow a woman and child to pass, then promptly resumed.

Steve blamed most of the current troubles on the police. 'The police have now got so good,' he said, 'that we're more constrained than before. We just don't have the time that we used to have. The moment a fight starts we're immediately surrounded by dogs and horses. That's why everyone has started using knives. I suppose it might sound stupid but because the policing has got so good we've got to the point where we have to inflict the greatest possible damage in the least amount of time, and the knife is the most efficient instrument for a quick injury. In fact these knifings – because there is so little time – have become quite symbolic. When someone gets knifed, it amounts to an important victory to the side that has done the knifing. If the policing was not so good, I'm sure the knifings would stop.'

People were leaving Yates's. Steve said it was time to get moving, and I followed him outside. Talking to Steve was a curious experience. Everything was exactly the way it was not meant to be. The police were bad because they were so good. Knifings were good because they had the potential to be so bad. The violence was good because it was so well organized. Crowd violence can be blamed not on the people causing it but on the ones stopping it. In themselves, these would be curious statements to consider. What made them particularly unusual was the way Steve presented them. He was rational and fluent, and had given much thought to the problems he was discussing, although he had not thought about the implications of the thing – that this was socially deviant conduct of the highest order, involving injuries and maiming and the destruction of property. I don't think he understood the implications; I don't think he would have acknowledged them as valid.

Everyone left Yates's and made his way on to the High Street. There were about a thousand people, milling around 'casually', hands in their pockets, looking at the ground. The idea was to look like you were *not* a member of a crowd, that you just happened to find yourself on the High Street – at the time that a thousand other people happened to have done the same.

The next London train was due at one forty-two, a matter of minutes, and it was known that the West Ham firm would be on it. The Manchester United firm intended to meet it and had a plan. From Yates's, the High Street led straight to the ramp of Piccadilly station, and, at the agreed time, everyone would charge up the ramp, burst through the station entrance and attack the

West Ham supporters as they were coming off the platform. I thought that the plan was preposterous, but, if it could be pulled off, it would be spectacular – in the sense of a spectacle that was extraordinary to behold. I tried to remember the station. The police had been there this morning when I arrived but not in numbers great enough to have stopped a thousand supporters crashing through the station's entrance with the momentum that would have built up and been sustained over the length of the High Street. And that was what had been described to me: that everyone would charge up the ramp at full speed. I remembered the shiny floors – I had noticed someone washing them – and imagined the fight that would break out. For some reason, a very vivid image of blood arose in my mind. The blood was deep red and had formed into a thick puddle and sat, swelling, jelly-like, on that shiny white floor. The image would not go away.

I found the plan breath-taking to think about – genuinely breath-taking in that I could detect my own anxiety in the way I was now breathing – but also exciting. I didn't want to miss it and intended to be as close to the front as I could get. I wanted to experience this thing fully.

A police car pulled up, stopped and drove away. I was sure that the policeman knew what was going on, but was surprised he didn't stay. There were no other police.

Another minute passed. Nothing happened. The street was busy with Saturday shoppers – families, older women all carrying Sainsbury's carrier bags – but no one knew the nature of the thing that was forming around them.

Another minute, and the supporters drifted into the middle of the street. There was still the studied casual look, but it couldn't be maintained. As the clusters of people came together, a crowd was being formed, and, as it was in the middle of the High Street, it was conspicuous and intrusive. The crowd had blocked the path of a bus, and the traffic behind it started to build up. Someone tooted his horn.

I found myself in the middle of the group, which was not where I wanted to be, and I tried to work my way to the front, but I was too late. The crowd was starting to move; it had started off in the direction of the station. It proceeded in a measured way, nothing frantic, at the pace of a steady walk. I could see the confidence felt then by everyone, believing now that they were actually going to pull this thing off. The pace accelerated – gradually. It increased a little more. Someone started to chant, 'Kill, kill, kill.' The chant was whispered at first, as though it were being said reluctantly. Then it was picked up by the others. The pace quickened to a jog, and then a faster jog, and then a run.

An old woman was knocked over, and two carrier bags of food spilled on to the pavement. There were still no police.

Half-way up the ramp, the group was at a full sprint: a thousand people, running hard, chanting loudly: 'KILL, KILL, KILL.' I was trying to calculate what was in store. The train from London would have arrived by now if it was on time, although it was possible that it was late and that we would burst through the station doors and find no one inside. But *if* it was on time, the West Ham supporters would be clearing the ticket barrier and heading for the main waiting area – that shiny floor where I kept seeing a thick, coagulating puddle of blood.

I couldn't see who was leading the group or what was up ahead. I had people on all sides of me and couldn't get past them, but we must have been within yards of the entrance. They were going to get away with it, I thought. It was about to happen. It would only be a few seconds more.

And then suddenly something had gone wrong. I crashed into the person in front of me: hard, bumping my nose. He had stopped and turned with cartoon-like speed, his legs whipping round, while the momentum of the run carried the rest of his body forward. He had a look of intense panic on his face, his hands flapping in the air, grabbing at anything, everything, me, the person next to me, the railing. His eyes were wild with fright. He was desperately trying to run back down the ramp. So were the others. I was turned round by the force of the people in front and then had to concentrate on not falling. I don't know what had happened; I could hardly think about it because we were running so hard. Someone was squealing: 'Dog! Dog! Dog!' I didn't understand this. The moment before they had been chanting 'Kill, kill, kill.' Now they were screaming: 'Dog! Dog! Dog!' It was only when I reached the bottom of the ramp that I understood what had occurred.

The police had known all along what was taking place and simply waited for it to unfold. They had judged the moment with precision and had placed two dog-handlers on the other side of the entrance to the station. As the first supporters pushed open the doors, they would have been greeted by two husky German shepherds going for their throats. Two dog-handlers – there were no other police – had turned back a chanting mob of a thousand people intent on violence.

The dog-handlers then came hurtling down the ramp. One supporter fell and the handler let the dog run over him. The dog went for the arm, biting into the flesh. I recognized the handler, a big man, with an Old Testament beard, whom I had seen on previous trips to Manchester. This was his beat, and he was very practised at it. He then jerked the dog up off the supporter and went after the next one, who had also tripped up, and the dog was allowed to run up over him, tearing noisily at his sleeve. And then he was off again.

The supporters had split up and were scattered in all directions. Other police arrived, but not in big numbers. This was the dog-handlers' show. I ran fast and hard – I was determined not to be part of it – and so I missed the appearance of the West Ham supporters. I did not notice them until they reached the bottom of the ramp.

There were about five hundred. They had walked down in

three columns. Once they reached the High Street, they stopped, still in formation. At the front was a big, broad-shouldered man, about thirty-five. This was Bill Gardiner. He stood there, feet planted apart, crossed his arms and waited. Next to him were his lieutenants, who had crossed their arms, their feet already apart, and waited. They were all dressed in the same manner: jeans, open leather jackets, T-shirts. Many had the same scar on their faces: the serrated hook across the cheeks, a knifing scar.

There were no shoppers or traffic, and the West Ham supporters remained in the middle of the High Street, waiting. People started throwing stones and bottles – arching high in the air, hurled from the different, scattered positions where the United supporters had found themselves – and the glass broke around the feet of the people in front. No one flinched. They stood there until the police had cleared away all the United supporters.

And then it was over. The police appeared with their horses and escorted the West Ham supporters to the ground, and that was that. But, according to the rules of engagement, West Ham had humiliated the supporters of Manchester United. The language – rich, as usual, in military metaphors – is important: the firm from East London had entered the city of Manchester and had taken it. They had made a point of showing that they could take whatever liberties they wanted to. They had walked into the city as if it had been their own.

I walked with the United supporters to Old Trafford. There were recriminations.

'We've been humiliated,' someone said. 'They're going to laugh at us now when they get back to London.'

'Fucking yobs,' someone else said. 'They had to start chanting when they went up the ramp.'

'We would have had them.'

'We should have had them.'

'But didn't you see them waiting for us?' someone said,

referring to that rather majestic moment in which Bill Gardiner stood his ground, flanked by his troops. 'They were waiting for us to charge. But no one would chance it. There was no one around.'

'This doesn't happen abroad. That's where we show what we're made of.'

'It didn't happen in Italy.'

'It didn't happen in Luxembourg.'

'In Spain, forty of us would have taken on fifteen hundred of those bastards.'

'Why can't we fuckin' do it? What's the matter with us?'

There were skirmishes throughout the day – outside the ground just before the match; outside the ground just after it. A tram ran from Old Trafford to Piccadilly station, and the West Ham supporters were put on it by the police. Sammy, knowing the routine, had taken a hundred of his 'troops' to one of the stops. He came charging down the stairs of the station, his lads just behind him, filling up the staircase, their chant – 'Manchester, la-la-la, Manchester, la-la-la' – echoing loudly. When the tram approached, Sammy ran up to it and pulled apart the doors with his hands. And then he stood back. The station was ringing with the noise. There were not many police, only two or three buried deep within the carriage and unable to get out.

'Come on,' Sammy was shouting, standing in front of the door, waiting for the supporters behind him to follow on down the staircase.

'Come on. We've got them.'

Only they didn't come. Sammy turned round angrily, incredulous that he was standing alone on the platform: 'What are you waiting for?' The doors closed and the tram left.

The moment had come and gone. It was not meaningful, except for me and only in one respect. Just before the tram pulled up, Sammy turned round and surveyed the supporters he had brought with him. He did a head count, one by one, looking everyone straight in the face. I was included in the head count. Sammy shook his head and cursed, realizing he had made a mistake. And then he looked at me again, stared, and counted me in. I was pleased.

What did I think I was doing?

PART TWO

BURY ST EDMUNDS

One British supporter, himself a referee, said that the ground outside the Stadium was littered with British National Front leaflets, some overprinted by the British National Party with their address. One witness spoke of passengers on the boat crossing the Channel with National Front insignia singing songs of hatred and exhibiting violence.

Mr John Smith, Chairman of Liverpool Football Club, spoke of how six members of Chelsea National Front had boasted to him of their part in provoking the violence and said that they seemed proud of their handiwork. Mr Bob Paisley, a former manager of Liverpool Football Club, said that he was forced to leave the Directors' Box at the start of the game as dozens of fans poured over the dividing wall and that the person next to him claimed that he was a Chelsea supporter and was wearing a National Front badge. A number of banners decorated with swastikas were recovered after the match, including one marked 'Liverpool Edgehill' . . . A banner with 'England for the English' and 'Europe for the English' was observed and a contingent of the National Front were clearly seen in Blocks 'X' and 'Y'. One party leaving Brussels main station was observed to be Londoners wearing Liverpool colours, carrying Union Flags and having National Front and swastika tattoos.

Mr Justice Popplewell
Final Report on the Deaths at
Heysel Stadium, January 1986

THE FIRST NATIONAL Front disco I attended was in Bury St Edmunds on an unseasonably warm evening in the middle of April. Bury St Edmunds is a highly ordered, middle-class town in East Anglia. It is known for its Georgian architecture and its rural ways, and I had decided beforehand that, following the disco, I would spend the night there. But around midnight it became evident that what I had planned for myself and what others had planned for me were not the same. It was around midnight that I found myself in the market square pushed up against a lamp-post, looking into the eyes of a young man named Dougie. Dougie, who was about my height, had gathered a great quantity of my cotton shirt in such a way that he had me standing on tip-toe, and every now and then, serving to reinforce the occasional phrase that Dougie wished to stress, I was lifted off the lamp-post and then pushed back sharply against it, knocking my head.

You like the National Front, don't you? Dougie was asking, stretching out his question to accommodate the full, painful rhythm of his lifting me up, bumping me back and knocking my head again.

Yes, Dougie, I said, I like the National Front very much.

But the point is, Dougie said, you really like us. He paused. Don't you?

Lift. Push. Bump.

Yes, Dougie, I really like the National Front.

I had grown fascinated by the tattoo on Dougie's forehead, right there in the middle, a small but detailed blue swastika.

And [*lift*] you are going to write nice things [*bump*] about us, aren't you? *Knock*.

Dougie had become a problem.

The evening was meant to be a good-natured Saturday-night outing, a party among friends, commemorating the opening of the Bury St Edmunds branch of the National Front and celebrating the twenty-first birthday of a new member. The party had been organized by Neil, the new chairman. It was an important event for Neil. This was his first National Front disco, and there would be members of the executive branch up from London to judge his performance. There was an approved way of holding such events, and Neil had worked hard to ensure that it was all done in the proper way. There was the party's climax, for instance. It was essential, as branch chairman, that you did not allow your lads to get too excited too early. A branch chairman would know not to do this. He would want the lads to get too excited – crowd frenzy was a valuable tool – but only briefly, right at the end, just before closing time. It was even permissible that some people might become a little violent – a little violence was an acceptable thing – but, again, only at the end. Any earlier, and the police would have to pay a visit. There was an understanding with the police of Bury St Edmunds, I was told: they didn't want to have to pay a visit.

But Dougie had become very excited very early. What's more, Dougie had become not a little violent, but very violent. Dougie had become a problem. And now this problem had a good part of my throat gathered into his fist.

There was another problem about Dougie: he was related to the new branch chairman; Dougie was Neil's brother.

I had met Neil and Dougie at a Cambridge United football match. Both were Chelsea supporters, and the match where we met had marked only the second time in its history that Chelsea had travelled to Cambridge. After the first match, there had been so much trouble – Chelsea supporters had 'done' Cambridge – that there had been a call to abolish the Cambridge team and ban football from the city.

Trouble was likely at the second match as well, and I made a point of getting into the Chelsea side of the ground. On the way over, I came upon a boy who had fallen on to a car bonnet, having stumbled into the street beforehand, stopping traffic. Blood was pouring from his throat, which someone had cut open with the serrated neck of a broken wine bottle. There was more fighting further down the Newmarket Road. I saw a fence being taken apart, the slats of wood being handed out as weapons. There were roving gangs of lads – six or seven in each – and every few minutes a new one appeared and then went chasing down one of the side-streets.

I entered the stands for the visiting supporters and ended up following a skinhead – big and brawny with a tight-fitting white T-shirt and fleshy biceps. His name, I would learn, was Cliff, which – sheer, unadorned, vaguely suggestive of danger – seemed entirely appropriate. The skinhead phase had long passed and, even here, in this crowd, Cliff stood out as a nostalgic anomaly, but Cliff had such an aggressive manner – the regulation braces and the heavy black boots and pockets full of twopences (their edges sharpened beforehand) to throw at the Cambridge supporters – that he seemed the most obvious person to befriend.

Once the match ended, I followed him outside the ground. He began panhandling to raise the money to pay for his fare home, and I offered him some change and introduced myself.

Why me? he wanted to know.

I didn't know what to say. And that was when he pointed to the badge attached to his braces. Is it because of this? he asked. Is that why you picked me?

And then, for the first time, I noticed a discreet little badge. It said: 'NF'.

Cliff was a drummer in a rock band (Have you heard of White Power music? I had not heard of White Power music) and an unemployed bricklayer. He was accompanied by several others, another feature about him I had failed to notice. One was Dougie. Dougie neither spoke nor smiled. He stared. His head, gaunt and darkened with exhaustion, could only have looked more like a skull if the skin had been peeled away. Another was Dougie's brother, Neil.

Neil concluded that I would want to visit his operation in Bury; he was just setting it up and there would be a party some time soon. I could come over, meet the lads. He would put me up himself.

I asked Neil for his number.

He wouldn't give it. He asked me for mine. He had to have mine – and my address, please – before he could give me any further information. There were people he would have to clear this with.

Somebody would be in touch.

And the following week, somebody was in touch. I received a large brown envelope. My name and address had been written out by hand. There was no indication of the contents or the sender except the postmark: Croydon.

Inside, I found three editions of *Bulldog*, printed in exclamatory red and black. *Bulldog* – its title invoking that highly expressive icon of English male culture – was the publication of the Young National Front. According to the banner at the bottom of the front page, it was the paper 'THEY WANT TO BAN.'

I picked up one and read – beneath the headline, 'SEX SLAVES! BLACK PIMPS FORCE WHITE GIRLS INTO PROSTITUTION' – a graphic account (beatings, kidnapping, torture, a bathtub full of spiders) of white prostitutes working for black pimps. There was an editorial.

'We hate what these Black animals are doing and we think that all of them should be locked up until such time as a National Front government can send them back to their own countries.'

I flipped through the pages. In each edition there were two regular columns. One was 'Rivers of Blood' – its title borrowed from Enoch Powell's speech predicting rivers of blood if the immigration of blacks into Britain was not stopped. 'Rivers of Blood' listed the incidents of racial injustice that had occurred the month before: a white youth had been killed by a 'Black bastard'; a race riot at a disco; an account of Savile Town, the multi-racial district of Dewsbury in Yorkshire, accompanied by a photograph of a member of the National Front kicking an Asian in the face. 'The trouble in Dewsbury,' the column concluded, 'will only get worse unless the Blacks are sent home. The choice is an easy one: repatriation or race war!'

The other column, entitled 'On the Football Front', took up the back page and was devoted to activities on the terraces. This is one of the letters to the football editor:

Dear *Bulldog*,
In issue 35 you printed an article on the racist 'boys' who support Newcastle United. The 'boys' were pleased to have been mentioned but they disagree strongly with *Bulldog*'s claim that they don't have as many racist 'boys' as Leeds, Chelsea or West Ham. In fact the 'boys' believe that they have more and that they are now the number one racist 'firm' in the country . . .
Yours sincerely,
Joe of the East Stand

This is another:

Dear *Bulldog*,
I buy your paper regularly but a lot of your reports are the same: it's always Leeds or Chelsea or Spurs or West Ham in

every issue. I follow Rochdale AFC and at every home match you can count on hearing racist chants and songs. The police have tried to stop us but to no avail. Recently they were stupid enough to send a Paki copper but he got so much abuse that he hasn't been seen at the Dale since. If you print this letter it will show people that there is NF support at the smaller grounds as well as the big ones.

Yours sincerely,

The Rochdale AFC National Front

From my reading of *Bulldog*, the member from the Rochdale National Front was unnecessarily worried about his minority status as a racist supporter from the provinces. In these three issues of *Bulldog*, there were accounts of racial abuse in Birmingham, Wolverhampton, Cardiff, Portsmouth and Folkestone Town, which wasn't in the league ('During a Southern League Cup match between Folkestone and Welling, the Folkestone fans threw bananas at the opposing Black players').

How was I to view these publications? I was surprised by how much I disliked receiving them. I found them repellent – spread across my kitchen table, having been delivered in the ordinary way, arriving with the morning letters and bills – and I was reluctant to touch them: it would be a few days before I was prepared to examine them again. I didn't believe that they were widely read: the writing inside was characterized by too much ranting; it was the hortatory hysteria of someone who wasn't being listened to. Even so, I was sure that many people shared its views, although I didn't think that I personally knew many of them. I was confident that my English friends didn't, but my English friends – met in Cambridge or London or Oxford – were of a different world. I was coming to wonder how much they knew about England.

The first time I heard the ape grunt – the barking sound that supporters make when a black player gets the ball – it was so foreign I couldn't figure out what it was. It was a deep, low rumbling, and I had trouble placing where it was coming from: from underneath the ground perhaps? That such a sound could be coming up from the ground was frightening. I thought: it's an earthquake, if only because that was the only sound – that low, bass drumming – that seemed at all comparable. I remember a friend visiting from the United States. He was here for a week and I wanted to show him the football terraces. There was a match at Millwall – the names alone evoked what I wanted him to see: Millwall at the Den on Cold Blow Lane. But there had been rain and the pitch was a swamp, and the match was cancelled. We crossed London and got to White City in time to watch Queen's Park Rangers. A black player touched the ball and the grunt started: uggh, uggh, uggh, uggh, uggh.

My friend turned to me and said: What is that curious sound?

I said nothing, but the grunt continued: uggh, uggh, uggh, uggh, uggh.

What is it? he asked again.

It's because a black player has the ball, I said. They are making an ape sound because a black player has the ball.

The looks that crossed my friend's face were so genuine and so unmediated – bewilderment, outrage, disgust, but mainly incomprehension: he couldn't understand it. The grunt continued: uggh, uggh, uggh, uggh, uggh. Both of us looked round. The grunt was coming not from a few lads, but, it seemed, from everyone on the terraces – old, young, fathers, whole families. Everywhere we looked we saw the ugly faces of men grunting, sticking out their lower jaws in their crude imitations of apes. Why was it so much worse here? I thought, appreciating suddenly the ironies of being in White City, having entered from South Africa Road – until finally the black player passed the ball on and the grunting stopped.

And then another black player got the ball and the grunt resumed.

My friend's face was still fixed in an expression of intense incomprehension. I couldn't explain it. I was embarrassed to be living in this country.

It's England, I said.

There were other items inside my brown parcel. One was a copy of *National Front News*, a more serious periodical, full of opinions about the National Health Service, British Rail, employment, crime figures and a piece on deer hunting entitled 'Stop this Barbaric Sport': a publication that had set out to tell a young man what to think. There was a compliments slip from Nationalist Books and a note wishing me luck with my writing about football supporters, hoping that the enclosed publications might help. It was signed 'Ian'.

'Ian' was Ian Anderson. I identified him from my copy of *National Front News*; its back page listed developments in the Party. Ian Anderson had a number of responsibilities. He was the Party's Deputy Chairman, the second in command. But he was also the head of the Branch Liaison Department. And he was the head of the Administration Department. *And* he was involved in the Activities Department, but of the Activities Department Ian Anderson was joint-head with a man named Joe Pearce (Joe Pearce was the Chairman of the Young National Front; he was also head of the Education and Training Department; *and* he was the principal organizer of the Instant Response Groups *and* the apparent 'genius' behind the Unemployed Activist Units). The National Directorate of the National Front – I learned this as well from my back page – had 'made a number of changes in the party administration designed to increase its effectiveness.' It seemed to me that there was an underlying purpose to this back page that was more than keeping people informed about what was happening in the Party; it was also to convey a reassuring message about the Party's organization: that it had one. The National Front was real, this page said; it was not an arbitrary convocation of loons on the fringe of society trying to get people to listen to it. It was a real party, with a real bureaucracy, with departments that needed running and managing.

My compliments slip had a telephone number. I wanted to know more about the National Front. I wanted to understand its relationship to football supporters.

I phoned Nationalist Books and the man who answered recognized my name. An eerie moment – was I already known among members of the National Front? – until I realized that the man who answered the phone was Ian Anderson. Ian Anderson was also, it seemed, in charge of the switchboard.

Mr Anderson was not very friendly, despite his encouraging note. Journalists made him nervous. It is possible that anyone not a member of the National Front made him nervous, but I wasn't to know that yet. At the time, I was writing for a Sunday newspaper that had been particularly unfriendly to Mr Anderson. In fact, no Sunday newspaper – or any other paper on any other day of the week – had succeeded in being particularly friendly to Mr Anderson. This was perhaps why Mr Anderson was a little unfriendly himself. And you can't really blame him: once you've had your teeth kicked in so many times you learn to close your mouth.

He wanted to know why I would be any different from the others. Why should he speak to me?

This was not a simple question: how do you reassure a racist militant that he doesn't arouse feelings of hostility in you without saying that you, too, are a racist militant? I'm not a racist militant and, besides, he would not have believed me if I had said that I was one. So I said only that I was different.

Yes, Mr Anderson persisted, but why should you be any different?

Because I am, I repeated.

The fact is I think I was different. I wasn't hostile to the National Front. I couldn't take it seriously: I really did regard it as a convocation of loons, although I probably didn't know enough to justify making such a judgement. When I came to England as a student, everyone took the National Front very seriously: opposing it was a popular cause, a rallying point at the college bar for articulate, intelligent, liberal-thinking people animated by their distaste for what the National Front represented. Intelligent liberal-thinking people are meant to show a tolerance for dissent, but the National Front was fascist and so intolerable that it made liberals behave as if they weren't liberals. This, I felt, was a tribute to the National Front. The National Front was evil. It was an evil of such an order that many of my friends believed that its members should be banished from society – imprisoned at the least; some wanted to see them maimed. Their feelings were that strong. This, too, was a tribute to the National Front. There was an element of fear in this, and not without cause: the local left-wing bookshop had been repeatedly fire-bombed, and it was said that this has been done by the National Front; there had also been National Front marches with Nazi banners that had ended with people being badly kicked in the head. For my friends, it would have been inconceivable that one might actually talk to a member of the National Front, let alone have a conversation. And that was why I was trying to have one. I was curious. I had a chance to meet the devil and I wanted to find out if he deserved his bad reputation.

I would have hoped, however, that the devil wasn't going to make his appearance in the shape of Ian Anderson. He was not a credible Satan figure. Photographs of him featured in the papers and broadsheets that Anderson himself had sent me: a tiny, tightlipped little man, dressed in a suit with an outsize tie, at the head of the marches, always surrounded by big boys in boots. I had come across an article by Anderson, 'Naughty but nice', a heavily ironic account of a coach journey ('There is no reason why a coach trip need be boring and dull') to a Sinn Fein gathering. The accompanying photograph showed a minibus surrounded by lads attacking it with bricks – one was on the bonnet smashing the windscreen with his Doc Martens. The caption was: 'Members of the public have meaningful dialogue with IRA supporters.'

It was becoming evident, though, that I was not going to have a dialogue, meaningful or not, with Mr Anderson. At least not on this phone call. Suddenly he broke off our conversation. We'll be in touch, he said abruptly. And then hung up.

He was true to his word. More publications arrived. As before, each was delivered in a plain brown envelope, my name and address written out by hand, no other markings except for the Croydon postmark. These publications were different from the first batch; these were for grown-ups. Mr Anderson must have believed that I was different, after all.

These had titles like *Nationalist Today* or *Heritage and Destiny*. Inside there were history lessons: on the anniversary of the fourteenth-century Peasants Revolt or the traditional British folk song or the achievements of the Vikings. There were intellectual appreciations: of Hilaire Belloc and William Morris. And a denunciation of Jacob Epstein and abstract art ('Epstein's work is not meaningless; it is sufficiently representational to project and reflect strong and racially alien aesthetics'). There was a four-part science series on racial inequality ('Professor Arthur Jensen's paper is a major breakthrough for the forces of science and reason over the opaque murk of Marxist, liberal and Levantine cant and ideologically inspired bigotry'). These publications, however distasteful their contents, were not unsophisticated and revealed how deliberate was the National Front's effort to recruit football supporters: *Bulldog* was a recruitment paper; it was down-market, the National Front trying to talk to the football supporter in his own language. I can see now that the National Front had modelled *Bulldog* on the *Sun* – on the publication that the lads read. The lads, it would seem, were not held in especially high regard.

And then, a few days later, I heard from Neil. He called me at home from a payphone in a pub. He understood, he said, that I had been speaking to a member of the executive board and that it looked likely that he would get approval for me to come along to Bury. The date for the party had been fixed, and it was only a few days away – Saturday, the fourteenth of April. Could I make it? He would meet me at the station. He insisted on putting me up for the night. I would be his guest.

I arrived early and watched Neil setting up. The party was being held at a pub which – in the optimistic belief that its management has changed – I will refer to as the Green Man. It was in the centre of town, and Neil had reserved it from six until closing time at eleven. He had stereo equipment, a collection of records and tapes, party streamers which he had already hung from the ceiling and a large cardboard box filled with packets of cheese-and-onion-flavoured crisps. It was a party. An ordinary Saturday night party in a pub.

The others, Neil said, very preoccupied, would be arriving from London shortly. And he kept repeating that. They'll be here any minute, he said only a few moments later.

It was evident that Neil was anxious. I wondered if it was evident to him that I was as well. For Neil the evening represented a chance to prove himself, and, if things went wrong, then his career as a fascist would advance no further. I had never thought of fascism as an endeavour characterized by its career prospects but that was what was at stake for Neil. Most National Front members whom I met later would be unemployed; many, it seemed to me, would remain unemployed for a very long time. Unlike the football supporters I was meeting, the rank and file membership of the National Front consisted mainly of people who felt, with some justice, that they had nowhere else to go. Neil was different: he worked in a meat-packing plant and had risen to the position of a middle-level supervisor. But it was clear that he believed he stood to gain more by the National Front than by anything he might do at his work.

I was less sure about my prospects: what would the evening mean for me if things went wrong? I had seen nothing to change my view about the National Front. I still couldn't take it seriously, but by that I mean that I couldn't take it seriously as a political party. I didn't see the political threat of fascism in Britain – at least not now and not from this lot. But that was armchair stuff. What I did take seriously was the National Front's bad press. I took its record of violence seriously. And that was what I found myself worrying about. I would be spending the night here, and I was not comfortable about what might be in store.

While Neil was hooking up the stereo, I went to the bar and chatted with members of the pub staff. I wondered how much they knew about what was going on. I ordered a pint of bitter and asked the barmaid what she thought about having a party for, well, you know – ? I couldn't bring myself to say the words 'National Front'; I thought it was something to be quiet about.

She didn't understand what I was asking. She thought I meant Neil and all his friends. Everyone knew Neil and his friends. They were regulars. And everyone liked Neil.

No, not Neil. But the others. The NF, I said finally. What do you think about holding a party for the National Front?

It's an honour, she said, now clearly understanding. It's an honour and a privilege.

This surprised me.

So she explained. The Green Man, she said, prided itself on being the most racialist pub in England. That was her word: racialist. There were other racialist pubs, she said. In fact, there were two more in Bury. But none was as consistently racialist as the Green Man. The Green Man, she continued, had never served a coloured person. No black or Paki had ever had a drink at the Green Man. And everyone who worked at the Green Man was proud of its record. It was also why everyone regarded it as a privilege to hold a party here for the National Front. They felt they had earned it.

No wogs, her partner behind the bar added, perhaps for clarification.

That's right, she said. No coloured people of any description.

I was surprised. I had not expected to hear racism expressed so explicitly by people working behind the bar of a pub – one owned by a brewery that was itself a public company. The fact was I hadn't expected to hear racism expressed so explicitly by people I had only just met, regardless of where they worked. I felt soiled by it, implicated because I couldn't imagine these things being said unless it was assumed that all of us, the bar staff and the National Front and *me*, thought the same. The barmaid was attractive – she had black hair and a soft oval face – and it was disconcerting trying to reconcile this face with the ugliness that came out of it.

We also, she said, don't serve Americans.

Oh, not you, she said quickly, registering my unease. We're serving you, aren't we? The Americans we don't like are the servicemen. We never serve the servicemen. We don't like them and don't like them here. We want them to take their aeroplanes and go back to America.

There were American air bases throughout East Anglia, and Bury St Edmunds must have been one of the towns the servicemen visited on leave. The National Front, I remembered, was against the American military presence in England. It was un-English.

Last night, her partner offered again, a Friday night, six American servicemen came in here and we wouldn't serve them. One was a nigger. They got very uppity and started to argue. It's a free country, they said, and I said that's right and that's why I'm not serving you. That made them even more angry so some of the lads had to take them outside and deal with them. They had a go at them up against the wall, just outside that door

140

there. If you step outside, you can still see the blood. There was a lot of blood.

I was having to think carefully about what I was hearing: I had spent fifteen minutes in an ordinary brewery pub in this perfectly ordered middle-class town and had been invited by the publican to look at the dried pool of blood just outside his front door.

More people arrived, and I was introduced to them as a journalist. This information was not accepted with the grace and interest that I would have liked. And then I spotted Cliff. An ugly face, but at least one I recognized. *Cliff,* I called out, relieved, grateful, expectant. But Cliff didn't answer. *Cliff,* I repeated. It is Cliff, isn't it? I asked myself. He was staring at me. He seemed to be refusing to remember me. And then he became very agitated.

What's he doing here? Cliff asked; he was looking for Neil. Who said *he* could come?

He found Neil and I watched as Neil tried to reassure him – telling him that it had been approved in London – but I could see that Cliff was unhappy. He looked at me, hard. 'I don't like him here. Why weren't we told that he'd be coming?'

I thought that now, after all, might be a good time to pop outside. I had no intention of looking at the wall and the blood that had dried on it, but I had decided that I wasn't ready, just yet, for the evening ahead and that I would do well to organize my thoughts.

What was I doing here? I looked at my watch. It was seven-forty. The last train to Cambridge would be leaving in about two minutes.

I crossed the street and sat on a wall. I sat there for a long time. It grew dark while I sat there. I was not prepared for this; that was evident. So I sat there and decided that I would have to prepare myself. I didn't know how I was going to do this. More guests arrived. Many, like Cliff, were cultural anomalies, skinheads, out of touch, not simply with what was current, but – everything. Life. The future. The world. A blond lad turned up. He was dressed in a black leather SS uniform. He had a red and black Nazi arm-band.

I was having a hard time persuading myself that this was just an ordinary pub party. Blond men in black SS uniforms with Nazi arm-bands do not show up at ordinary pub parties. Inside, the not-so-ordinary-pub-party-goers were starting to chant.

> *Bury skinheads we are here*
> *Shag your women and drink your beer.*
> Sieg Heil! Sieg Heil!
> Sieg Heil! Sieg Heil!

It was dark. By now my train must have been half-way to Cambridge. I was not sitting in it. I was sitting on a wall listening to people chant *sieg heil*. There was, I decided, no choice. I would have to re-enter the pub, but would make sure that I then got very, very drunk.

The pub was packed with people. I went straight to the bar and ordered three pints, which I lined up, one in front of the other, on the beer mat. I would make it to the end of the evening. I did not know where I would be when that time came, but this way, it might not matter.

Mid-way through my first pint, I found that someone had decided to befriend me. Neither of us knew why. I was, in his view, from the media, and he had made a rule of never speaking to the media. But having permitted himself to speak to me, he had some difficulty stopping. I was about to discover that, wherever I went in the pub, my new companion would always be there, next to me, telling me that he never spoke to anyone from the media. He was round and covered with fuzzy hair. His name was Phil Andrews.

Phil Andrews was in his early thirties and over the course of a decade had lived a life of several extremes. He had trained as a policeman, but gave it up. He then became a militant communist, but gave that up, too. And now, for a while at least, he had become a career fascist. He had just been asked to help run the Young National Front, an important position – its aim was to recruit new members from schools and colleges, traditionally the 'breeding grounds' of the left – and Phil must have been picked for the job because he knew so much about the other side.

None of Phil's recruits would have been at tonight's gathering. It was not a collegiate crowd. Everyone here would have been a *Bulldog* reader, drawn from the football grounds. I had heard that the football grounds were ideal for recruiting new members – Ian Anderson had said that there was nowhere else in Britain where you would find so much discontented youth in one place – but the problem, having brought them together, was to keep them from fighting. Neil had said the same thing at the start of the evening: his task, as the chairman, was to keep the Chelsea and West Ham supporters from having a go at each other.

My new fuzzy friend Phil was disgusted by football violence – or at least he put up a good show of disgust. According to Phil, it was all of the government's making. The government had the power to stop the violence if it wanted to, Phil believed, but it hadn't because it was in its interest to keep the violence going. It was in its interest to turn working people against each other. It deflected working people from having to address the real problems of their lives.

Spoken, I thought, like a true Marxist. There must be some comfort in being able to reuse, in his new capacity as a member of the extreme right, many of the old arguments that he had developed when a member of the extreme left. But Phil was manifestly upset about football violence – the more he talked about it the more distressed he became – and he wasn't about to be interrupted.

He was upset, for instance, that the National Front was always being blamed for crowd violence, which, he repeated, he found disgusting. The National Front was blamed for the riots in France and the deaths at Heysel.

One day, Phil said, there will be riots all over Britain. Those will be organized by the NF. But not now. People are always saying that the NF is responsible for the football riots. But what would possibly be the point? Even if we could organize riots of this kind, what would we get out of them? Why would we want to organize riots in Europe?

Phil wanted me to understand this point – it was a complex one – and so he repeated it: Even if we could organize riots of this kind, what would be the point?

Phil then repeated it again.

I looked around the room. It had filled up with Clifflookalikes, and Neil was playing the music – now at a fairly high volume – that was the most appropriate for heavy black boots. It was an antiquated, numbingly monotoned derivative of punk that consisted almost wholly of a crushing, unchanging percussion and an equally crushing, unchanging electric guitar. It had got the lads dancing, although at first there were not many – eight, maybe ten.

The way they danced was intensely physical: they all huddled together in the middle of the room, and, rubbing each other's head with one hand – most were shaved on top – and holding themselves closely together with the other, they jumped up and down. Each tune was played at the same brutal and breathless speed, and the lads, to keep up, had to do a lot of jumping. In fact, I don't recall ever having seen people jump up and down so fast, especially people who were tied together in such a peculiar knot, with their arms and hands this way and that. The tune ended, the lads bent over, breathing heavily, Neil put on something else which my untutored ear was unable to distinguish from the last thing he had taken off, and the lads were off again: they clasped each other, rubbed their heads a bit and started jumping up and down. This looked distinctly ridiculous, but was apparently the thing that everyone had in mind when they talked about an NF disco. Somewhere in the middle was the birthday boy. The NF disco, I remembered, was also a birthday party.

There were women present, girl-friends mainly, who had also retained an affection for the punk style – bleached jeans and T-shirts, their hair cropped short except for a flattened duck-tail at the back. I learned later that the women were even more anachronistic than the men and that their hair-style was in fact pre-punk. They were called 'suedeheads'. The women sat at the far end of the pub, smoking cigarettes. They did not join in the bouncing and the clasping and the rubbing. The bouncing and the clasping and the rubbing were distinctly boys' concerns. The boys danced; the girls watched.

Disgusting rabble, Phil said, muttering quietly. Skinhead riff-raff. They don't know what the National Front is really about. They don't understand the message.

Another record, and more dancing. The rest of the night was clearly going to consist of lads drinking large quantities of lager and shaking it all up violently in the middle of the room. I then noticed that, stationed at several points around the pub – forming an outer circle around the knot of dancing lads – was a number of well-dressed men.

I was surprised I hadn't seen them before. They were different from anyone else in the pub. They were wearing flannel trousers and jackets and had neat executive haircuts. Several were here with their girl-friends, but they were different from the ones sitting in the back. The girl-friends were dressed in a style that could be called 'sensible'. One had a silk scarf and a cashmere jumper. Another was dressed in jeans, but the jeans were expensive and highly flattering. They stood alongside their partners, resting on their arms.

These were the visitors from London.

That some had come with their girl-friends suggested that they, like the others, regarded the evening as an event, an entertainment, a Saturday night out, but they did not appear to be enjoying themselves – at least not yet. Unlike Phil – who was still at my side, and by now drinking very heavily, and reminding me that he didn't speak to the media – none of the London visitors was touching alcohol. They were drinking mineral water or Coke or nothing at all. They were also not dancing and didn't look like they were about to begin. They were not even talking – neither between themselves nor with their girl-friends. They just stood there, looking on.

I recognized one of these urbane visitors. His name was Nick Griffin. All the others from the executive branch, including Ian Anderson, might well have been there, but it was Nick Griffin I spotted and ended up watching. He seemed to have a role in managing the evening's activities.

Nick Griffin was not in fact from London. He lived nearby, in the Suffolk countryside. The National Front was always having to change its base of operations, and for a while it would be run from a converted barn on Nick Griffin's family's property. I got through to the family once. They might well have been farmers, landowners certainly, affluent enough – you could hear it in their accents – to have sent their son to Cambridge, and they were now involved in helping him out in his career as a fascist.

The son was a well-mannered young man with an intelligent face. He had a politician's good looks and an attractive manner. Like the others from London, he was different from – in Phil Andrews's phrase – the rabble bouncing up and down in the middle of the room. In fact, it was evident that Nick Griffin had no intention of being seen near them. He spent the evening against a wall, watching, inconspicuous, and the only time he spoke was when he walked over to Neil, which he did every now and then, and whispered an instruction. Then he returned to his position against the wall. His girl-friend – pretty and blonde and utterly expressionless – stood beside him and never said a word.

There was some talk about playing the White Power music. In Nick Griffin's view, it was too early to play the White Power music. The White Power music should be played only at the end.

I was feeling the need to wander round. My friend Phil was starting to become importunate. He was now very, very drunk, and very, very determined to tell me how he never spoke to the media. Why, he wanted to know, was he speaking to me? Why, I wanted to ask him, won't you stop then? Phil was bothered that, in his opinion, I had not understood the observation that he had made earlier in the evening, even though he had made it several times. This was his observation that, even if it was in the National Front's power to organize riots on the continent, what would be the point? And so he asked the question again. He asked: Even if it was in the National Front's power to organize riots on the continent, what would be the point?

I told him I agreed. I believed him. You are right, I said, there is no point; the National Front could not possibly have organized those disturbances. The National Front, I added, has been unfairly blamed.

You see the point? he asked.

Really, I said. I see the point.

Phil followed me. I should have known. I went to the bar for another drink, paid and turned round: Phil was there. I went to the loo and when I opened the door I almost knocked Phil over. When I stepped outside to get some air, Phil stumbled along after me.

I did not want to talk to Phil any more. I didn't want to be impolite, but I wanted him to go away.

It was time, I said, that I spoke to some of the lads. It was essential to my research.

There were many more dancing now – perhaps thirty.

Fucking skinheads, he said. They're all lobotomized. Ignore them. What I want you to understand is this. Even if . . . Even if . . . The riots, that is. Even if . . .

And he stopped.

I spotted the boy whose birthday the occasion was notionally honouring.

How do you feel? I asked.

Wonderful, he said. I'm very happy.

How old are you?

Twenty-one, he said.

And was this how you wanted to spend your twenty-first birthday?

It couldn't have been better.

Do you know many of the people here? I asked.

Hardly anyone, he said and then started giggling uncontrollably. He stopped only when he realized that I was the journalist that he had heard the others mention. I was surprised he realized much at all. I don't know what chemicals were in his body, but there must have been many and his body did not seem to be particularly accustomed to housing them. He had been dancing hard, bouncing up and down, and was covered in sweat. The pupils of his eyes had contracted to tiny little dots.

You're the repoyta, aren't you?

Amphetamines, I figured. Speed has this effect.

You *are* the repoyta, he said. I knew it!

And then he grew very excited. He was convinced that he was going to be written about. He grew so excited he started to bounce up and down. I'm going to be in the papers, he said, bouncing higher and higher. I'm going to be in the papers, he said, still bouncing, until finally, ecstatic, he bounced out of range, through the crowd, over a table, and somewhere on to the other side of the pub.

I turned round and there was Phil Andrews. He was still trying to finish the sentence that he had begun the last time I saw him. He was having some difficulty focusing. He was pointing vaguely. He wanted badly to tell me something. I thought I knew what it was that he wanted to say.

Even if, he said, and stopped.

He was not going to reach the end. Nature, in a sense, had finally silenced him. I was pretty sure that he was about to vomit.

I started moving around, confident that Phil couldn't keep up. I moved from one conversation to another. People were telling me things.

I was told that they were an organized army; that football had brought them together; that they were creating a police force; that they tried to take over the places they visited.

I was told that they were warriors.

I was told that the banks were run by Jews and that the banks ran the country; that the number of Jews killed in the Holocaust was vastly exaggerated.

I was told that the Labour Party was a shambles; that the Conservative Party was a shambles; that all Americans soldiers should leave Britain.

One member told me the cities should be 'deracinated' – that was the word he used – and that we should all return to our natural element. The man who said this was another one wearing a Nazi arm-band. He was a member of the League of St George.

More militant and more extreme, he assured me, than the National Front, the League of St George was against all modern technology. It advocated a form of agrarian socialism. Modern man, he said, has been uprooted from the soil and placed in an artificial concrete world.

It's a view, I told him, that sounds like the one held by the Khmer Rouge.

Precisely, the man from the League of St George said. And he then said it again: Yes, precisely. He nodded and grinned. It was a very sinister grin.

There was no longer a centre of the room where people were dancing, because everyone was dancing everywhere. On the far side, some of the new members had started in on their football chants, just as Neil had feared. These appeared to be West Ham supporters. They were then answered, from the other side of the room, by Chelsea supporters. A contrapuntal chorus of West Ham and Chelsea songs followed, one that sent Neil scurrying through his record collection. It was time to change the music, and Neil looked over to Nick Griffin.

Nick Griffin nodded. It was time to play the White Power music.

Most of the songs Neil then played were by a group called White Noise; Skrewdriver and Brutal Attack were among the others. None of the songs was played on any of the established radio stations or sold in any of the conventional shops. It was a mail-order or a cash-in-hand music trade, and from the titles you could see why: 'Young, British and White'; 'England Belongs to Me'; 'Shove the Dove'; 'England' and 'British Justice'. These were the lyrics of 'The Voice of Britain':

> *Our old people cannot walk the streets alone.*
> *They fought for this nation, and this is what they get back.*
> *They risked their lives for Britain, and now Britain belongs to*
> *   aliens.*
> *It's about time the British went and took it back.*

> *This is the voice of Britain.*
> *You'd better believe it.*
> *This is the voice of Britain*
> *C'mon and fly the flag now.*

> *It's time to have a go at the TV and the papers*
> *And all the media Zionists who'd like to keep us quiet.*
> *They're trying to bleed our country,*
> *They're the leeches of the nation.*
> *But we're going to stand and fight.*

> *This is the voice of Britain.*
> *You'd better believe it.*
> *This is the voice of Britain*
> *C'mon and fly the flag now.*

The music was delivered with the same numbing, crushing percussion that had characterized everything else that had been played that evening, and most of the lyrics of the songs that followed were lost to me, disappearing into a high decibel static. The only reason I can quote the words from 'The Voice of Britain' is that they were reprinted in a 'White Noise' pamphlet that was being passed round, no doubt to aid understanding. There was one refrain I could follow, and that was because it was played repeatedly, and because, each time, everyone joined in. It seemed to be the theme song.

> *Two pints of lager and a packet of crisps.*
> *Wogs out! White power!*
> *Wogs out! White power!*
> *Wogs out! White power!*

It was interesting to contemplate that the high-point of the evening was organized around this simple declaration of needs: a lad needed his lager; a lad needed his packet of crisps; a lad needed his wog.

Nick Griffin indicated that the volume should be turned up further, and the music was now brutally loud. The room was hot and filled with smoke and smelled of dope. The air had grown heavy and damp. Sixty or seventy lads were in the middle of the room, clasped together, bouncing up and down, rubbing their hands over each other's heads and chanting in unison:

> *Wogs out! White power!*
> *Wogs out! White power!*
> *Wogs out! White power!*

They had taken off their shirts and were stripped to the waist, their braces dangling by their sides, knocking against their legs: sixty or seventy pale, narrow chests, covered in perspiration, pressed tightly together. They were bouncing so vigorously that they all fell over, tumbling on top of each other. I thought someone was hurt – a table had been knocked over – but they all clambered up over each other and, with difficulty, resumed their dancing. They fell over again, wet and hot. I don't know if it was the drink or the drugs or the delirium of the dancing or that chorus, over and over again, but there was a menacing feeling in the air – sexual and dangerous. The people in the crush were not in control – the business of falling over was not intended and no one was finding it funny, as people might in a spirit of drunken merriment. Some of the lads appeared to be in a trance.

I looked at the women, sitting in the dark, smoking cigarette after cigarette, none of them dancing. Something was happening that they didn't understand. They were embarrassed. One was giggling. Their boy-friends were in the middle of the room, pressed against each other, virtually undressed, heaving and bouncing.

Louder, Nick Griffin was shouting to Neil, but Neil couldn't hear him, and Griffin had to cross the room. I could not follow the exchange, but it seemed that Neil was being asked to turn up the volume, but that the volume couldn't be made any louder. The volume was turned up as high as it would go.

There appeared to be more well-dressed men than before, but I don't think that could be right. Is it possible that more would have shown up just at the party's end – its climax? They formed a discernible circle. For the last fifteen minutes, none of them had moved; no one had gone to the loo or got another drink. They stood transfixed, studying the group.

Neil had taken to repeating the theme song. Once it had finished, he merely replaced the needle and started again.

> *Two pints of lager and a packet of crisps.*
> *Wogs out! White power!*

Wogs out! White power!
Wogs out! White power!
Wogs out! White power!

And then the whole thing was over. Dougie, suddenly, went berserk. There was some screaming on the other side of the pub, and I looked up and saw Dougie swinging a bar stool above his head. Somebody went down, and a table full of glasses got knocked over. He picked up a chair and raised that above his head, but lost his balance and crashed into a table. There was more broken glass.

Nick Griffin went over and stopped the record and turned off the stereo. The party had ended. I spotted Phil in the corner. He had passed out and was leaning against the wall, seated on the floor.

DOUGIE, DOUGIE, DOUGIE.

It was Neil speaking. He was whispering: gentle, comforting, reassuring.

Dougie, Dougie, Dougie.

I am still not sure what happened between Dougie's swinging a chair over his head and Dougie's pinning me against a lamp-post. Having your head bumped against a lamp-post concentrates the mind wonderfully, however much it might jar its container. I am very clear about the moments when I was in Dougie's grasp because I was thinking about each one with some care. I was thinking about the look in Dougie's eyes – not a nice look and one that suggested that my prospects of being Dougie's friend were very small. I was also thinking about the words Dougie's brother, Neil, was saying. Having seen me being banged against the lamp-post, Neil had intervened.

Dougie, Dougie, Dougie.

Neil had a very gentle manner, and it seemed to be producing the desired effect. Dougie had stopped banging me against the lamp-post and was now listening. It was as if Neil was calling out to someone who was very far away and not in view – at the end, possibly, of a very long tunnel.

Dougie, Neil said, there is no need for that now, is there?

Dougie had turned his head to his brother. He was very attentive.

Dougie, Neil said, this man is a nice man. He's a friend. He is one of us. If you let go of this nice man, Neil continued, then we can all go off and have another drink, and, if you're good, I'll let you throw a brick through the Indian restaurant.

Throwing bricks through the window of the Indian restaurant or the Indian food shop or, occasionally, an Indian family's home was, I learned, a common late-night pastime. Dougie grinned – a toothy, stupid grin – and he let me go.

I'm not sure what happened later. I followed along, crisscrossing the town of Bury St Edmunds, stumblingly, going from house to house, most of them fairly run-down terraces, meeting new people, including three men in black SS uniforms. I know that I had fulfilled my promise of getting very drunk and had, additionally, supplemented the liquid toxins with whatever else was to hand. And there seemed to have been many other toxins to hand. And then blank. Nothing. I have no memory of anything. At some point, late the next morning, I woke up, feeling very unpleasant, and found myself in a damp two-up two-down. It was where Neil and Dougie lived, a squat with no heating and a broken window – through which, I assumed, they had first entered. There was only one bed and I, the guest, had been given it. On the floor around me had slept more than twenty skinheads, the rabble of the pub. They were still asleep. The room had a powerful smell about it.

Neil woke me up. He was offering me a can of lager for breakfast. There were several cases of Harp lager stacked, I now noticed, at the foot of the bed, and he wanted to know if I wanted one.

I left later in the afternoon.

Thereafter I followed the National Front casually, believing that there was something more I needed to discover. I contacted Nick Griffin several times, attended some marches, listened to the speeches afterwards. More party magazines and newspapers were sent to me – not to my home; I had moved; but care of the office where I worked – but I learned recently that the staff was so offended to receive them that the publications were all sent back with rude cover notes. In fact, I had already gained my most important insight into the National Front – there, that night at its disco – and it had little to do with its politics or its membership. It was its attitude towards the crowd.

I am sure that Ian Anderson was right when he said that the football stadium was his ideal recruiting ground, but he would also have known that it provided a special kind of member, one already experienced, if not trained, in how to become part of a crowd, sometimes a violent one, even if it was not politically directed. And he would also have known that the crowd is a revolutionary party's most powerful weapon. On paper, it would have seemed so straightforward, and so many of the National Front's activities – its discos, its marches, its propaganda – were designed to recreate the crowd among its members and then make it political. But it isn't straightforward, and in the end the young, well-dressed executives of National Front were not very good at their task – they were there to lead, but few were following. But, although incompetent, they were not ignorant. They understood something about the workings of the crowd; they respected it. They knew that its potential – its rare, raw, uncontrollable power – was in all of us, even if it was so persistently elusive.

CAMBRIDGE

The thousands stand and chant. Around them in the world, people ride escalators going up and sneak secret glances at the faces coming down. People dangle tea-bags over hot water in white cups. Cars run silently on the autobahns, streaks of painted light. People sit at desks and stare at office walls. They smell their shirts and drop them in the hamper. People bind themselves into numbered seats and fly across time zones and high cirrus and deep night, knowing there is something they've forgotten to do.

The future belongs to crowds.

Don DeLillo
Mao II (1991)

I WANT TO describe the experience of waiting for a goal.

In January 1990, I attended an evening match played by Cambridge United, in the small, exposed Abbey Stadium on the edge of town. The match was one of the final rounds of the FA Cup, a knock-out competition that the Cambridge team – at the time in the Fourth Division – had survived longer than its supporters could have reasonably expected. The match was a replay: three days before Cambridge United had met Millwall for the first time, making the historic journey to the Den, and had come away with a draw. Tonight's match would decide which team went into the quarter-finals. No Fourth Division team had got beyond the quarter-finals.

I entered the ground and found myself among the supporters pressed up against the fence near the half-way line. It took some minutes before I could get to a position where I could watch the game without being obstructed, and once there I retained possession of my spot by holding on to the perimeter rail. I was on my own. On my left was a man of about fifty, a face full of friendly creases, smelling strongly of American cigarettes, with ash eyebrows and tobacco-stained teeth. Behind me were three lads – one, to keep his balance, rested his forearm on my shoulders. On my right was a woman with her boy-friend; she was in her twenties with short blonde hair and was pressed into my side. Others – children, police, the stadium stewards – were having to squeeze past constantly, as access to the pitch was through a locked gate in front of me.

I was not a supporter of the Cambridge team; I was there out of curiosity (it was Millwall's first visit to the city), but I surprised myself by how engaged I became by the match. In a matter of minutes, I was cheering, even singing, along with everyone else – my voice, slightly high-pitched, as foreign sounding to me as the voices around me. I groaned when the crowd groaned, and when it surged in one direction, and we all had to tumble with it, I instinctively reached out for the people near me, clinging to stay upright. And when the crowd surged back again and we all tumbled back with it, I found that these same people were reaching out for me. Having just walked in from the street, I had stepped into a situation of unusual intimacy, and while I hadn't said more than a few words to the people near me – we were pressed too closely together to have a conversation – something was being communicated between us. Something, I felt, was being communicated between everyone there: just about every member of that crowd of nine thousand people was pressed closely against someone else, and was held, as we were held, tightly together, waiting for a goal.

In the opening minutes, it seemed that we might see one. Millwall was then in the First Division, but it was the Cambridge team that was dominating the game, although not with much finesse. Its players were aggressive and had little style, but they were tenacious and seldom lost possession of the ball. They were the ones making the shots on goal. In the first three minutes, the Millwall goalkeeper had to make two dramatic saves, including one in which he got his hand up to send the ball inches over the net at the last possible moment. Two minutes later, the ball was slammed against the post. Ten minutes later, another was slammed against the crossbar.

I watched the goalkeeper. His name was Keith Branagan, and

160

this was his first match against Cambridge, his former team, since it had traded him to Millwall for a large sum of money – the largest that the Cambridge club had got for one of its players. There might have been a hidden agenda – Branagan out to show his former supporters what they had lost – although it was more likely that, being an exceptional goalkeeper, he simply played exceptionally. With Cambridge United firing so insistently at the goal, Branagan was emerging as the most conspicuous talent on the pitch. After a while I felt there was more to it: that there was some mysterious force at work around his goal – something greater than Branagan's talent – that was preventing the ball from entering it. I felt that the ball would never enter the net and that it would be unnatural if it did.

There was no score in the first half, and during the interval everyone on the terraces relaxed visibly. There was more room; without the excitement, the supporters seemed to diminish in size. They had stopped moving around, and there was no need to cling to anyone for support. To have touched someone now would have been wrong. A conversation would have been possible, but a conversation did not seem right either. I had nothing more than the most perfunctory exchanges with the people near me. Friends and partners were the only ones speaking. Strangers had become strangers again. Our privacy had been reclaimed.

The game resumed.

The second half started off in the same spirit as the first forty-five minutes – brutal and ineffective. United's play was relentless, but it was difficult to see how, at this pace, its players would last out the match. They were very physical – and responsible for most of the fouls – and if they didn't score within the first fifteen minutes I didn't believe that they would score later. They would be exhausted; they would be lucky to hold on to a goal-less draw. That was what it would be: another goal-less draw.

But I was wrong. After twenty-five minutes, Cambridge had

not let up. Another shot bounced off the post – that had been the fourth – followed by another dramatic save by the Millwall goalkeeper.

The game, so far, was what I had learned to describe as good English football. There was nothing unusual about it or the crowd. In fact, although the match was an important one for the Cambridge side, it was, in every other respect, a provincial affair, an ordinary night out in the middle of the week in January. Even the size of the crowd was ordinary – if not less than ordinary: the Abbey Stadium is the smallest in the league, its capacity no more than twenty per cent of the larger First Division grounds. And yet, there was little that was actually ordinary about the experience.

It is not uncommon, in any sport, to see spectators behaving in a way that would be uncharacteristic of them in any other context: embracing, shouting, swearing, kissing, dancing in jubilation. It is the thrill of the sport, and expressing the thrill is as important as witnessing it. But there is no sport in which the act of being a spectator is as *constantly* physical as watching a game of English football on the terraces. The physicalness is insistent; any observer not familiar with the game would say that it is outright brutal. In fact, those who do not find it brutal are those so familiar with the traditions of attending an English football match, so certain in the knowledge of what is expected of them, that they are incapable of seeing how deviant their behaviour is – even in the most ordinary things. The first time I attended White Hart Lane on my own, everyone made for the exit within seconds of the match ending: I looked at the thing and couldn't imagine an exit more dangerous – an impossibly narrow passageway with very steep stairs on the other side. There was no waiting; there was also no choice, and this peculiar mad rush of people actually lifted me up off my feet and carried me forward. I had no control over where I was going. *Stampede* was the word that came to mind. I was forced up against the barrier, danger looming on the other side, was crushed against it, wriggled sideways to keep from bruising my ribs, and then, just as suddenly, was popped out, stumbling, as the others around me stumbled, to keep from falling down the remaining stairs. I looked up behind me: everyone was grimacing and swearing; someone, having been elbowed in the face, was threatening to throw a punch. What was this all about? This was not an important moment in the game: it was the act of leaving it. This, I thought, is the way animals behave, but the thought was not a metaphoric one. This was genuinely the way animals behave – herd animals. Sheep behave this way – cattle, horses.

At the heart of any discussion about crowds is the moment when many, many different people cease being many, many different people and become only one thing – a crowd. There is the phrase, becoming 'one with the crowd'. In part, it is a matter of language: when the actions of diverse individuals are similar and coherent enough that you must describe them as the actions of one body, with a singular subject and a singular verb. They are . . . It is . . . The many people are . . . The crowd is . . . The English football game expects the spectator to become *one* with the crowd; in a good football game, a game with 'atmosphere', the spectator assumes it: it is one of the things he has paid for. But, even here, it is more than an ordinary crowd experience.

It is an experience of constant physical contact and one that the terraces are designed to concentrate. The terraces look like animal pens and, like animal pens, provide only the most elementary accommodation: a gate that is locked shut after the spectators are admitted; a fence to keep them from leaving the area or spilling on to the pitch; a place for essential refreshment – to deal with elementary thirst and hunger; a place to pee and shit. I recall attending the Den at Millwall, the single toilet facility overflowing, and my feet slapping around in the urine that came pouring down the concrete steps of the terrace, the crush so great that I had to clinch my toes to keep my shoes from being pulled off, horrified by the prospect of my woollen socks soaking up this cascading pungent liquid still warm and steaming in the cold air. The conditions are appalling but essential: it is understood that anything more civilized would diffuse the experience. It seems fitting that, in some grounds, once all the supporters have left in their herd-like stampede, the terraces are cleaned by being hosed down: again, not just the images but the essential details are those of an animal pen. That is what the terraces offer, not just the crowd experience but the herd experience with more intensity than any other sport, with more intensity than any other moment in a person's life – week after week.

Here, in Cambridge, on a Tuesday night, me a stranger among strangers: the physicalness was constant; it was inescapable – unless you literally escaped by leaving. You could feel, and you had no choice but to feel, every important moment of play – through the crowd. A shot on goal was a felt experience. With each effort, the crowd audibly drew in its breath, and then, after another athletic save, exhaled with equal exaggeration. And each time, the people around me expanded, their rib cages noticeably inflating, and we were pressed more closely together. They had tensed up – their arm muscles flexed slightly and their bodies stiffened, or they might stretch their necks forward, trying to determine in the strange, shadowless electronic night-light if this shot was the shot that would result in a goal. You could feel the anticipation of the crowd on all sides of your body as a series of sensations.

Physical contact to this extent is unusual in any culture. In England, where touch is not a social custom and where even a handshake can be regarded as intrusive, contact of this kind is exceptional – unless you become a member of the crowd.

When I arrived at this match, coming straight from a day of working in an office, my head busy with office thoughts and concerns that were distinctly my own, I was not, and could not imagine becoming, 'one' with any crowd. It was windy and cold and that biting easterly weather was felt by *me* personally – in *my* bones. I was, in what I was sensing and thinking, completely intact as an individual. And it was *me*, an individual, who was then crushed on all sides by strangers, noticing their features, their peculiarities, their smells – *except* that, once the match began, something changed.

As the match progressed, I found that I was developing a craving for a goal. As its promises and failures continued to be expressed through the bodies of the people pressed against me, I had a feeling akin to an appetite, increasingly more intense, of anticipation, waiting for, hoping for, wanting one of those shots to get past the Millwall goalkeeper. The business of watching the match had started to exclude other thoughts. It was involving so many aspects of my person – what I saw, smelled, said, sang, moaned, what I was feeling up and down my body – that I was becoming a different person from the one who had entered the ground: I was ceasing to be me. There wasn't one moment when I stopped noticing myself; there was only a realization that for a period of time I hadn't been. The match had succeeded in dominating my senses and had raised me, who had never given a serious thought to the fate of Cambridge United, to a state of very heightened feeling.

And then the game – having succeeded in apprehending me so – played with me as it played with everyone else. It teased and manipulated and encouraged and frustrated. It had engendered this heightened feeling and, equally, the expectation that it would be satisfied: that there would be gratification – or not. That the team would score – or be scored against. That there would be victory – or defeat. Climax – or disappointment. *Release*. But what happens when all that energy, concentrated so deep into the heart of the heart of the crowd, is not let go?

At ninety minutes, there was the whistle. There was no score. There would be extra time.

Cambridge United had advanced to this stage in the FA Cup by drawing with three of its opponents. With one, there had been three replays before a positive result was achieved. The team was accustomed to extra time. Not scoring – themselves or their opponents – was a feature of their play.

Not scoring is a feature of the game itself. Neither winning nor losing is another. Four matches were played on the preceding Sunday. In the match between Norwich City and Liverpool, the result was a goal-less draw. Between Bristol City and Bolton Wanderers, it was a one-one draw. Manchester United scored one goal and beat Hereford United one-nil. Everton beat Sheffield Wednesday by an own goal – victory was a mistake. The day before there had been eight games in which no goal was scored. There had been ten matches in which the final result was a draw. The preceding weekend there had been twelve.

People attend football matches in the belief that they, like the spectator of any other sport, will see either victory or defeat; they accept it as their condition that they will see neither. They accept that they will not witness a goal being scored. A goal *is* an unnatural event. There are so many obstacles: the offside rule, the congestion in the penalty box, the narrowness of the goal itself, the training of the keeper and his defenders. But then, such is the game and its merciless punishment of its spectators, that even when the unnatural occurs and a goal is scored, they can never be sure that they have seen it. It is one of the fallacies of the game that there is no thrill greater than watching the scoring of a goal; it is one of the facts that most people miss it. The goal itself is a see-through box of threads, and unless you are looking upon it from up high or into it from straight on or viewing it with the benefit of television cameras, you cannot tell when the ball has actually gone through and scored – until it has hit the back of the net. In every goal except the penalty kick, there is a small period of perception when there is neither goal nor no goal: dead time. Dead time is not a long time in clock-time – there is the moment when the ball *appears* to be about to cross the line, and, *later*, there is the moment when it definitively hits or fails to hit the back of the net – but in any kind of emotional chronology it can seem endless. Here in Cambridge, watched on all sides by supporters desperate to see a goal, wanting to beat this magical goalkeeper and the mysterious gravitational field he had established around himself, five shots were on target. Five shots that – especially from our exaggerated position, at midfield, level with the players – were visually indistinguishable from shots that had crossed the line. And again, each time, the sheer physical sensation: I could feel everyone round me tightening up, like a spring, triggered for release. Except that there was no release. There was no goal. The ball did not hit the back of the net: the shots had gone wide.

And, when, finally, there is a goal?

Some time ago, I attended a Scottish Cup Final at Hampden Park between the two Glasgow teams, Celtic and Rangers. There were sixty-six thousand supporters, one half in blue, uncompromisingly Protestant, and the other half in green, uncompromisingly Catholic. I stood on the Celtic side. The terraces were enclosed by chain-link fences, topped by four rows of barbed wire curving back in the direction of the spectators. The message was clear: the herd would not be going over the top. At the bottom of each aisle was a gate that led on to the pitch. The gate was locked shut. Behind each gate stood three policemen, their backs to the pitch: throughout the game they watched only the crowd. Only the supervisor had the key, and he had to be called over when a gate needed to be opened. The gates would have to be opened twice.

Rangers scored the first goal before the first half was over.

Then, at the outset of the second half, Rangers scored again. With fifty minutes gone, Celtic was behind two-nil.

It was early days – I had not been to many matches – and I had no way of measuring what I was seeing. I knew that this spectacle – the stadium full of sectarian intensity, sixty-six thousand supporters, half in blue, half in green – was unlike any sporting event I had ever attended. With hindsight, I can see that I did not appreciate the weight, the *gravitas*, of the occasion: Rangers and Celtic; Protestant and Catholic; the Cup Final. And Celtic losing two-nil.

The Celtic goal, when it came, came quickly – there was an opportunity; it was taken – but it was difficult to say what had occurred. It had happened with such speed that no one knew who had made the shot or, even, at first, that a shot had been made. There was silence – stunned, incredulous silence. Dead time, frozen time, no time, neither goal nor no goal. No one could register the fact of it, as if sixty-six thousand people were playing the moment over again in their minds, checking their perceptions: was that a goal? is there a penalty? is the flag up? is the ball in the net? Proof: the ball is in the net. Check again: yes, it is there. The ball is in the net. The unnatural deed is done. The goal is a fact.

And then, after the silence, the explosion. There was room and space around me, and the crowd, erupting, swelling, rose inches into the air. A stranger, who moments before had looked menacing and aggressive, grabbed both my hands. Another one embraced me. I turned and was kissed on the cheek. I was embraced again. Everybody was in motion, when suddenly the movement was more than what I understood and I was tumbling forward, everyone was tumbling forward, falling down the steps of the terrace. I rolled down several steps – five, six – and when I looked up there was no one standing. Everyone had fallen and yet the celebrations continued. People got up on to their knees and were shouting. Still jubilant, there were others, rolling around, kicking their feet in the air, screaming with bliss, as though in a fit.

The police unlocked the gates and came running up the aisles. I thought there had been trouble, and it was only later that I realized that the police had rushed up to collect the injured. There were five stretchers. One supporter broke his leg. Another, from the way he was writhing and grabbing his side, appeared to have bruised or broken his ribs. The other three supporters had head injuries. One was unconscious.

The police returned to their positions at the bottom of the aisles and locked the gates.

In the ninetieth minute, at the moment when defeat appeared inevitable, Celtic scored another goal. Again, could I have appreciated the significance? Rangers and Celtic; Protestant and Catholic; the Cup Final. And Celtic had equalized in the last minute of normal time.

It was the second time that the police had to unlock the gates. Once again, there were injuries, so many that there were not enough stretchers. Several people were taken off on folding metal chairs – the back of the chair held by one policeman, the legs by another, the injured supporter flopped over it, head dangling dangerously. Others were placed on the advertising placards that encircle the pitch. One casualty disappeared atop a promotion for Marlboro Lights.

The police returned to their positions at the bottom of the aisles. The gates were locked.

Nothing like this happens at any other sporting event – anywhere.

I offer one other illustration from another Scottish Cup Final, also between Rangers and Celtic, and also played at Hampden Park in Glasgow. The crowd had worked itself into such a state that by the end of the match thousands had run on to the pitch and proceeded to uproot the goal posts. The newspaper account said that:

Mounted constables arrived, and in the mêlée that followed more than 50 persons were injured. When the barricading was broken down, the rioters piled the debris, poured whisky over it and set the wood ablaze. The flames spread to the pay-boxes, which were only 20 yards from a large tenement of dwellings. Great alarm prevailed, particularly when the firemen were attacked by the mob, and prevented from extinguishing the fire, for no sooner had they run out the hose than the crowd jumped on it, and, cutting it with knives and stones, rendered the efforts of the firemen useless.

The wooden seats caught fire and went up in flames. More police arrived, but when a supporter was arrested, the rest of crowd responded angrily, rescuing the arrested man, stabbing two policemen and injuring many others. The fighting continued. It spilled out of the ground, and every street lamp in the area was broken. A constable was stabbed in the face.

There are two points about this act of violence that are of interest: first, it is the first recorded incident of serious crowd trouble in the history of football. It took place in April 1909. Previous incidents had been mainly small acts of vandalism directed at officials for cancelling a match, or attacks on referees for making bad decisions. This was the first crowd riot: the Scottish football league was twenty years old.

The second point is the apparent cause: for the second Saturday in succession, the match between Rangers and Celtic had not produced a result; for the second Saturday, the match had ended in a draw. The crowd could not endure another match ending without victory or defeat – without release.

The first period of extra time ended, and there were still no goals. One fifteen-minute period remained, but I was resigned to a draw. I'm sure that the nine thousand Cambridge supporters were resigned as well.

Everyone except the members of Cambridge United team itself. They were playing as if they believed they could win; they appeared not to have realized that they did not have the stamina to carry on, that their style – consisting of long passes, pitch-length sprints and maximum exertion – was a particularly exhausting one. After one period of extra time and no substitutions, it would have been reasonable to have played defensively, to have accepted a draw. Instead the Cambridge United players appeared more determined: more long balls, more pitch-length sprints, more brutal exertion. They had drawn upon some inexplicable reserve of adrenalin, and mid-way through the final period of extra time, United looked like it might score.

It began with a corner. The wind, which had been severe all night, was now blowing with the force of a gale, and the ball, kicked high, had got caught and hung in the air. Everyone could see the prospect of the goal – again that physical appetite, wanting that goal, craving it – and the ball dropped for a perfect header. And the perfect diving save.

There was another corner, on the opposite side, and although not directly against the wind, it could not take advantage of it. But it was a good kick, headed on for another chance and – another impressive save, this one pushing the ball over the net.

There was another corner. And so it went on. There were six corners. One side, then the next; one side, then the next. Each time the expectation of a goal grew greater. But each save or deflected pass or blocked header merely confirmed what I had already been convinced of: there would be no score.

In the last minutes, the Millwall keeper started stalling for time. Even he had accepted the draw, not wanting to ruin the chance now, with so little time remaining, of a replay. He dribbled the ball round the penalty box, ventured to its outer edge, returned, and then out to the edge again, where he passed the ball on, turned and returned to his goal. He did not realize that the ball was about to be passed straight back to him.

So when the goal finally came, it was a fluke, a mistake, a miscalculation with no time remaining to correct it: a back pass to Millwall's goalkeeper when he wasn't there to receive it. You could hear the Millwall players screaming. A sloppy ball, overstruck and misdirected, rolled slowly, slowly, slowly into the goal. And then time ran out. Millwall had beaten Millwall by scoring against itself.

The expected jubilation followed. It didn't matter how the goal was got; what mattered was that there was one. Cambridge United would be going on to the quarter-finals.

I made my way back to my car. It was illegally parked outside a petrol station on the Newmarket Road, and when I got to it I discovered that, by a surprising coincidence, the car parked next to mine, also illegally, belonged to the very man who had been standing next to me in the ground – the one with the wrinkled face and the strong smell of American cigarettes. We acknowledged each other in a friendly sort of way, but one involving the smallest possible physical gesture. I think I raised an eyebrow, my left one, slightly. I think he might have lowered his chin, just. And that was right: a conversation now – even a simple greeting – would have been hugely out of place.

DAWES ROAD, FULHAM

I was reading the morning newspapers in the coffeehouse in Ober Sankt Veit. I can still feel the indignation that overwhelmed me when I took hold of the *Reichspost*. There had been a shooting in Burgenland, workers had been killed. The court had acquitted the murderers. The judgement was designated, no, trumpeted, as a 'just verdict' in the organ of the government party. It was that mockery of any sense of justice rather than the acquittal itself that triggered an enormous excitement in the workers of Vienna. From all parts of the city, the workers marched in closed processions to the Palace of Justice, which with its sheer name embodied injustice for them. It was a completely spontaneous reaction, I personally felt just how spontaneous. Taking my bicycle, I zoomed into the city and joined the procession.

The workers, usually well disciplined, trusting their Social Democratic leaders, and content that Vienna was ruled by them in an exemplary fashion, were acting *without* their leaders on that day. When they set fire to the Palace of Justice, Mayor Seitz, standing on a fire engine, tried to block their way with his right hand raised high. His gesture was futile: the Palace of Justice was *burning*. The police were ordered to shoot, ninety people were killed.

That was forty-six years ago, and the excitement of that day still lies in my bones. It was the closest thing to a revolution that I had physically experienced. A hundred pages would not suffice to describe what I saw. Since then, I have known very precisely that I need not read a single word about what happened during the storming of the Bastille. I became a part of the crowd, I dissolved into it fully, I did not feel the least resistance to what it did. I am surprised that I was nevertheless able to grasp all the concrete details occurring before my eyes.

Elias Canetti
The Conscience of Words (1976)

WHAT HAPPENS WHEN it goes off?

It was around one o'clock, and Robert wanted to show me; he wanted me to see the event close up. Something was going to happen, and Robert didn't want me to miss it. Since eleven that morning, the Manchester United supporters had been gathering at the Manor House – a large, rambling Victorian pub and snooker club in north London – and there were now so many people that the pub had run out of glasses. People were standing on the snooker table because there was no more room on the floor, and others were shouting for drinks from outside because they couldn't get through the door. And then, in an instant, the pub was empty, and everyone was in the street, heading up the Seven Sisters Road, on their way to Tottenham.

Everyone except Sammy, who wouldn't be showing up.

Sammy, Robert was whispering, is said to have killed a man, and there are people out to get him. They will always be out to get him – this year, next year, for ever. Whether he did it or not doesn't matter. They *think* he did it.

The pace was brisk, and Robert held on to my sleeve, tugging me along, urging me on, guide and bodyguard, making sure that I was in front, that I wouldn't miss what was going to happen, and, at the same time, looking out for trouble.

They'll come at you from nowhere, Robert said. Snipers. Knife merchants. They cut you up and then they're gone.

The police appeared – vans, accelerators pressed melodramatically to the floor, their engines whining, coming up from the side-street where they had been waiting for the United supporters – and everyone stepped up the pace slightly in response.

On our right were tower blocks. On our left were tower blocks. It could be Warsaw or a suburb of Moscow, except that everything else was so inimitably characteristic of north London – the film of filth that settled on your skin and the grime from the exhaust fumes and the litter slapped by the wind up against the walls. We passed a doctor's surgery, its doors and windows boarded up, and several buildings black from smoke, with bits of things spread out on the pavement in front: a broken plastic chair, a bed sheet, a pink rubber boot, crinkly empty packets of all kinds – crisps, peanuts, nappies, digestive biscuits, the yellow tissue paper of a cheeseburger. There were bits of plastic – red plastic, clear plastic, white plastic, plastic cups, plastic containers – and food tins and drink tins and endless cigarette butts. Across the street, there was an ice cream van, and I spotted a prostitute hiding behind it, sitting on a low wall, out of view.

Fast now, Robert said, shooing me along, telling me to keep up.

We pressed on, a steady pace, past shops that had been locked away behind metal shutters and wire-mesh cages, small shops, all of them single units – fish'n'chips, kebabs, motor parts, take-away chicken, a café open six a.m. to four p.m., a sandwich shop, a belt shop, a shoe repair shop, new and used furniture bought and sold, GOOD BUYS, a newsagent, another shoe repair shop, an evangelist church, life insurance, women's clothing, cans of household paint (only white emulsion, a lorry-load of white emulsion) – and we then crossed the entrance to the Seven Sisters underground station.

That's where it happened, Robert said. That's where the man was killed.

A supporter's back had been broken, and Robert described him twitching and moaning, legs flapping, unable to stand up.

It was very, very bad, Robert said, and it was probably because I had never heard Robert describe anything he had seen as very, very bad – when I would have described virtually everything he had seen as very, very bad – that I knew this use of 'very, very bad' to be a terrible understatement. Two hundred people were involved in a fight on the escalator leading down to the trains, and with Tottenham fans racing up the moving stairs as the Manchester United fans came racing down, someone hit the emergency stop button, and everyone tumbled. Several people were knocked unconscious, and there were many bones broken – arms, legs, the floppy man with his crushed vertebrae – and the traffic along the Seven Sisters Road was backed up from the ambulances that were called in. At the bottom, once everyone had got up, was the dead man.

That's why Sammy is not here today, Robert said. It doesn't matter that it was never proved in court. He can never come to Tottenham again.

The Seven Sisters Road ended in a T-junction just past the tube station, and the long line of United supporters bent round to the left, going up the High Road in the direction of White Hart Lane. And then, on the other side of the street, I saw them: the Tottenham supporters, hundreds, more than a thousand, as many, certainly, as had arrived that morning from Manchester. They, like the police, had been waiting for the United supporters, and – this was why Robert kept pushing me up to the front – the United supporters had known they would be there.

Be ready, Robert said, whispering again, as if the supporters on the other side of the High Road might hear his instructions above the noises of the traffic and the police who were filling up the street with their vehicles and animals.

Any moment now, Robert said. And the walk-run was now verging on a sprint, the two parties, spread across several blocks of the High Road, moving in tandem, trying to get ahead of the police, waiting for the moment to cross.

A dog-handler came racing up alongside the pavement and cut across our path – eight of us now at the front of the crowd, Robert seeming to lead it. The dog-handler was out of breath. He knew what was going on, all the police did, and he would have been dispatched to get to the head of the group to slow it down and prevent it from getting beyond control. He was agitated and jumpy and you could see in his eyes that he knew that at any moment he might find himself in the middle of a riot. He had grabbed his dog by the collar so that, with his other hand, he could use the full length of his chain-leash like a whip.

Get back, he shouted, swinging his chain-leash above his head, cowboy style. Get back, and suddenly my face was stung – a sharp, bright pain across my jaw. The dog-handler had taken to snapping his chain-leash into the faces of the supporters, including my own. I was indignant and shouted at the policeman by his badge number.

We're just minding our own business, I said, we're just minding our own business on our way to a football match. What gives you the fuckin' right to hit me?

He twisted round to look at me, and his face betrayed an expression of bewilderment and incomprehension, and I could see that he couldn't make sense of what he had just heard: an American shouting out his badge number.

Tell him you're from the press, someone shouted at me from behind my shoulder. Tell him you're going to report him for police brutality.

The policeman dropped his chain-leash to his side and trotted along, led by his dog, and continued staring back at me, his head still twisted round.

Go on, the others were now shouting, tell him you're going to report him.

I have gone too far, I remember thinking. I have let myself become one of them. Here I am, being whipped by a policeman, arguing with him, being urged on by the supporters behind me – by the supporters behind me? By the one thousand supporters behind me: here I am at the front of a crowd, among the people leading it. And then something happened behind us – somebody had crossed the street – and the two long lines, the United supporters on one side, the Tottenham supporters on the other, momentarily converged, a roar going up.

Watch out now, Robert said, watch out for knives. It's going to go off.

But it didn't go off, and it was unclear what had happened – a loss of nerve? – when a supporter appeared, running hard, straight down the middle of the High Road, chased by two policemen, and one caught his heel and the supporter fell and rolled and covered his head, and, just as we passed him, I saw his chin popped backwards by a policeman's boot and then knocked forward as he was kicked by another policeman from behind.

There was another incident further back, but I couldn't see it – the lines of supporters on either side of the street seemed to stretch for a half a mile – and the roar went up again, and everyone turned, ready, but then nothing happened.

Any moment now, Robert was repeating, any moment. He was watchful, waiting for that instant when the thousand United supporters straggling along the High Road would change and know to act in a different way, in unison, as a crowd – as a *violent* crowd. I could see that Robert was actually judging each moment, weighing it, and that the time was not right yet, and that the time was still not right, but that it would be right shortly.

Any moment now, Robert said again.

Something was going to happen, but it was evident that whatever happened would have to involve the police. Had Robert

179

anticipated the police? There were too many – not so many that they were not outnumbered by the supporters – but enough that, having placed themselves down the middle of this road, having positioned their dogs and horses and vans between the two groups of supporters, the police would have to be attacked first. They were in the way – deliberately. It seemed to me that it was one thing to fight those who wanted to fight. It was a different thing to fight those who wanted to arrest you. This was not done. You don't attack the police – unless, it follows, you are able to beat them up so effectively that it is then impossible to get arrested. But this, too, was not done: you don't beat up the police. Scattered along this long street, I now realized, were around two thousand people working themselves into a state so heightened that it would allow them to attack the police. They were daring themselves, provoking themselves, asking, as Robert was asking, if this moment was the one that would set them all off.

This road, this ordinary north London thoroughfare, the most direct route into the city, the A10, the very one that led straight back to my home in Cambridge, had taken on a powerful meaning. It separated the supporters of Tottenham from those of Manchester. It separated both from the police. But it also separated them from the experience they were all trying to have. And they knew it. To remain on the pavement was lawful. To step off it was to enter lawlessness. The divide was almost a physical thing. I looked back, taking in the length of this line, this border, and it was as if I could see the lads pressing up against it, testing it, stretching it, wanting to break through it but being unable to do so – *just*. Someone stepped aggressively into the street, but the others whom he was hoping would follow remained on the pavement, and he hesitated, and, having hesitated, lost his nerve, withdrew and disappeared. Someone from the other side did the same – venturing out but finding himself alone – and retreated. This street – such a simple thing – was the line that needed to be crossed for this crowd to become a violent one.

THESE ARE THE things that are said about crowds.

A crowd is mindless.

A crowd is primitive; it is barbaric; it is childish.

A crowd is fickle, capricious, unpredictable. A crowd is a dirty people without a name (Clarendon). A crowd is a beast without a name (Gabriel Tarde). A crowd is a wild animal (Alexander Hamilton, Hippolyte Taine, Scipio Sighele). A crowd is like a flock of sheep (Plato), like a pack of wolves (Plato), like a horse – tame when in the harness, dangerous when set free. A crowd is like a fire burning out of control, destroying everything in its way, including finally itself (Thomas Carlyle). A crowd is in a fever, in delirium, in a state of hypnosis (Gustave LeBon). A crowd reveals our Darwinian selves, primal hordes suddenly liberated by the sway of the pack. A crowd reveals our Freudian selves, regressing to a state of elemental, primitive urgency. A crowd killed Socrates; a crowd killed Jesus. A crowd kills – in the Bastille, at the Commune, in front of the Winter Palace, in the streets of Vienna, down a dirt road in Mississippi or Soweto.

And who do we find in a crowd? Trouble-makers, riff-raff, vagrants and criminals (Taine). The morbidly nervous, excitable and the half-deranged (LeBon). The scum that boils up to the surface of the cauldron of a city (Gibbon). Both honorary barbarians (Hitler) and the vulgar working class who want nothing more than bread and circuses (Hitler). We find people driven by the impulses of the spinal cord and not the brain (LeBon). We find people who have abandoned intelligence, discrimination, judgement, and, unable to think for themselves, are vulnerable to agitators, outside influences, infiltrators, communists, fascists, racists, nationalists, phalangists and spies. We find people with a thirst for obedience (LeBon), an appetite to serve (Freud).

181

A crowd needs to be ruled. A crowd needs its patriarch – its despotic father, chief, tyrant, emperor, commander. It wants its Hitler, its Mussolini. A crowd is like a patient to a doctor, the hypnotized to the hypnotist. A crowd is a rabble – to be manipulated, controlled, *roused*.

A crowd is not us.

Whose metaphors are these? They come from Freud, Burke, the historians of the French revolution, our nineteenth-century heritage, our newspapers. Who is telling us what a crowd is *like*? It is not the crowd – the crowd does not tell us its histories; it is the observers of the crowd, listening to each other as much as to the shouting outside their windows: Edmund Burke, removed in London, weighing the gravity of a revolution that he sees only through other people's eyes. Hippolyte Taine, preparing lectures in Oxford, where he reads in the English papers of the violence of the Commune and fears for his family and his property in Paris. Gustave LeBon, the 'father of crowd theory', eleventh-hour sociologist, effortless plagiarist, lifting passages from Scipio Sighele, Gabriel Tarde and (inevitably) Hippolyte Taine (it is possible that the only crowd seen by the father of crowd theory was in Paris on a shopping day). Freud, two years after the great crowd massacres of the Great War, the streets outside his window already alive with the sounds of restless nationalism and anti-Semitism, advancing his own theories about the crowd and its leaders, based (inevitably) on the work of the 'justly famous' Gustave LeBon.

The history of the behaviour of crowds is a history of fear: of being a victim, of losing property, of a terror (and of *the* Terror) so powerful that it needs a name – to be accounted for, distorted into intelligibility, made safe. The history of the behaviour of crowds is one of explanations. It has given us the politics of violence and its sociology. It has provided us with the models of revolution and the ego-ideal. It has shown us cause and effect, the details of oppression, the brutalities, the injustices, the prisons and the torture, the price of bread, the loss of land, the inequities of exploitative taxation, the mechanical contrivances and contraptions of a dehumanizing modernity. Crowd theory makes sense of the crowd and its violence, as if, as in a scientific experiment, the right conditions could and always will produce the same results. Crowd theory tells us *why* – relentlessly, breathlessly, noisily, as if by shouting the reasons loudly enough the terror can be explained away. But crowd theory rarely tells us *what:* what happens when it goes off; what the terror is like; what it feels like to participate in it, to be its creator.

I have a recent photograph depicting a crowd incident in the seaside city of Split in Yugoslavia. I will describe it.

The crowd, all men, fills the frame. It consists of Croatian nationalists who have surrounded a tank that has been sent in among army troops to restore order. The photographer, uncredited, is positioned above the crowd – perhaps perched atop a vehicle travelling alongside or else crouched on the balcony of a nearby flat. Some of the protesters are pressed up against the tank, so closely that, panicking, they are having to pull themselves out of its way. They are the only ones moving. The others are still. Their stillness is sudden and compelling. In another context, they could be described as onlookers or members of an audience: their faces have the same expressions – expectant, slack-mouthed, not just judgement but the act of judging suspended or deferred – that we are used to seeing in any sporting crowd, waiting for something to happen. Or not. They, too, are waiting for something to happen. Or not.

Five men have just climbed on to the tank. There is a sixth man, out of view, about to leap on board – we see only his arms extended as he reaches out for support – and another, a seventh, still on the street, who is afraid of being left behind and is prepared to climb on from the front. The others are more circumspect and have avoided the gun turret, knowing that, to disarm the tank, they would have to do it from the rear, as though coming up behind a snake and grabbing it below the head. The men are neat and clean-shaven, except for one who has a moustache. He was the first to reach the top of the tank, although he is now being pulled back by his jacket – the seam joining the sleeves is starting to come undone – by a man who is eager to get to what he has in his hands. It is the head of the tank commander. The man with the moustache has reached down into the tank and pulled out the commander by his head: his hands cover the commander's face – his thumbs are pressed deep into his eyes – and he is yanking him out by his chin. It is possible to complete the metaphor: having taken the snake from behind the head, the man, wanting to disarm it properly, has now reached into its mouth to pull out each one of its fangs.

A brave act? Or a crowd act?

The newspaper reports that one soldier died in Split that day. We can imagine that the fatality was the tank commander. As I write, there are accounts of terrible killings in Yugoslavia – dismemberments, a disembowelment. We are accustomed to the journalist's scrutinies of the excesses of human conduct; they provide us with the material of our entertainments, the stuff of our newspapers, our television news, our films. We have no illusions about the potential depravities of our nature, except that rarely, despite our modern sophistication, do we admit that these depravities are genuinely our own: yours, mine. We know how the mob behaves, once in a frenzy. But, even today, the mob is not us. It is easy to dismiss an incident of crowd violence in Yugoslavia; it is an unstable state; it is not ours. It is even easier to dismiss an incident in South Africa or India, countries that, removed in both geography and culture, are manifestly not us: it makes sense – does it not? – that there, among the 'underdeveloped', the 'underprivileged' the 'uncivilized', the 'Primitive' (our nineteenth-century metaphors re-emerge) there would be mob violence. But it is as easy to dismiss the violence outside the doors of our homes. Here, now, in England, in London, down a side-street, not far from the centre, there is a crowd assembling: but that crowd, we will insist, is not us. Here, now, in the provinces, a bank holiday weekend, just before closing time, there is another crowd assembling which the police cannot control: but that crowd, too, is not us.

On 31 March 1990, a march on Downing Street to protest against the Poll Tax turned into a riot that injured 132 people, crippled twenty police horses, damaged forty shops and destroyed millions of pounds' worth of property. Forty thousand people joined the march. How many were among the rioters? The rioters filled Trafalgar Square and controlled the centre of the capital for more than three hours. How many rioters were there? Three thousand? Five? Ten? England, my newspaper told me the next day, is a civilized country. How could this have happened? Was it not because ringleaders, of dubious politics, infiltrated and influenced the crowd? Was it not instigated by the riff-raff of our society, the marginal elements, the anarchists, the small-time revolutionaries, the anti-parliamentarian militants? The language of the prosecution, when the arrested were brought before a magistrate, could have been Burke's – or Taine's or LeBon's. The crowd, it seems, is still not us.

Two years before, on 19 March 1988, a silver Volkswagen Passat was driven into a funeral procession on its way from St Agnes's Church to the Milltown Cemetery in Belfast – the dead man, thirty-year-old Kevin Brady, had been killed three days before by a deranged Unionist assassin. The driver and his companion, two army corporals not in uniform, were surrounded and trapped by the mourners, pulled out of their vehicle, beaten, stripped of their clothing and thrown over a wall, bundled into a taxi, shot and abandoned on a piece of waste land.

A brave act? Or a crowd act?

There were two thousand mourners. Some were members of the IRA; many, we can assume, were sympathizers. Most, however, were *also* responsible members of a community: taxi-drivers; shopkeepers; people with jobs, with families; owners of property. The killings themselves took place amid detached houses, family cars in driveways, a park – the suburbs. How were the members of this procession perceived? They were all terrorists, according to Tom King, then Secretary of State for Northern Ireland, capable of unknown 'depths of evil'. They were a 'depraved and perverted people', according to the spokesman from the Royal Ulster Constabulary. They were starved animals in a Roman arena (the *Sunday Telegraph*), animals in a frenzy of hatred (the *Independent*), a tribe capable of eating you alive (the *Sunday Times*). 'There seem to be no depths,' Margaret Thatcher said, 'to which *these* people will not sink.' They were thugs, terrorists, primitive bully-boys, IRA rabble, 'baying for blood'. And, within a week, the search was on for the leaders (there are always leaders) – the IRA 'godfathers' who had turned this crowd into 'a mob of seventeenth-century assassins prepared to impale their enemy on spikes.'

Let us indulge in an exercise of imaginative projection. You are in a procession to mourn a friend, perhaps a relative, murdered by the same act of violence that has just killed three people and injured sixty others. Before you join the procession, you are body-searched for weapons. The march begins. Thirty minutes later, a car appears speeding dangerously, driving against the direction of the procession. There is no other traffic. Its lights are on; its horn blaring. As it approaches, its speed seems to increase and it actually drives up on to the pavement alongside you, heading straight for a group of children. They leap out of the way; the car stops, reverses and blocks the path of the hearse itself. Someone shouts: 'It's the peelers, the peelers.' Someone else shouts, 'We've got the Rod. They're Brits, they're Brits' – and the shout is taken up by the others around you, as the car, still in front of the hearse, is now boxed in – one in front, two behind – by the other vehicles in the procession. You are frightened. Everyone is frightened as two thousand people – naturally? – close round the car. People are banging on its side; someone is on the roof, when the driver emerges, climbing out of the window, trying to get away, flourishing a hand-gun – a *hand-gun*?

Every crowd knows the laws it transgresses, and every member of that crowd would have known that they were about to deprive two men of their lives. Are you confident that you would have stopped short of killing them?

The crowd is not us. It never is. Again two years before; this time, April and May 1986: Saturday after Saturday, I was outside News International's printing plant in Wapping when hundreds of people were injured during crowd rioting. I *thought* I had witnessed a process by which previously rational adults – policemen, print-workers with mortgages and pension funds and families – suddenly behaved in a highly irrational way. But I was wrong. The violence, I always read the next day, had been the work of outsiders, anarchists and agitators. One year before, May 1985: (the chronology is so arbitrary, but so patterned): the deaths at Heysel stadium; they were not the doings of anyone from Liverpool. Reliable authorities – a mayor, a former referee, a director of the football club – inform us that the National Front was responsible: and not the members from Liverpool but from *London*. One year before, this time 1984. The violence surrounding the miners' strike: infiltrators, Militant Tendency, the lunatic socialist fringe. And even football violence itself: it is not the ordinary supporter, but a minority of trouble-makers, bad apples, villains and criminals – descriptions I kept repeating when on the last day of the season, four hours after running up the High Road to Tottenham with the lads from Manchester, I watched the trouble at King's Cross, trouble involving supporters from many clubs – London ones returning to the city, provincial ones on their way home. There were crowd fights – crude charges, medieval in their primitiveness – in every direction I looked. The traffic was stopped for an hour, and still the fighting went on.

Down the side-streets, there was further violence. There was a fight on York Way; another one up the Pentonville Road; yet another broke out on the steps of the Underground station. I heard sirens in the distance and realized that there was more trouble at the nearby Euston Station. I flagged down a taxi and drove back and forth along the Euston Road. There were now police, fire engines, ambulances, helicopters – and still the fighting continued. It was difficult to estimate the number of people involved, because the violence was spread out over such a large area, but it ran into the thousands.

But these thousands were not us.

It is worth re-examining the photograph from Yugoslavia.

I am intrigued by what I continue to find. I note that the men are well-dressed – two are wearing fashionable leather jackets; one, a suit and tie – and that it is likely that they have jobs, perhaps well-paid jobs in an office or a shop. I note that they are mature adults – with handsome, attractive faces; one has a stylish haircut. I note the high calculation of their act – coming up behind the hatch and pulling out an armed man. It is bold, but thought out, the risks weighed. Studying this scene on the tank, *in medias res,* I can infer the order of events that led to it: that the crowd, having surrounded the tank, found itself unable to commit the next act – an unequivocally criminal one, antisocial, lawless – and then one man, the man with the moustache, scaled the tank. He was not a leader, or at least not a leader in the sense that we believe crowds to be governed by leaders. He was not there to cajole, persuade, exhort, enjoin, hypnotize or *rouse,* and it is unlikely that the crowd would have responded to him if he had tried. Although he will be seen by the authorities as responsible – he is *there,* after all, in view – he has no influence over the crowd. He is merely the first to cross an important boundary of behaviour, a tacit boundary that, recognized by everyone there, separates one kind of conduct from another. He is prepared to commit this 'threshold' act – an act which, created by the crowd, would have been impossible without the crowd, even though the crowd itself is not prepared to follow: *yet*.

Every crowd has a threshold; all crowds are *initially* held in place by boundaries of some kind. There are rules that say: this much, but no more. A march has a route and a destination. A picket line is precisely itself: an arrangement of points that cannot be crossed. A political rally: there is the politician, the rally's event, at its centre. A parade, a protest, a procession: there is the police escort, the pavement, the street, the overwhelming fact of the surrounding property. The crowd can be here, but not there. There is form in an experience that tends towards abandon. I have described the relentless physicalness of the terraces and how they concentrate the spectator experience: that of existing so intensely in the present that it is possible for an individual, briefly, to cease being an individual, to disappear into the power of numbers – the strength of them, the emotion of belonging to them. And yet again: it is formlessness in a contrivance of form. Being a spectator is an insistently structured experience: there is a ticket that confers exclusivity; there are gates that govern what is possible here, inside; what is not possible there, outside. The demarcations are reinforced by the architecture itself. The face that a stadium, of uniform concrete or brick, presents to the outside world is blank and unexpressive: nothing is said, nothing admitted. The face that it presents to itself is an enclosure of faces – faces packed as tightly as bodies will allow, design at its most expressive: everything is possible here. Outside, one experience; inside, another; outside again, and the crowd experience, like the match which governs it, is terminated: there is an ending, closure, a point when the crowd can be designated as having ceased to exist. In every crowd, there is something – with form – to contain the inherently formless nature of the crowd itself, to control what is potentially uncontrollable.

And when the threshold is crossed, the form abandoned?

There in the streets of Tottenham I watched the faces, concentrating, as moment by moment everyone tried to build up the confidence or the intensity or simply the strength of feeling that would allow them to step over the high boundary that separated them from where they wanted to be. The idea was, figuratively, literally, historically, an act of transgression: to step (*gressare*) across (*trans*) what was forbidden to cross. Everything militated against crossing it. Every act of every day, every law that had been learned, respected and obeyed, enforced and reinforced, every inculcated custom of conduct, was preventing them from finally taking the step.

Again, the photograph in Split. The man with the moustache has been followed up on to the tank by five or six others. These men are not LeBon's morbidly nervous, half-deranged masses nor are they Gibbon's urban scum; they are ordinary, ordinarily responsible members of society, except in this one crucial respect: they have now done what is not done and cannot return to the orderly crowd standing round watching them. Having crossed this line, they are now outside the civilization they have left behind. On the face of one, the man pulling at the jacket of the one with the moustache, wanting also to get to the tank commander, is a look of terrible excitement. It is not panic or fear or anger or revenge. It is exhilaration.

There cannot be many moments in a person's life when what is civilized ceases to be, when the structures of continuity – job, shelter, routine, responsibility, choice, right, wrong, the state of being a citizen – disappear. English, the great mapping language of imperialism, has no verb which is the antithesis of to civilize, no word to describe the act of un-making the rules that citizens have made. Our lives do not admit the prospect, are organized to exclude it. Our day consists of patterns of conduct that hold us intact. My place in a civilized society, my place as a citizen, derives from an arrangement of agreements and routines. My day is heavily patterned: I wake, pee, eat, shit, shower, dress, travel to work, write my letters, make my phone calls, pay my bills, attend to my diary, drink coffee, pee, talk, lunch, run errands, catch my train, arrive home, have dinner, drink, pee, am entertained, fuck, pee, clean teeth, sleep. I have a house, a shelter. I leave it in the morning and return to it in the evening: it is there – a material fact, not simply reassuring but reinforcing in its familiarity. I own it by virtue of an agreement between me, my place of work, the bank and the law of the land. I am a collector, not in a refined sense but a fundamental one – my photographs, my articles of clothing, my pieces of furniture (arranged so), my library of books (arranged so), my friends and loved ones (arranged so), my idea of my life made smooth and comfortable by regular use, my papers, my work, my idea of me. I surround myself with things, prop myself up with property, fill up my space with stuff: I *personalize* it; I make it *intimate*; I make it *mine*.

I have so many images for it – this state of being a citizen, of being civilized. I see it as a net that holds me in place, keeps me from falling. I see it as a fabric – a network of individual threads, intertwined, pulled tight – that keeps me warm, that I can wrap around both me and others. I see it as property, a house, a structure, a made thing, walls to keep out the cold, a door to keep out the unwanted, a roof to protect me from the night and its terrible undifferentiated darkness:

But I see it, too, as a weight. I see it as a barrier, an obstacle between me and something I don't know or understand. I see it as a mediator, a filter that allows only certain kinds of experience through. And I am attracted to the moments when it disappears, even if briefly, especially if briefly: when the fabric tears, the net breaks, the house burns – the metaphors are arbitrary. This line, again; this boundary: I am compelled, *exhilarated*, by what I find on the other side. I am excited by it; I know no excitement

191

greater. It is there – on the edge of an experience which is by its nature antisocial, anti-civilized, anti-*civilizing* – that you find what Susan Sontag describes as our 'flair' (the word is so attractively casual) for high temperature visionary obsession: exalted experiences that by their intensity, their risk, their threat of self-immolation exclude the possibility of all other thought except the experience itself, incinerate self-consciousness, transcend (or obliterate?) our sense of the personal, of individuality, of being an individual in any way. What are these experiences? There are so few; they are so intolerable. Religious ecstasy. Sexual excess (insistent, unforgiving). Pain (inflicting it, having it inflicted) – pain so great that it is impossible to experience anything except pain, pain as an absolute of feeling. Arson. Certain drugs. Criminal violence. Being in a crowd. And – greater still – being in a crowd in an act of violence. Nothingness is what you find there. Nothingness in its beauty, its simplicity, its nihilistic purity.

A FINAL IMAGE: a December match against Chelsea. All morning long, the supporters have been gathering at the Lion and Lamb, a red-brick Irish pub near Euston Station, arriving, once again, according to a calculatedly staggered schedule – by hired coaches arranged during the week, vans and minibuses that have avoided the major motorways, private cars. Both rooms of the pub are crowded – steamy and sweaty and unpleasant – and the floor is covered with a gooey mix of beer and mud and wetness. It is impossible to move. I try briefly to get a drink but never reach the bar. At around one-thirty, the principal figures accounted for, the group sets off, the manner of its leaving by now a ritual known even to me. The pub is evacuated, glass breaking as pints of beer are simply dropped, and a crush of people instantaneously fills up the small street outside, a preposterous number in a preposterous hurry – no one wanting to be left behind – and then turns into the main Euston

Road, spreading out, kerb to kerb, blocking the traffic in both directions, everyone organized and united and feeling the high energy and jubilant authority of suddenly being a crowd.

They avoid the Underground at Euston Station (too many police) and march to the next one, Euston Square, entering it as one – placards, posters, stools being picked up and swept along *en route*, no barricade or turnstile an impediment – everyone chanting now, the group's euphoria building, no one buying a ticket, no one being stopped or challenged, and board the train that happens to be waiting at the bottom of the escalator, holding open the doors to prevent its leaving until everyone is inside.

But the train does not move.

The doors close finally, but the train remains at the platform. It is waiting; the driver is waiting – for something; for some sign; in all likelihood, for the police. Every carriage, front to back, is filled with supporters. Every seat is filled; every aisle, entrance or bit of space – for standing, sitting, squatting, holding on – has been taken. This is rush-hour closeness, an intolerable number of people pressed tightly together. The train has become hot and unbearably uncomfortable. Someone pushes the button to open the doors but they don't open. The supporters start shouting. They pound the windows. They try rocking the carriage from side to side.

And then the train starts and rapidly attains full speed. It passes through the first Underground station, Great Portland Street, without stopping. It passes through Baker Street and through the next one, Edgware Road, and it is apparent that the train is not going to stop, and that, with all other traffic cleared off the line, the train is going straight to Chelsea (*if* that's where it is going). I watch the faces of two passengers, a couple in their late fifties, modestly dressed, the man in a duffel coat, shopping bags at their feet, whose Saturday outing was ruined the moment they made the mistake of boarding this particular train. They appear too uncomfortable to make themselves conspicuous by objecting to where they are being taken, and sit anxiously looking side to side. Notting Hill Gate appears and disappears in a blur.

The train finally stops at Fulham Broadway, the station near the ground, and there is, despite the preparation – the elaborate routes into London, the expensive hire vehicles, the strategies of evasion – nothing to see but members of the Metropolitan Police. There are rows and rows of them. They are the only people on the platform; they have taken over the station. They appear, once we finally reach the top of the stairs, to be the only people waiting outside as well, but then, amid the police and the horses – a helicopter is noisily overhead – the pushing and the jostling, I hear someone say that he sees 'their lads'.

In the confusion around the entrance to the ground, the police line momentarily falls apart, and I notice a short, red-haired lad from Chelsea has slipped in among the Manchester supporters. He is following one, walking closely behind him, stride for stride. He taps him on the shoulder and, as the supporter turns round, fells him by an act of decisive violence: a heavy object, an iron bar or a weight that the red-haired fellow is holding in both his fists, is raised so suddenly, rammed with such force into the supporter's Adam's apple, that he is lifted off his feet, rising several inches into the air, and then falls backwards and collapses. When I look for the Chelsea supporter, he is gone, disappeared into the crowd.

Inside the ground, the policing continues but at a distance: there is a line of police along the bottom of the terraces, on the other side of the perimeter fence; there is another line at the top, along the uppermost row, looking down; and there are clusters on either side, in the stands left empty to provide a buffer between the home and visiting supporters. The police, it would appear, are happy to keep the area surrounded but reluctant to enter it themselves. Inside it, Chelsea supporters have 'infiltrated' and, like the little urban terrorist who surprised the United fan from behind, are conducting a discreet campaign of highly targeted violence – most of it unobserved by the police. I suspect, in fact, that the police are happy to 'unobserve' the violence: there is the sense that anything that occurs within the perimeters of the net they have formed is tolerable provided it doesn't slip through and get out into the open; but there is also the sense that anyone who gets hurt probably deserves it – for being there.

The effect is unpleasant. The experience of the whole match is unpleasant – nasty, unsettling. It is cold and windy: there is grit in my eyes, and I can feel it in my hair and underneath my clothes. There is constant movement: too many people have been admitted – a familiar ploy, to get them off the streets – which makes it difficult to do more than try to remain upright and fight for a view of the match. Every now and then, there is another little *snap*-violent disturbance effected by one of these runt-like infiltrators: everyone cranes his neck to have a look at the thing that has happened; you can never quite see it. Moments later, there is another incident somewhere else, and everyone cranes his neck in that direction. And so it goes on. Someone has taken to throwing spark plugs, and a supporter near me is struck in the head by one, slicing his forehead. It is uneasy and claustrophic. There is mention of a stabbing, but I don't see it, and it would be in keeping that there would be one, but also that there wouldn't be one, that it would have simply felt appropriate that someone should have been stabbed by now.

Towards the end of the match I spot the red-haired Chelsea supporter. I had thought that he would be among those who had infiltrated the visitors' stands. I watch him. His face, even though cheerfully freckled, is hard and unforgiving. He has the familiar crescent cheek, the encrusted scar from being knifed. He is small – he comes about half-way up my chest – but his smallness is not a liability or a weakness: it serves only to make him compact and spring-like and immediately menacing. He is an unhappy thing to look at, a little entrepreneurial machine of small-time violence. When he comes closer, working his way through the terraces, and passes in front of me – he is an arm's length away – I feel an urge to take him from behind by the neck and squeeze him until his breathing stops. The urge is a real one, I am convinced, and not a violent fantasy, and as he walks out of my reach, I regret I have done nothing.

By the end of the match, everyone is restless and frustrated; the 'atmosphere' is charged in some manner, as though by electricity or some kind of pressure in the air. I have grown irritated. I want to be warm. I want to be home. I am tired of standing and of the policing and have got a chill from the cold and damp of the night air, and am unhappy about the prospect of being held back, crushed up against lads smelling of bad food and bad drink and the bad indigestion that is the result, while waiting for the streets to be cleared of rival supporters. I resolve that I will figure out a way of slipping through the police line.

A policeman reaches out for me, looking as though he wants to stop me, but then lets me pass. I am on the other side. I am free to go. I am very relieved.

I recognize the person walking next to me; he is a Manchester supporter. I surmise that he must have done what I just did: he, too, has slipped through the police line, by himself, looking very solemn and very thoughtful – the last person in the world who could cause trouble.

I carry on. I spot Robert. How did Robert, of all people, succeed in getting past the police?

Behind Robert is another lad. This one, also by himself, is also terribly serious in manner: preoccupied, distracted. This is suspicious. Then there is another, until finally it occurs to me that they are all emerging from the ground in the same manner, having separated so that they can sneak through the police line one by one. There is a momentary indecisiveness and then they start down the Fulham Road, not wanting to hang about, not walking too fast, everyone maintaining the I-am-on-my-own-and-not-about-to-start-trouble look. I can't tell how much of this has been planned; the feeling is of overwhelming spontaneity. A crowd is forming, and the effect is of something coming alive. I can see more people joining up, attracted by the familiar, powerful magnetism of numbers, but they don't seem like additions: they don't seem to come from the outside, but from within the crowd itself. You can feel it growing, as though this crowd, this thing, this creature were some kind of biological entity, multiplying in the way cells multiply, expanding from the centre.

I follow, not wanting to miss out. I don't know why they are going in this particular direction but I am determined to be there – wherever 'there' might turn out to be. I have forgotten that a moment ago I was ready to go home. I am no longer tired or irritable or cold, but, like everyone around me, alive to the possibility that something is going to happen.

There are faces I haven't seen before – older faces, supporters in their mid-thirties and early forties, veterans of violence, old hands who have turned up because it is a match against Chelsea. The experience is manifestly so familiar to them that they have an eerie ease and knowingness. They are canny and savvy and know not to say a word.

The group – still fairly disparate, unhurried, deliberately casual – strolls silently round the Fulham Broadway, going behind the Underground station by way of a side-street. The police, concentrated near the entrance, have dogs and horses and a small fleet of vans. Everyone knows that, having got this far, he must not be detected. It is a ludicrous effect: as if a thousand people, having just burgled the back of a house, are now leaving on tiptoe through the living-room, while the owner sleeps in front of the television. It would take only one policemen to spot what is going on. But no policeman notices. Each step increases the expectation that they're going to get away with it. I catch sight of a street name – Vanston Place. I don't know the area and find that I am looking for reference points. Everyone bears to the right. I follow. And then they turn sharply to the left, a quick left. They have done it: the Fulham Broadway is behind us.

I don't see any Chelsea supporters. But I understand enough to know that I don't see any police either. *That* is what matters: that the police are behind us, receding with each step, mistakenly positioned on every Underground platform between here and Euston Station, waiting for the violent supporters who will never appear. The realization is intoxicating. Nobody says a thing – the silence of the group is uncompromising – but you can see it in the faces.

We are free, the faces are saying.

We have got past the police, the faces believe.

We cannot be stopped now.

All day long a crowd has been trying to form, and all day long it has been prevented from doing so. It has been cribbed and frustrated and contained. The experience of the day has been one of being boxed in: the pub in the morning; the train at Euston Square; the platform at Fulham Broadway where everyone was frisked, scrutinized, surrounded and then escorted to the ground. They were boxed in during the match – literally a box, its sides made of the heavy steel fences of the enclosed terraces. Throughout, the containment has been absolute. At every moment, there have been limits.

And now there is none.

The pace picks up. I can feel the pressure to go faster, an implicit imperative, coming from no one in particular, coming from everyone, a shared instinct for the heat and the strength of feeling, knowing that the faster the group goes the more coherent it becomes, the more powerful, the more intense the sensations. The casual stroll becomes a brisk walk and then a jog. Everyone is jogging in formation, tightly compressed, silent.

I am enjoying this. I am excited by it. Something is going to happen: the crowd has an appetite, and the appetite will have to be fed; there is a craving for release. A crowd, already so committed, is not going to disperse easily. It has momentum: unstoppable momentum.

I catch sight of a street name – Dawes Road. I press on, going a little faster, wanting to get to the very front, while repeating the name of the street as I run. I recognize the familiar high-street businesses – a Ladbrokes, a Lloyds Bank, a building society, a shop selling fruit and vegetables – but they could be anywhere. I could be anywhere.

It is getting congested. I am on the pavement, which is filled with supporters, and I am having difficulty getting any closer to the front. There are more supporters on the other side of the street as well, on the opposite pavement, and some running between the cars.

For the first time I hear shouting, although it is some distance away. It is a football chant, but I can't make out what is being said. I am surprised by the sound. Someone says: 'Their lads.' These words seem slightly intrusive – *their lads* – and they echo round in my head. The shouting, I then understand, comes from Chelsea supporters. What does this mean? That we are being chased by Chelsea supporters? I find the idea thrilling. The crowd has a purpose: the Chelsea supporters have provided one. Actually I find many things in the idea. I also find it frightening: there are no police; this is about to become ugly. And I find it confusing. How, at this point, can the Chelsea supporters be *behind* us? I look back but see little: only members of the Manchester crowd, who seemed to have swelled now, a bloated presence, filling the full width of Dawes Road. I can't see beyond them. I can't tell if anyone is chasing us, but I hear them. Yes, the chanting is definitely Chelsea's.

Yes, someone else says, it's their lads.

I press forward. I don't want to get caught from behind in a fight, but to get any closer to the front I have to push people out of the way. I inadvertently make someone stumble, but he doesn't fall. He swears at me, and I mumble an apology, and when I look up again I see the most astonishing sight: it is Sammy. Sammy is at the front of the group. Where did he come from?

I remember Sammy in the pub that morning, but I haven't seen him since. It seems fitting that as this crowd came into being he would emerge out of it, pushed up to the front, created by the crowd. I feel reassured seeing him. I watch him. He is jogging steadily, his little lieutenants by his side. He has noted that the Chelsea supporters are behind us – he turns his head every three or four steps – but the prospect does not disturb him. Sammy does not look unhappy. Something is going to happen – that's his look; he knows it's going to go off.

Even so, I still don't understand: where have the Chelsea supporters come from? It is as if they have materialized out of our footprints. There was the police barrier; the police at Fulham Broadway; the quick route through the back streets. But nowhere were there Chelsea supporters. Something is missing. Is it possible that the United supporters set out in this direction knowing they were going to be followed? But how could they have known that? Were the Chelsea supporters in hiding, waiting for them to pass? Did I miss them?

I continue watching Sammy – in control, still checking behind him, judging how close the Chelsea supporters are. Everything, his manner suggests, is going to plan. And then the thought occurs to me: yes, it *is* going to plan. It is an improbable notion, but it makes sense of everything. It has been planned. Riots are meant to be spontaneous and sudden: you don't control the uncontrollable. Crowd violence is never planned – or is it? Is it possible to have a riot by appointment?

I want to ask, but things are moving very fast. Sammy, having been offered control, is exercising it. The pace quickens. I am running hard, too hard to catch sight of anything. There are shops, but they are unfamiliar. I don't even recognize the high street standards. It is a strange sensation: I feel as though I am running in a tunnel. Along the peripheries of my vision is a blurry darkness, the light – from a sign or a window or a headlamp from a car – is intermittent and unfocused. I am having to concentrate on the back of Sammy's head; I have hooked my gaze there so that I can be dragged along by it, so that I won't stumble or fall. The chanting of the Chelsea supporters is louder – progressively louder. They are getting closer.

Someone says: They are on our tails.

Sammy presses on. Stay together, he calls out; it is the first thing he has said. Stay close together, he repeats.

I still can't see any Chelsea supporters, but I believe that I can *feel* them. They are just behind the last members of the Manchester crowd, keeping pace but also distance, maintaining a buffer.

Streets start appearing rapidly on our right. I catch the name of one, but then forget it. There are more streets. For some reason, there are many. Every fifteen or twenty yards, it seems, there is another one. I notice Sammy noticing them. He seems to be looking for a particular one. There is a strategy at work but I am not understanding it. Sammy then shouts something – he has discovered the street he wants – and the crowd, sprinting now, runs with him. He leads us round the first corner. Then a quick right: after ten yards, there is another corner. And, surprisingly, another quick right. Three small streets, and then we are back to where we started from, except in one crucial respect: before we were being chased; now, having looped round, we are the ones chasing.

Later, looking at a map, I will discover that Dawes Road passes through the area at an angle, cutting diagonally across the other streets, breaking them into small residential triangles, making it possible for Sammy to run round one rapidly enough to be able to re-emerge directly behind the Chelsea supporters.

It is the first time I have seen them, but it is, I think, only the younger ones I see, the ones hanging back, at the rear of the crowd, bouncing in and out of my vision. I can take in little more than vague figures, the occasional face, a look of panic as someone turns round to see what is chasing him down from behind. The pavement ends, we enter the street, cross it, the pavement begins. I see this because I am watching my feet, everyone pressed so closely together and moving so fast that I don't want to fall. But I don't know how many streets we have passed. I perceive them not as facts, but as symptoms of movement. Where is the traffic?

It goes on. I was convinced that, having looped round, the momentum would carry us straight into the violence, but it doesn't. It is a chase, and the chase continues, pressing against this barrier, this threshold, the act of transgression moments away, but no one prepared to undertake it: on and on and on and nothing is happening. I am being held back, restricted, leashed. The buildings around me, although hardly discernible, have a weightiness about them: they are shadowy and dark and oppressive. I find that I am noticing them – more than I am noticing the supporters. I want the buildings not to be there. It is as if the street were no longer wide or large enough for me. The buildings have become aggressive physical facts, constricting and overbearing. Something has got to give way, something has got to give.

And when it does, it is property.

There is glass breaking: it is a window. I hear it, I don't see it, but the effect is sensational – literally sensational: it fills the senses, reverberates inside me, as though a blast of voltage has passed through my limbs. Something has burst, erupted. There is another sound: the soft, crushed sound of a windscreen shattering. The sensation of hearing this is intensely gratifying. There is another muted crash, another windscreen. And then everywhere, glass is breaking. It is property that is being destroyed first, in order to help us across this barrier: *property*, the symbol of shelter, the fact of the law.

And then they are gone. They go over the crest. There is the roar, and then everyone flies – as though beyond gravity – into violence. They are lawless. Nothing will stop them except the physical force of the police. Or incapacitating injury.

I will not describe the violence because what I want to depict is this precise moment in its complete sensual intensity – before chronology allows the moment to evolve into its consequences. What has occurred? What has happened when a crowd goes over the edge – or the cliff: the metaphors, though hackneyed, are revealing.

This is the way they talk about it.

They talk about the crack, the buzz and the fix. They talk about having to have it, of being unable to forget it when they do, of not wanting to forget it – ever. They talk about being sustained by it, telling and retelling what happened and what it felt like. They talk about it with the pride of the privileged, of those who have had, seen, felt, been through something that other people have not. They talk about it in the way that another generation talked about drugs or drink or both, except that they also use both drugs and drink. One lad, a publican, talks about it as though it were a chemical thing, or a hormonal spray or some kind of intoxicating gas – once it's in the air, once an act of violence has been committed, other acts will follow inevitably – necessarily.

And how would I talk about it?

I think of consciousness as having to be aware of the present on a multiplicity of levels. The human mind is never at rest in the present; it is always roving, recalling, remembering, selecting, adding, forgetting. Sitting in this room as I write my mind is accommodating so many different activities at once: it encompasses this sentence as I write it; it has already composed the next one; it has completed this book and it has, at the same time, not completed it; it has never completed it. It accommodates the state of the kitchen; the sounds of the birds outside; the quality of the light; the items that I must address later in the day – tonight, this weekend, next month, when I am old. It has, over the time it has taken me to write this paragraph so far, addressed my relationship with the bank, with my family; noted the eye make-up that my sister wears on national holidays, recalled a death; lingered upon a sad memory. Human consciousness exists on far more levels than consciousness itself could represent. This is our reality; our humanness: the thousand million stimulants of the moment, the indiscriminate mass of motion that the mind is constantly engaging, disengaging, abandoning, retrieving.

I am attracted to the moment when consciousness ceases: the moments of survival, of animal intensity, of violence, when there is no multiplicity, no potential for different levels of thought: there is only one – the present in its absoluteness.

Violence is one of the most intensely lived experiences and, for those capable of giving themselves over to it, is one of the most intense pleasures. There on the streets of Fulham, I felt, as the group passed over its metaphorical cliff, that I had literally become weightless. I had abandoned gravity, was greater than it. I felt myself to be hovering above myself, capable of perceiving everything in slow motion and overwhelming detail. I realized later that I was on a druggy high, in a state of adrenalin euphoria. And for the first time I am able to understand the words they use to describe it. That crowd violence was their drug.

What was it like for me? An experience of absolute completeness.

PART THREE

DÜSSELDORF

The disaster of the 9th March, 1946 . . . occurred at Burnden Park, Bolton, the home ground of the famous Bolton Wanderers Football Club, on the occasion of a Cup-Tie between the Wanderers and Stoke City. Disaster it was, for it brought death to 33 persons and injuries to the hundreds of the crowd assembled on the ground. The disaster was unique. There was no collapse of a structure: it was the first example in the history of football following of serious casualties inflicted by a crowd upon itself . . .

One of the deepest impressions left upon my mind from the enquiry is how simple and how easy it is for a dangerous situation to arise in a crowded enclosure. It happens again and again without fatal or even injurious consequences. But its danger is that it requires so little additional influences – an involuntary sway, an exciting moment, a comparatively small addition to the crowd, the failure of one part of the barrier – to translate the danger into terms of death and injuries. The pastime of football watching is on the increase and the chances of danger among the crowds are rising.

Moelwyn Hughes
Report of an Enquiry into the Disaster at the
BoltonWanderers Football Ground (24 May 1946)

I MET DJ at an Italian restaurant in April 1988 in Woodford Green, a leafy district of outer London not far from Epping Forest. The restaurant had candles and linen table-cloths; in the corner, a piano player was singing early Bee Gees tunes with a Mediterranean accent. The restaurant was DJ's choice, and he was a regular customer; he had an account.

I had heard about DJ from a friend, a television journalist who, having produced a story about West Ham's Inter-City Firm, had become friends with the supporters and remained in touch. He wanted me to meet DJ. DJ was, according to my friend, one of West Ham's 'Top Men', but was also someone who wanted to do something new. He wanted to be a photo-journalist and make his name taking pictures of crowd trouble. My friend thought we might be able to work together and so he arranged a dinner between the three of us. He also asked another friend to come along, the managing director of a photo agency.

DJ's crowd was extraordinary, even by the standards set by the supporters I had met. My friend mentioned Kelly, a very small man interested in only very big crimes. My friend asked me if I remembered the Leicester prison break-out in 1986. That was the one in which a helicopter flew into the grounds during the exercise period and whisked off two inmates. Kelly was the pilot of the helicopter.

My friend also described a Sunday excursion to the beach. Someone had hired a coach – as became apparent later, cash was never a problem – and fifty or sixty members of the firm headed out of East London for the coast. They were near Clacton-on-Sea when my friend decided that he had seen enough. He announced that he was getting off the bus then and there unless the supporters stopped what they were doing. They got angry. They pouted. They called my friend a spoil-sport. But finally they stopped.

It had started shortly after setting out. Most people on the bus were in a state of moderate brainlessness – there had been drink and dope and cocaine – when, after passing a hospital for the mentally ill, they spotted a woman on the roadside, looking for a lift. They told the driver to stop.

She was about seventeen, wearing a night-dress, and had escaped from the hospital. Her thinking facilities were severely impaired – she couldn't see straight or talk properly or move with any kind of grace – but she was a sexual being and responded to the attention that was paid her. The supporters gathered round: they tickled her, played with her nipples, rubbed her clitoris, stripped off her clothes and placed her naked on the floor in the aisle between the seats. They were waving their penises in her face. Someone had urinated on her. They were about to rape her – one of the supporters, crouched between her legs, was holding his erection in his hand – when my friend stopped the coach and asked to get off.

They drove on through the morning and reached Great Yarmouth in the early afternoon and entered the first pub they saw. They were in a mood for trouble. Everyone ordered up a big lunch and then hurled the various items of it at each other – a food fight involving pies, pub lasagne, whipped potatoes, the basic hot lunch menu. They were thrown out. They entered another pub, which was filled with 'squaddies', troops from the local RAF air bases, a feature of East Anglia. A fight began, one involving nearly seventy people – chairs, bottles, tables, a bench; the supporters got away before the police arrived.

They entered a third pub.

By this time the local constabulary was looking for them. In addition to the pub disturbances, they were spending money that was 'moody'. It was counterfeit. Their trail was easy to follow.

Through all this, they retained the girl. They hadn't raped her, but kept her on as a mascot of sorts – a plaything.

The bus driver had been following many of these antics from the car-park and had decided that he had seen enough. He started up the engine and pulled out into the street. Unknown to him, three West Ham supporters were asleep in the back. They had passed out earlier from any possible combination of drugs, but one of them was alert enough to register that the bus was moving and he woke up the other two. The driver would have been startled to hear their voices. They offered him a choice: either he returned the bus to the parking lot or they would set it alight: they would torch it.

The point about my first meeting with DJ, however, was not to learn about West Ham supporters; it was to see if DJ could make it as a photographer. By the time we sat down at our table – we had cocktails first – the managing director of the photo agency had already agreed to put up the money for DJ's film and processing just to see what she got back. The European Championship was to be held in Germany that summer and would be the first of several 'hooli-fests'. Ever since the Heysel Stadium deaths, the England team was always accompanied by many journalists when it went abroad – as many journalists as supporters, sometimes – eager to capture the next instance of violence.

The European Championship would also mark the first time, since crowd trouble had become recognized as not only an English but a European problem, that the notorious supporters of so many different countries – the Germans, the Dutch, the Italians as well as the English – would be in the same place. England was scheduled to play Holland in its second match in Düsseldorf, and, as the border with Holland was but a few minutes away, a large number of Dutch supporters would be attending. England was not scheduled to play Germany, unless it got through the first round, but German supporters would be everywhere. DJ knew there would be trouble and wanted to be taking pictures of it. It would be the start of his new career.

Even so, he seemed to be prospering in his old career, although I was not certain what it was exactly. Import-export, he said at one point, and it did seem to be a trade of some kind. He had returned that very morning from Bangkok, where he had done some 'deal' involving children's clothes and had 'cleared', he said, a thousand pounds. I could not imagine how this worked, but I didn't get a chance to ask him about it until the end of our meal.

Underpants, DJ then explained. He had come back with suitcases full of children's underpants.

You trade in children's underpants? I asked. It sounded a little unsavoury.

Among many other products.

And then, perhaps feeling a little defensive, he listed them. They included watches, fashion accessories, men's suits, women's and children's clothing, shoes and cars. For some time he did a line in Mercedes. The travel involved in trade of this kind was considerable, and DJ mentioned that, in the last year alone, he had been to Hong Kong, Taiwan, Tel Aviv, Manila, Cairo, Luxembourg, Mexico City and Los Angeles. He liked to travel; it was important to him. He said that even this morning, just off the flight from Bangkok, he had phoned his travel agent – after so much work, it was time for a holiday – hoping to arrange a little trip, leaving tomorrow perhaps, to Sun City in Southern Africa. The idea of Sun City appealed to him and he described its attractions. I don't know if he went. I suspect that the holiday was described in the same spirit that informed his homilies about the virtues of the economic practices of the Conservative Party and the philosophy of Margaret Thatcher: he knew the liberal politics of his new media friends.

He paused to admire the label of the jacket I was wearing. He was putting on a good show. Before the evening was finished, he would mention the house he had just sold. He would also say something about the Jag he wanted to buy, the movement of his investments on the stock market, the races at Newmarket and his drive there in a Mercedes along the Six Mile Bottom Road, the automatic speedometer fixed to 135 miles per hour, throwing empty champagne bottles out the window. DJ was twenty-three years old.

The managing director of the photo agency arranged to give DJ some photography lessons, and he and I agreed to meet for a drink at a later date. The bill for the meal was £120; DJ insisted on putting it on his account.

DJ and I met several times before the European Championship. He had been a football supporter since the age of ten and had stories to tell. Some of these involved the lads from Manchester United. I was amused to learn how far Sammy's reputation extended. Among West Ham supporters he was known as 'Steamin' Sammy' because he was always the first one from Manchester United to 'steam into trouble'. On one occasion, Sammy's spectacles were seized and displayed as a trophy behind the bar at the Builders' Arms, one of the West Ham pubs, and when Sammy, nearly blind, wandered into the pub later that day, he was set upon. DJ was also on the train from Manchester in which Roy Downes was beaten up and nearly killed. According to DJ, however, the trouble started when Roy threw a cup of hot tea at Bill Gardiner, West Ham's famous 'Top Man'.

As we drove through London together, DJ would recall the

spots where great liberties had been taken – 'taking liberties', a recurrent DJ phrase, was one of the more serious of possible misdemeanours and involved violating the territorial claims of a rival. At one time, he alluded to his scars. And although I would later hear his friends describe him as an animal – 'Lunar the Lunatic' was one of his nicknames – DJ's talk was not dominated by the subject of football violence. His agenda was more complicated.

DJ was different from most other West Ham supporters. For a start, he was Jewish – he mentioned getting 'nicked on Yom Kippur on a West Ham away' – and, although he spoke in a flat East London accent, I came to suspect that it was cultivated. He mentioned once that he had been to a small public school, and, when I pressed him on the point, I discovered that he had five A-levels. He spoke French. He read regularly, mainly non-fiction dealing with social issues: police, crime, development problems in the inner city. I also learned – the information was admitted reluctantly – that his family, although of a working-class background, was well off and that his father had a successful furniture factory somewhere in the East End. His brother worked for an investment company in New York. Later, I would see that DJ was a conspicuous spender, known also among friends as 'Bags-of-money', although it was my belief that the money had been earned by DJ himself, that it never came from his father. It was my hunch that DJ was conducting some kind of private rebellion against his upbringing.

DJ was an eccentric, and my sense of journalism told me that the details of his life justified spending more time with him. But there were other reasons, too.

I began work on this book because I wanted to know why young males in England were rioting every Saturday, and, although I knew very little about the game of football and only a little more about the people who attended it, I thought that my ignorance might not be such a bad thing. I believed that by entering an experience of this kind unencumbered – by history or tradition or even the habits of a Saturday afternoon – I might see it in a clearer way than someone for whom it was a familiar feature of the culture. I wasn't interested in questions of right or wrong, and I didn't ask them. I wanted to get close to the violence – very close, as close as I could possibly get – because I thought that this way I would find out how it worked.

I was surprised by what I found; moreover, because I came away with a knowledge I had not possessed before, I was also grateful, and surprised by that as well. I had not expected the violence to be so pleasurable. I would have assumed, if I had thought to think about it, that the violence would be exciting – in the way that a traffic accident is exciting – but the pure elemental pleasure was of an intensity that was unlike anything I had foreseen or experienced before. But it was not just any violence. It wasn't random violence or Saturday night violence or fights in the pub; it was crowd violence – that was the one that mattered: the very particular workings of the violence of numbers.

This is, if you like, the answer to the hundred-dollar question: why do young males riot every Saturday? They do it for the same reason that another generation drank too much, or smoked dope, or took hallucinogenic drugs, or behaved badly or rebelliously. Violence is their antisocial kick, their mind-altering experience, an adrenalin-induced euphoria that might be all the more powerful because it is generated by the body itself, with, I was convinced, many of the same addictive qualities that characterize synthetically-produced drugs.

I understood this and was convinced by it, but was still not satisfied. Why this kind of antisocial conduct? I couldn't separate the end – this exhilaration – from the means that got people to it; I couldn't treat it as this generation's thing, its rock and roll. There are endless precedents for extreme forms of behaviour – especially violence – but not for organized violence, not for violence pitched at achieving this kind of frenzied high: the crowd high. This was unusual. And, amid all the different factors that contribute to why an assembly of people becomes a crowd and then, ultimately, a violent one, there is almost invariably a political or economic cause of some kind, even if the cause is cosmetic or rhetorical – a grievance or an injustice or at least a hardened feeling of social frustration – and I couldn't get away from the starkness of the conclusion I kept reaching: that there was no cause for the violence; no 'reason' for it at all. If anything there were 'unreasons': rather than economic hardship or political frustration, there was economic plenty and an untroubled, even complacent faith in a free market and nationalistic politics that was proud of both its comforts and its selfishness.

I couldn't believe that what I saw was all there was.

This was where DJ came in. In the figure of DJ I had the fundamental contradiction at its most concentrated. He had so many things going for him – education, intelligence, an awareness of the world, money, initiative, a strong and supportive family. Even if he had had no interest in crowd violence, he would have been a fairly exceptional member of his generation. Here was someone on whom the social order of the day had bestowed so many advantages and opportunities that he would have to go out of his way not to be successful in society. Implicit in my thinking was the liberal commonplace that those who 'turn against society' – I felt that destroying its property and inflicting injury on its members could be described as 'turning against society' – have been denied access to it. This wasn't true of DJ. DJ, I hoped, could teach me.

I had started to feel troubled by the fear that I didn't know enough, even though by now I had been going around with violent people for about four years. My anxiety went hand-in-hand with my belief that what I saw couldn't possibly be

216

everything, and I grew convinced that I needed to do more research. By restricting myself to only what I could witness, I was sure that I wasn't getting the whole picture.

I STARTED SUBSCRIBING to a press service run out of the Old Bailey. The easiest thing *not* to miss, it seemed to me, was what appeared before a judge in the criminal courts, and the service, run by a group of young copy-writers, would be an insurance policy of sorts. It produced stories on the day – they arrived by fax – which were always a little over-written and over-packed with detail so that journalists could pick and choose according to the needs of their papers. The first story was much like any other. It was an account of the prosecution's case against John Johnstone.

John Johnstone belonged to a large group of Millwall supporters who, after attending an afternoon match against Crystal Palace, boarded the train to Charing Cross in London. The journey is only ten minutes, but during it Johnstone became violent. According to the prosecution, Johnstone approached one of the ordinary, paying passengers and ripped the newspaper that he was reading out of his hands. He then punched him repeatedly in the face. A ticket collector intervened, and Johnstone turned on him.

Word of the trouble reached the driver, who radioed on ahead to the Transport Police at Charing Cross, and John Johnstone and his friends – there were six in all – were apprehended when they arrived. They were not held for long, however, and were soon free to carry on with their plans for the evening.

These plans were not ambitious. In fact, Johnstone and his friends never ventured further than three hundred yards from the station where their evening began. Their first stop was the McDonald's on the Strand. They were there for only a few moments before Johnstone pulled out a knife and threatened a skinhead who was eating a hamburger. When another skinhead appeared, one of Johnstone's friends walked up to him and poked him in the eye.

Johnstone and his friends made their way to Trafalgar Square, stopping briefly at the Admiral Nelson Pub on Northumberland Avenue, where they posed as doormen, charging people money to enter, threatening them if they didn't pay. When they finally reached Trafalgar Square, there was more trouble, occasioned by a man with a spider-tattoo in the middle of his forehead. Johnstone and his friends found a spider-tattoo to be an intolerable thing, and so they beat the man up.

They made their way back to Charing Cross Station, where one of Johnstone's mates, Gary Greaves, hit a young man across the face – a stranger, standing on his own – and knocked him down. Greaves then kicked the man in the head, and the others joined in. A coach driver and his wife, parked nearby, waiting to pick up passengers from a train arriving later in the evening, witnessed the violence and felt compelled to try to stop it. And, to an extent, they succeeded – the lads abandoned the man on the ground – but they then turned on the coach driver and his wife, and both of them, man and woman, were badly beaten.

I don't know how long Johnstone and his friends remained at Charing Cross. The next sighting was in the Underground station. The Charing Cross Underground station is large and complex, a network of passageways connecting the three tube stops at Trafalgar Square, Charing Cross and the Embankment. Near the steps of the Embankment they met up with Terry Burns. Terry Burns was with friends, and they were panicky and frightened, having run into the Underground to flee a fight that had broken out at a Covent Garden pub. I infer from the prosecution's depiction that the West End, on this Saturday night, was a menacing place to be. There is no mention of the much larger group of Millwall supporters from whom Johnstone and his friends were separated when they arrived in London. It is likely that, if the larger group was not involved in the fight that

Terry Burns and his friends were fleeing from, then it would have been in another fight not far from there. There would have been many gangs of football supporters that night in the West End.

As it turns out, Terry Burns was a West Ham supporter. Johnstone and his friends had been looking for football supporters all evening, knowing that they were about, and would have been frustrated at continuing to meet up only with skinheads, men with non-conformist tattoos, strangers, bus drivers and lonely British Rail commuters. It must have been an exciting thing finally to find some genuine football supporters. I am sure, as well, that Johnstone detected the panic and fear that Terry Burns felt – it would have been apparent in his face; it would have been a presence like a smell – and Johnstone would have found this to be exciting as well. The result was violence of an altogether different order.

Johnstone and his friends charged into the strangers, stabbing one in the neck and arm. Burns fled and ran out of the station and up into Villiers Street. According to the prosecution, Johnstone then ran after him, shouting, 'Kill the bastard', his friends not far behind. They caught up with him in the street, and the group sprinted through Covent Garden in pursuit. They were chanting 'Millwall' over and over again. Terry Burns was unable to run fast enough – the Millwall supporters were directly behind him – and he tried to escape through a side street that turned out to be a dead end. The only detail we have is of a bicycle – Terry Burns picked it up to defend himself – but I imagine the bowel-seizing terror that Burns must have felt on realizing that he was cornered. I imagine him casting round for a way out – the door bells, the wall – before he picked up the nearest thing to hand, this unmanageable shield of spokes and tubes, to fend off what he knew would come pounding down the pavement in a moment's time.

Terry Burns died. He was stabbed six times. Each stabbing punctured the heart.

*

Terry Burns was not killed by a crowd; he was killed by a gang; but the distinction between crowd and gang violence is probably not meaningful in this case: it was only by chance that John Johnstone and his mates were separated from the crowd of Millwall supporters. The killing, however, wasn't in itself of interest. It was the quality of the evening – the desultory episodic nature of the violence and the sense of boredom that characterized it: this was violence of the most extreme kind, because there was nothing else to do.

The individuals also interested me. Why were they so bored?

John Johnstone was from Lewisham – a London suburb – and was working as a decorator at the height of the housing boom. His pockets would have been full of twenty- and fifty-pound notes. Although he was only twenty-one, he had a highly patterned criminal record. At the age of sixteen, he was convicted for causing actual bodily harm; at seventeen, for threatening behaviour; at eighteen, again for threatening behaviour; at twenty, for carrying a jack-knife. His mate, Trevor Dunn, also had a criminal record; he, too, was from the London suburbs, working as a successful decorator. Gary Greaves, twenty-seven, had his own business.

In the end, murder charges against all the supporters were dropped. John Johnstone was convicted of affray, two assaults and possessing an offensive weapon. He was sentenced to three years in prison.

It doesn't seem like much – a man was killed, after all – but in the eyes of the law Terry Burns's murderer has never been found. In fact, John Johnstone's sentence was, given the nature of the convictions, fairly severe: in the past, it is unlikely that he would have been put away for longer than two months. The longer three-year sentence was in keeping with the attitude that had come to characterize the judiciary's approach to football 'hooligans': to ensure that they were given the most severe sentences possible; to make them 'examples' to their peers.

Earlier in the year, two of Chelsea's so-called 'generals' – Stephen Hickmott, then thirty-one, and Terry Last, twenty-four – were each sentenced to ten years in prison, having been found guilty of conspiracy to fight and cause affray. Hickmott, who ran his own courier business, was, like his Millwall counterparts, from the suburbs (Tunbridge Wells); Last worked as a clerk for a solicitor in the city. The others arrested with them included a decorator, a chef, a builder and a Falklands War veteran – a former Royal Navy submariner.

Around this same time, I had also begun subscribing to a newspaper clipping service. Every two days, a package arrived, and I was surprised by how many clippings I found inside. There were usually between fifty and hundred, but sometimes many more.

Most were from small town and county papers, reporting the violence that had occurred at the local match that Saturday. For the first month or so, I went through every story, but it was too much to take in. I didn't know what to do with the information. I thought about discontinuing my subscription, but felt that wouldn't be right – that it would amount to choosing to neglect what was out there, to ignoring the historical facts. Even so, I had lost any desire to go through the stuff. I'm not sure when I stopped the service, but it wasn't until I had filled three large boxes – they are still stacked on top of each other in my study, most of the envelopes, with their detailed accounts of the violence of the week, still unopened.

Recently, I plucked one out at random; the envelope was dated 19 May 1987 and the clippings inside described the events of the preceding week. The 1987 season was not particularly remarkable for trouble. The deaths at Heysel Stadium, the fire at Bradford, the rioting at Luton between Millwall supporters and the police: all that had already occurred; *that* was history. This was the end of the football season. It was an ordinary football weekend. It was also ten days after the punitive, let-this-be-an-example sentencing of Stephen Hickmott and Terry Last.

Of the seventy or so clippings inside, only two were from national newspapers: the *Guardian* which described scuffles along the sea-front in Brighton following a match with Crystal Palace, and the *Daily Mail* which reported that a fan, aged nineteen, had required twenty stitches after 'his throat was slashed by thugs before the Everton-Manchester City match.' Everything else was from the provincial papers.

One was the *Wrexham Evening Leader*. There had been violence at a Sunday League game at Gresford in north Wales. The Sunday League is amateur football, played between pub teams, and this was its Wrexham Lager Cup semi-final involving the Cambrian Vaults and the Saughall Institute at Chester. It is unclear how the trouble began, but once under way it became very violent: there were 150 injuries, most incurred from people being kicked or head-butted. One man was struck over the head with a corner post; another had his leg broken. Even the coach of the Saughall Institute football club was involved: an amateur video caught him throwing a brick into the crowd and striking someone on the head. Of the eleven people convicted of affray – the sentences ranged from three months to two years – all but one had previous convictions involving violence.

There was trouble in Huddersfield just outside Leeds. Leeds fans had gathered at the Wharf pub to celebrate their team's winning the match that secured it a place in the league promotion play-offs. Later in the evening members of a Rastafarian reggae band passed by on their way to buy fish and chips in the centre of town. On seeing them, the Leeds supporters emptied into the streets and surrounded the band and started chanting '*sieg heil*' while making the Nazi salute. A beer glass was crushed into the face of one of the band members; four others were stabbed. When an ambulance appeared, the Leeds supporters refused to let it through, and one of the band members came close to dying from loss of blood.

In Bournemouth, supporters, after roaming from pub to pub, took over the Royal Exeter Hotel, smashed its windows, set fire to deck-chairs and then stoned the police and the fire-service vehicles that had been called in to stop the trouble (*Southampton Southern Evening Echo*). Members of the Robstart Football Club from Stockwell, another amateur team, were involved in a brawl at the Cabot Court pub in Weston-super-Mare. There were fifty-six arrests. In Southend, Wolves' supporters 'ran riot', and there was a 'clash' at Filbert Street following the match between Leicester City and Coventry.

In Peterborough, 150 Derby supporters, having stopped briefly in the city centre for petrol, attacked a group of local youths, punching one so hard that when he hit the ground his skull broke. In Southport, Bangor City football fans occupied one end of the stand and then jumped up and down until they destroyed it, whereupon they attacked the officials on the pitch. In a match between two non-league teams, Gillingham and Chelmsford City, twenty-one-year-old Anthony Robertson was arrested during crowd trouble that resulted in him being caught spraying ammonia in the eyes of a rival supporter and then knocking a local policeman against the wall, kicking him and injuring his shoulder. And in Bolton, supporters, described by the local journalist as 'howling demi-brains' displaying 'all the courage of a magpie with a sparrow's egg,' assaulted Middlesbrough fans at the Green Tavern where they were having a drink and then went on to attack nothing less than the Burnden Park police station, where one climbed a floodlight pole and cut the electrical cables into the station.

This list is already too long; in fact, it is only a partial one. It also excludes the packets that arrived around the same time – the ones postmarked 8 May, 13 May, 15 May, 20 May and 27 May. They are still unopened. The arrests and trials of the metropolitan centres are well represented by the agencies of the news media already located there. These stories are an indication of what doesn't get in the news; this is what Saturday afternoon in Britain is really like.

There is one further story that is worth citing. It is from the *Oldham Evening Chronicle* and involves two Irish sales reps, Neil Watson and Terry Moore, old friends, and long-standing Oldham Athletic supporters, who regularly flew into Manchester for a match. They made a weekend of it: a hotel, a meal and a drink on the Friday night. This match was against Leeds United, and both men had spent the evening at the bar of the Royton Hotel just outside the city. Just after closing time, they met up with a number of Leeds supporters and were attacked. Terry Moore was punched repeatedly in the face and fell to the ground unconscious, where he was then kicked in the head six or seven times. Terry Moore has a rare blood type, and this was used as evidence: forensic tests showed that it was this particular blood type that was to be found on one of the supporter's shoes, socks, trousers, T-shirt and hair. There had been a lot of blood. After the incident, the Leeds supporters went off but they returned a short time later. This is one of the details that is so compelling: they had come back in order to resume kicking Terry Moore's head. This was done six or seven more times; Terry Moore hadn't moved; he was still unconscious. He still hasn't moved. For twelve days, he was in a coma. When he emerged from it, he was paralysed and had lost his ability to speak.

I WAS UNABLE to accompany DJ to Germany for the 1988 European Championship – I would be going later – but he phoned me on the Friday he arrived. He then phoned me regularly thereafter to keep me informed of the trouble. There seemed to be a great deal of it – most of it between English and German supporters – and several of DJ's West Ham friends had already been arrested. And then, shortly after England's first match against Ireland, the press got what it had been waiting for – a terrible riot, with tear-gas and scenes of spectacular violence. DJ sent back his first batch of film on a late-night flight to London.

The next England match was in Düsseldorf – it was the dreaded one against Holland – and I flew over on a special flight added to accommodate the press. The British sports minister – a small man who spent much of his time talking about imprisoning male members of the working class under the age of thirty – sat in the front row. The flight was sold out; every seat had been taken by cameramen, photographers, columnists and free-lancers of various descriptions. Three members of an Australian film crew, having heard that I knew a real hooligan, followed my taxi into the city.

The city looked like Beirut. The green cars of the police were everywhere. There was a water cannon and a windowless bus for mass arrests. There were policemen – armed, wearing helmets – on every corner. But there were also as many journalists. A Central Television crew was interviewing a 'hooligan'. Later I would spot several supporters from Manchester United, including Daft Donald, the supporter armed with mace and chains and Stanley knives who, on his way to the match in Turin, had never got past Nice: Daft Donald had granted an 'exclusive interview' to the German correspondent of the BBC.

In the event, I never met up with DJ: Robert, another West Ham friend, was arrested that night, and DJ would spend most of the evening trying to rescue him. I ended up befriending a lad from Grimsby.

Grimsby, as I came to think of him, entered my life through a mix of fear and boredom: fear, because for the first time, journalists were being treated with a great deal of aggression – I saw a photographer badly hurt when supporters beat his nose in with his own camera – and I felt safer in company; and boredom, because it became apparent that, despite all the promises, the Dutch and the English supporters were not going to exterminate themselves in the riot of the century. This was partly due to the

German police, who, caught out on the first night when violence erupted between English and local supporters, were not going to get caught out again. After the match, the Düsseldorf police had succeeded in corralling most of the 'difficult' English supporters in the railway station. That was where I befriended Grimsby. I used an old crumpled press pass that I found in my wallet to slip through the police and search out a bar.

Grimsby decided I was acceptable because I was writing a book. I was not, therefore, a journalist – nothing, in his view, could be more contemptible. I was an author (Grimsby's mother was a schoolteacher, and such distinctions were important). And that was how I would be introduced throughout the rest of the evening: an author; *not* a journalist. He always added the important qualifier.

I can't say that there was anything special about Grimsby – no trait or feature that I hadn't already seen countless times in countless others – except that, no matter how many times I met the specimen, I was always surprised to see what one of them would do next. It was predictable, but, in its very uninhibited excess, it was more than I could ever get used to. I was never able to become entirely accustomed to the lad character in its expressive mode.

Grimsby entered that mode the moment we got into the taxi. The driver, a woman, was reluctant to accept the fare and before setting out she turned to Grimsby and, in English, established the rules that would govern our journey if we were to reach our destination: there would be no smoking, no open windows, no bad behaviour. My companion promptly lit a cigarette, opened the window and let fly a string of abuse – 'cow', 'cunt', 'Nazi whore' – that stopped only when the taxi finally stopped and we were ordered out.

The exchange established a pattern for the rest of the evening. We didn't stay long at the bar we found – a working man's place filled with what I judged to be a pretty rough crowd – because

Grimsby had taken to chanting 'Heil Hitler'. I ushered him out. There were similar encounters later, including one in a restaurant with a Dutch supporter in his mid-fifties who was eating dinner with his three sons. As he was the only Dutch supporter there, Grimsby took it upon himself to walk across the room, interrupt the family's meal, lean over and call the father a wanker, while jerking his hand up and down in his face, as though masturbating into it. He made a fizzy foaming sound with his mouth. Then he called the father a fuckface; a fucking fuckface wanker; and finally a Dutch shitbag cunt of a coward.

Grimsby believed that he needed to prove his cultural superiority to every foreigner he met; I had forgotten just how violent the violent nationalism of the English football supporter could be, and being in Germany had made him vigorously nationalistic. There was also the war: the one 'we' won. Although he was only twenty years old – Grimsby worked as a lorry driver, making deliveries for a local brewery – his talk was almost exclusively about World War Two: it provided him with the images and the history to attach his nationalism to. He wanted to fight the war all over again. The viciousness of the Germans, the spinelessness of the Dutch, the bulldog bravery of the English: these were tenets of a fundamental belief, and Grimsby would be an unhappy man if he couldn't go into a battle of some kind to illustrate that they were more – that they were in fact incontestable verities of national character.

We ended up at a bar called the Orangenbaum, which, if it wasn't Dutch to begin with, was certainly Dutch now. This was the thing that Grimsby had been looking for, and he flew into the crowd, pushing and shoving, ready to punch the first person who responded with even a modicum of aggression. I stayed outside. The bar was crowded but I could see everything through the open doors. Behind me were the German police. They had been following Grimsby for some time. But it seemed that nothing, yet again, was going to happen. The Dutch supporters were large, big-boned meaty sorts of fellows who seemed capable of absorbing anything that was hurled at them – including Grimsby who, although he sallied into them at full speed, was merely embraced and offered a beer. Grimsby did not want to drink the beer of the enemy.

Finally, after an interminable amount of friendliness, someone responded aggressively to one of Grimsby's provocations and, with the nation's reputation at stake, fists were momentarily flying. Actually I was exhausted by that late hour, and so bored and indifferent that I am not certain that anyone did respond; it might have been a lamp-post. It was possible that Grimsby had reached the point where he had started punching a small functional article of urban architecture. Grimsby was then arrested.

For reasons that remain a mystery to me, I argued with the police and – against the interests of Germany, Britain and European harmony – dissuaded them from carting Grimsby off to jail, provided that I would take him in my care and return him to where he was staying.

He was staying, as such, at the railway station. I left him there at about three in the morning. He found an empty bench, but before settling in he started shouting 'England' at the top of his voice. This woke up some of the supporters sleeping on the ground nearby, who cursed him, but Grimsby persisted: he repeated the name of his country, over and over again. His arms had dropped to his side and his torso was tilted slightly forward. He was in a peculiar nationalist stupor – no longer noticing me or, I suspect, much of anything else – and so I slipped off and set out for my hotel. The sound of 'England' echoed off the buildings. I imagined returning in the morning and finding Grimsby still there, his voice grown hoarse, croaking noiselessly. As I walked on, his chant grew quieter until it disappeared behind the shouting of other England supporters in other parts of the city.

It was a long walk to my hotel, and over the course of it I watched the gaggles of English supporters, weaving drunkenly through the streets, chanting their crude phrase of nationalistic belligerence, until, one by one, they all started to drop away. At one point, I paused and followed a group as it struggled across a square. The square was a large one, and I didn't think that the group was going to make it. Everyone was clinging to consciousness by the thinnest of threads. They were singing 'Rule Britannia', holding on to each other's shoulders, now mainly for support, in what must have started out as a conga-style singalong. And then one supporter fell off. He collapsed, crumpled and didn't move. Two more followed. Finally only three supporters remained and, seeing that they were alone, they stretched out on the ground and went to sleep.

The city was at last growing quiet. Everywhere you could see the bodies of English supporters. In the strange, shadowy, lamp-lit light, they looked like sacks of rubbish, strewn randomly across the pavements, under bus shelters, heaved atop park benches and under the bushes of the city's squares.

Grimsby gave me his phone number and his address, but I never contacted him. I was not persuaded that, by spending more time in his company, I would discover hidden depths in his character. I did not think that there would be any surprises. In Grimsby, what I saw was all there was.

DJ, I thought, was different, and I made a point of staying in touch. He had made his debut as a photographer – two of his pictures appeared in a prominent American weekly magazine. In July he asked if I wanted to join him and his friends for a trip to the boating regatta at Henley-on-Thames. He had hired a Daimler and a driver and would bring along ice buckets filled with bottles of champagne. The idea was that DJ and members of the Inter-City Firm would mingle among the home counties crowd.

At the last minute, however, there was a problem: DJ had to fly to Greece. There were business difficulties, and no time to waste. He needed to get a flight that evening, and we were able to meet for a drink as he made his way to the airport. DJ could spare thirty minutes. The trouble seemed to involve some friends, fellow supporters of West Ham, who needed help.

The next time I heard from DJ it was through his father. It was the first time we had spoken and he wanted me to explain why his son, who, the father believed, was involved professionally in my own work in some way, had just been arrested in Greece on charges of passing counterfeit money.

I couldn't explain. I knew that there was a lot of counterfeit money about. I had heard people mention an operation in Manchester that printed American dollars: the bills were sold on to a small network of 'friends' (almost exclusively football supporters) who then went abroad – often to remote outposts unused to tourists – to exchange the counterfeit money for real money. I even saw some of the currency once – the 'moody money'. It was a fifty-dollar bill that, to me, looked like any other fifty-dollar bill. I would happily have accepted it. It was then put against a real American fifty-dollar bill, which was alike in every respect, except size: the counterfeit note was *marginally* larger than the real one.

I wasn't in a position to know what had happened in DJ's case, except that I understood that the charges were serious. Two others were in jail with him: Martin Roche and Andrew Cross, both West Ham supporters. Andrew Cross had been the first one arrested: the night before there had been a dispute between him and Martin Roche, and Cross was beaten up; the next day, he was caught exchanging counterfeit fifty-dollar bills and led the authorities to Martin Roche's hotel room. It was where DJ was staying. Outside, on the ground below the balcony of their room, a wallet was found; it was full of moody money. In the hotel's safe, there was another wallet; it held ten thousand pounds worth of Greek drachmas. There were also two passports; one was DJ's.

I got my first letter at the end of July. It was articulate and careful and remarkably cheerful; in a surprising way, prison life suited DJ – a closed society with a number of systems in place that a crafty operator could learn to master. He had set himself up as the resident prison cook, doing deals for dishes, and had established an effective but complicated route to the local supermarket. He was still in import-export.

A few weeks later, I received my second letter. A trial date had not been set, but DJ was hopeful that he would be out in time for the next Millwall match in October: 'That might be a good one for you,' he wrote, recalling that the last time he went, a team of twenty people in jeans and trainers had arrested a number of supporters from West Ham after provoking a fight, having pretended to be from Millwall. He mentioned that he was practising his French and learning Greek and improving his cooking. By now he had the prison guards in his employ, doing his shopping.

But the situation was grave. Three Egyptians in prison with him were also up for trading in counterfeit currency – in their case, American traveller's cheques. For the ringleader, the prosecution had asked for a life sentence.

I WANTED TO attend DJ's trial, but months passed and no court date was set. In the meantime, I resumed my contact with Tom Melody.

I had met Tom the previous year in Turkey during one of the qualifying matches for the European Championship. He was the landlord of the Bridge, a pub in Croydon, and four of his regular customers – Dave, Mark, Gary and Harry, all Chelsea supporters – had put up the money to take Tom along on the trip to Turkey with them. In the event, one lad, Gary, was apprehended after tearing up some Turkish money, and Tom and

I got to know each other trying to prevent the Turkish authorities from using the full force of their military might against him, however much Gary might have deserved it.

I next saw Tom at the Leatherhead Recreational Park in Surrey. Tom's pub had a football team which, despite the sheer volume of alcohol that its players carried in their bloodstreams, had reached the final of a London competition. Tom asked me to come along.

The event began with only one policeman. He had been called out in response to an appeal from a driver whose bus had been stolen: the pub's supporters had come by bus, which one of the lads had taken for a joy-ride. The policeman was polite and stood on the edge of the pitch facing the stands, asking the clandestine joy-rider to return the keys and urging the others to 'desist' from their hooligan conduct. He was pelted with eggs.

Two panda cars appeared; more police were then called out after the Bridge supporters' club embarked on their banana attack. The rival team was from north London and its players were black; so, too, were the supporters, who were not lads, like the lot from the Bridge, but mainly families – parents, brothers and sisters – who were well-dressed, dignified and serious. The bananas were meant for them. So, too, were the copies of *National Front News*, which Mark, a skinny, highly nervous zealot of fascism, had entered the visitors' section to sell. By the end of the match the lone bobby had been supplanted by three hundred hardened riot police. It was the first time that riot police had appeared at the Leatherhead Recreational Park in Surrey.

We returned to the Bridge for Sunday-afternoon celebrations: Tom Melody had prepared home-made sausage rolls, barbecued hamburgers and grilled sardines. The girl-friends and wives and families – kept away from the match itself; a lad outing – were welcomed here, and this was where I met Harry and his family.

It was impossible not to like Harry. He resembled the lion in the Wizard of Oz, with a walrus handlebar moustache and goofy affectionate eyes. He had an easy, infectious laugh, and a line in witty repartee. His wife, short and affectionate, was irrepressibly cheerful. She was also very forthcoming. She was happy to analyse her husband's 'eccentric' behaviour, although she did not fully understand it. It had started, she said, around his twenty-fifth birthday. Before then, he had never been in trouble. He had never *even* been arrested: she stressed the idea, as if it were now impossible to contemplate. He had a good job – Harry is a self-employed brick-layer – and they were about to have their second child, when something in him changed and Harry, in her words, became a wild man. She laughed uproariously. She couldn't take it too seriously, which was probably a good thing: she viewed the regular trips to the police station or the magistrates court with a droll, ironic detachment. Harry looked at me and shrugged, but said nothing. He had one of his daughters clinging to his leg. She was standing on his shoes, with her arms wrapped round his thigh.

Since that time, Tom closed the pub. I discovered this when I tried to reach him shortly after DJ's arrest and was unable to get him on the phone. The line was dead. I drove down to Croydon to investigate and was told by the newsagent across the street that Tom had simply walked away one day, but that he had a new pub, the Axe on the far edge of Hackney, in East London.

The Axe turned out to be a large, dark Victorian monstrosity, several storeys high and costing more than a quarter of a million pounds; Tom had bought it. A Rolls-Royce was parked in front, the only car in view. Was this Tom's as well? I announced myself and, although I had phoned beforehand, was made to wait forty-five minutes before Tom appeared. The last time I had seen Tom he was wearing the friendly fuzzy jumper that I had always seen him in. He was now dressed in a tailored black suit. He had an immaculately pressed white shirt and a dark silk tie. He had large diamond cuff-links and gold rings on his fingers.

We talked openly, but not entirely comfortably, and Tom never smiled. His eyes were always shifting, fixing on various spots just over my shoulder and then moving on. Behind me was a mother with a baby. Tom snapped his fingers and bowed his head in her direction. He had many people working for him. She was fetched.

No babies.

She pleaded.

No babies.

But her man was expected any minute. It was raining outside.

No babies, he repeated, but he was already distracted and looking past her. She had become invisible.

Someone else appeared, asking if a bloke whose twenty-fifth birthday was next month could be served. Tom, apparently, had set up his own age limit for drinking.

Permission denied.

Someone else asked for a snakebite – a notorious alcoholic combination of lager and cider.

Permission denied.

There was some kind of deal going on in the corner. A black man was involved. Tom pointed in the direction of the corner, and the black man was removed. Tom, I discovered later, did not like black men. He also didn't like Asians.

I was finding this all a bit much to take in, when Lorraine appeared. I was introduced. Lorraine did not acknowledge the introduction. Lorraine was not interested in me; Lorraine wanted me to show the good grace to disappear. Lorraine, Tom informed me, was Norwegian. She had attractive high cheekbones, long blonde hair that had been plaited at the back and she was dressed in black leather. Everything about Lorraine expressed one thing: sex. This one thing was expressed with considerable power. Lorraine wanted to go upstairs, but Tom was not ready. Tom, still watchful, said: Not yet.

Lorraine, however, didn't move.

Later, Tom said, a hint of irritation emerging in his voice. He was busy. Couldn't she see that he was busy? He told her to go upstairs and wait. He would join her.

Lorraine went upstairs.

Tom had left the Bridge in Croydon, he finally got around to explaining, because he couldn't take it any longer: he had had too much trouble from 'young people'. It was a recurrent phrase. Every week, the pub got trashed by 'young people'. There was not a Friday or Saturday night without violence, and, when there wasn't violence, there was theft: he couldn't hire a young person who didn't end up robbing the till.

So he moved to a new area. In his eyes, East London was 'up and coming', a good investment, an area filling up with people from the City. It was where Tom wanted to be.

And then the first fight broke out. Ten patrol cars and five vans appeared, but the police never made it past the door. Tom mentioned catching the arm of one lad just as he was about to crack an officer over the head with a heavy motorcycle chain. The police were then chased outside, where their vehicles were overturned. By the end of the evening, the Hackney Fire and Rescue Emergency Service was involved – a van had burst into flames, and many policemen were injured. One officer was in a coma. Tom had been in business for two days.

Perhaps, he wondered aloud, he had misjudged the area after all. He then discovered – he had been in business for all of six days – that a petition, signed by more than two thousand local people, had been submitted to the Council demanding that the pub be closed down permanently.

'Something is happening to young people,' Tom said. That phrase again. 'There is something crazy about them. The old East London no longer exists – everyone can see that. Everyone except young people, who still believe in the East London code of violence. They all want to be East London gang leaders, living out East London myths of fighting.'

To my mind, what Tom was finding in East London was no different from what he had left behind in Croydon or what I had found in Manchester, Liverpool, Leeds, Bradford or Cambridge. Whatever it was that Tom was finding wrong with young people was not confined to specific districts in his *A–Z*. His difficulties were not, in fact, with any set of 'young people' in particular but with *all* young people. This was why Tom would not admit anyone under the age of twenty-five into his pub – English law allows eighteen-year-olds to drink – because he was hoping, in effect, to ban the entire generation. He would have preferred to have set the age limit at thirty. He would have been happiest if he could have made it thirty-five.

I asked about the lads from Croydon.

For a while, the lads from Croydon had stuck with him, Tom said. There were problems, however. By the end of the evening, they were so drunk they could get home only by taxi. Hackney to Croydon is a long run, and the fare was more than twenty pounds, but the lads were so abusive and threatening that no one would take on the job. On one occasion they beat up their own driver and then, seeing that he was too hurt to carry on, pushed him out of the door and stole his car.

I asked about Harry.

Tom shook his head. Harry was in jail. He had been convicted of affray – four counts.

The first conviction resulted from a Friday night visit to the Cartoon, a Croydon rock pub. Harry had gone there after work with his friend Martin, a short, compact, intense man who said little – I had met him once – and who had aspirations to be a professional boxer.

On this particular night, Martin and Harry were not admitted to the pub. The place was full, and so the two of them went round the corner to another one. I don't know how long they were there, but when they returned the Cartoon was still crowded, the entrance blocked by three people – two bouncers and the landlord. Harry knew the landlord and asked if he would wait where he was for a minute or two – he had something for him – and went off to retrieve it. Harry walked to his van parked across the street and returned with a spade. He used it to hit the landlord – twice, a full swing, *crack*, against the side of the head. Then he hit both doormen. He then picked up a park bench, lifted it over his shoulders and threw it through the window. Shattered glass was everywhere. The pub was packed, and the people inside started screaming and ran for the door. In the crush, there were several injuries. Harry waited until the pub was empty, entered it, picked up a stool and used it to smash the bottles of spirits and beer, the glass doors of the refrigerators and the wine bottles inside. Then he threw the stool into the mirror behind the bar. He turned, picked up a chair and smashed it against a table. He picked up another chair and did the same. And then he walked home and went to bed.

The next morning, on waking for work, he realized that he had left his van by the pub. When he returned to pick it up, the police were waiting.

The second conviction also involved his friend Martin. Martin had been working as a bouncer, but was unexpectedly fired, and the incident filled Harry with so much indignation that he felt it demanded some kind of retribution. It was the same routine. The spade; a rubbish bin (this time) thrown through the window; the broken bottles inside, the mirror, the chairs. When he left the place, every bottle was broken and the carpet was inches deep with drink. Harry then walked home and went to bed.

He was not arrested and for two months stayed out of the way of the police. And then something else happened.

This time it involved Mark – the skinny salesman of *National Front News*. Mark was on his way home, the hour already past closing time, and having run out of cigarettes, noticed that the local Turkish restaurant was still busy – a private party of some kind – and knocked on the door to see if he could get a packet of

Benson & Hedges. The private party was being held by the police – a celebration thrown for the local CID – and the detective who answered the door recognized Mark. He obliged the request, fetched the cigarettes, but couldn't resist a little rudeness. 'You've got your fags,' he was reported to have said. 'Now, hurry up, you cunt, and get the fuck out of here.' Mark was offended. He described the incident and the offence that he had suffered to Harry, who was indignant, and, vowing revenge, led Mark back to the restaurant, where he forced open the door with his shoulder and then shouted abuse at the people inside for having insulted his friend. Harry did not realize that the party was being held by the police – a little detail Mark had neglected to mention – but by then it was too late. Harry was already into his routine – the spade, the furniture through the window, the broken bottles and so on. In the fight that ensued, Harry wrestled one of the policemen to the ground, lifted him up by the chest and then head-butted him – inflicting a hair-line crack across the forehead. With the blow, the policeman must have lost consciousness if only because he seemed to offer so little resistance to what Harry did next: he grabbed the policeman by his ears, lifted his head up to his own face and sucked on one of the policeman's eyes, lifting it out of the socket until he felt it pop behind his teeth. Then he bit it off.

Harry rolled off the policeman, stood up and walked home.

I have come to conclude that Harry existed as two people. I don't believe that he was schizophrenic – no more than any of the other lads – but I do think that he had cultivated behaviour of this kind to such a point of refinement that he could effortlessly achieve the state of mind where it was possible to be almost limitlessly violent: I say almost because, while biting out the eye of a policeman strikes me as about as violent as a person can get – exceeding even Shakespeare in his own excesses; after all, Gloucester had his eyes pulled out by hand – Harry did not kill the man. He knew the state he wanted, and then, once in this state, his various goals achieved – no other object or person against which to be violent, the subject exhausted, the restaurant emptied, every breakable item destroyed – Harry grew calm again, resumed his lion-hearted Wizard of Oz manner and returned to being a friendly lovable sort of guy.

Harry was hungry and so he went home and persuaded his wife that, with the children asleep, she could join him for something to eat. She agreed, steadfast supporter, ignoring the fact that his T-shirt had soaked up so much blood that it stuck to the skin on his chest. And so they slipped out and went round the corner for a basket of legs and thighs at the Kentucky Fried Chicken.

And there they sat, nothing to hide, a bright light overhead, the two of them, husband and wife, huddled round a formica table-top mounted on a plastic podium, eating chicken with their fingers, in full view of the High Street. By the time they had finished, the place was surrounded by police. It was as if Harry were a terrorist or a bank robber. The police, having closed down the street in both directions, stopped all traffic and pedestrians from entering the area. Harry was arrested.

Tom later offered to help me find Harry, and in fact I would eventually meet up with him again. But I had heard enough. I never asked him about the fourth conviction. I wasn't interested. I was watching my clippings file come alive – over and over again in the flesh, the same desultory violence – and it was starting to make me feel very uncomfortable. I was no longer feeling anxious that I didn't know enough.

DJ'S TRIAL WAS finally set for 13 April 1989 and was to be held in a small, one-room open court-house along the waterfront on the island of Rhodes. His entourage of family, friends and legal advisers numbered ten people, and fell into two teams.

The first team consisted of people with money and social standing and was led by DJ's mother. For a number of legal reasons, I will refer to her as Mrs DJ. Mrs DJ was a large woman of Italian descent with a propensity to over-heat and to talk too much: by her own admission, she was a bad listener. Her admiration for her son was of the unquestioning kind, reinforced by her conviction that he was his father's favourite – it was the rebel in DJ that everyone seemed to be drawn to – although she was always made a little uncomfortable by the company he kept. Mrs DJ put it this way. Everybody is welcome in my house, she said, *everybody*. And my son knows the kind of people who are not. London, she said, amplifying the point, is a very large city, and there are many people in it. There is no need to meet all of them.

Martin Roche, DJ's co-defendant, was not someone she had met. Martin Roche was not, she added, someone she would ever have met.

Mrs DJ's team put up at the Grand Hotel Astir, a large establishment, which, judging from the number of *Daily Mail* readers I found eating breakfast on my first morning there, catered mainly to package holidays from Britain. I sat next to Mrs DJ, who pointed to the people nearby. There was a family from Liverpool and another from Manchester: you could tell, I was told, by their accents. In fact most of them were from the north, and I didn't need to be told, I was told, what kind of people they were. Can you believe it, Mrs DJ asked me, *sotto voce*, that there were people sitting in this breakfast room who still had their toilets out in the garden and who regarded this hotel as luxurious because they had something to flush? That was why, she added, you will always find them here in the restaurant at meal-times: they actually regard this cooking as good food. It was true, she said for emphasis and then apologized: the accommodation had been arranged at very short notice. She reassured me that she knew that I was different and that, like her, I was used to international travel.

The other important member of Mrs DJ's team was her elder

son and his American wife, whom, for the same legal reasons, I will refer to as DJ the elder and DJ the sister-in-law. DJ the elder and DJ the sister-in-law were never separated; on the contrary, they were invariably to be found holding hands. They did this without the least sign of affection – as though it wasn't a hand one of them was holding but a carrier bag. Affection, I concluded, wasn't the point; holding hands was the equivalent of a badge or a uniform: it identified them as their own unit – a team within the team.

DJ the elder looked about as different from his younger brother as an elder brother could: whereas DJ was tall and broad-shouldered, DJ the elder was short and small-framed and looked not unlike a tiny version of the young Paul Simon. Whereas DJ spoke in a flat, East-London accent, DJ the elder, having recently moved to New York, had obviously been under considerable pressure to abandon the way he had been brought up to speak in favour of a coarse twang that was somewhere between Brooklyn and Boston and as exaggerated as a jumbo hot dog. And whereas DJ's professional activities were, if described generously, 'unconventional', DJ the elder was nothing less than the straightest and the most narrow, having secured a position in a small firm specializing in international commodities. DJ the elder wanted me to understand that he was successful.

The team proper was completed by Alexandros Lykourasous, *the* most prominent lawyer in Greece, currently involved in defending the president of the country against accusations arising out of a recent banking and bribery scandal. Lykourasous was tall, moustachioed and charismatically flamboyant: the perfect trial lawyer, married to an actress, a poet in his spare time, a devoted reader of Patrick Leigh Fermor, a high-society figure of considerable power. He was accompanied by an assistant and they had both flown in from Athens earlier in the week.

The second team was led by Michelle. Michelle was DJ's fiancée – blonde, attractive, quick-witted and incapable of being surprised by what the world revealed next. She had come with her father, Jim. Jim had made the trip for the simple reason that he could not conceive of remaining behind when such an important matter was being decided. His love for his daughter, which was simple and absolute, extended naturally and uncritically to the man she wanted to marry. Jim was large-boned and solid and very dependable. He had very big hands and chunky large fingers, and spent much of his time, hunched over, staring at them, saying nothing. Beside him you would find Robert.

Robert was the friend who had been arrested during the European Championship in Germany: he was the reason DJ and I never met up. Robert had in fact only left Germany a short while before, having served nine months of a prison sentence, living on a diet of brown bread and vegetable soup and subscribing to a daily routine whose highlight was sleeping for fourteen hours at the end of it. He had been convicted of damaging a police car, which he said he didn't do, and I'm inclined to believe he didn't. When apprehended, Robert was regaining consciousness after having been ambushed by German supporters armed with crowbars, golf clubs, knives and flares, and had been hit so powerfully in the chest that he thought he had been killed. He blacked out. As Robert told stories of this kind I found myself actively wishing to protect him: he wasn't built to withstand anything more physical than a slap across the face. Although he was in his twenties, he could pass for fourteen. He was slight and delicate and punishingly shy. Being in Greece, particularly in the company of DJ's family, had rendered him particularly uncomfortable. Out of an evident need for reassurance and direction, he tended to look over at Michelle's father and be influenced by whatever he happened to be doing. If Jim loosened his tie, Robert loosened his; if Jim sat down, Robert followed; if Jim thought it was acceptable to have a beer, then Robert ordered one as well. By the end of my stay there, Robert was completing Jim's sentences before he reached the end of them himself.

I had, in these two teams, the two lives of DJ.

There was a third team, the one supporting Martin Roche. It included his wife, a skinny freckled woman – not unlike Sissy Spacek on a diet – who was an expert in the cheque racket (stealing cheque-books, buying goods, returning the goods for cash); their eighteen-month-old baby; and his grandmother. Martin Roche had sandy hair and pop-star good looks that were marred by his hardened, chillingly unexpressive eyes and by a ruby crescent across his cheek, a deep knife wound that had been inflicted when he was pinned to the ground and autographed by a number of Arsenal supporters. The scar was very conspicuous and was commented upon by the judge. So, too, were the five convictions that the court discovered on Martin Roche's record. The court failed to discover, however, that Martin Roche was not Martin Roche: the passport bearing that name was one of many false documents supporting several different identities. The identity of Martin Roche had been chosen because it had so few convictions attached to it. The name, however, that stuck in my mind was the nickname that he was known by in London: the knife merchant.

Martin Roche had neither an Athens lawyer nor a support-team whose members were dressed up in elegant suits and ties, nor for that matter a suit and tie for himself. But he was in a better way than the third defendant, Andrew Cross, the one who brought the police round to Martin and DJ's hotel. Andrew Cross had no support of any kind and every evening was obliged to wash the one shirt he possessed. His mother, who was not present, had refused Cross's request for a loan of a hundred pounds and reprimanded him for having reminded her of his existence. She would be happiest, she was reported to have said, if Cross was sent down for a very long time and never returned to England.

The trial lasted two days. On the first morning, DJ and Martin Roche entered the witness box shoving each other. Martin had called DJ a cunt; DJ told Martin to fuck off. They were close to blows; by lunch time those blows were delivered, and DJ's lip was ruptured and his nose broken and his beautiful Valentino suit badly stained: before the judge, their two faces were now equal. By evening they were being kept in separate cells. The next day, I noticed bruising along Andrew Cross's neck during his cross-examination. Someone had tried to strangle him.

There was a break for lunch, and the two teams – Mrs DJ's and Michelle's – went out looking for a place to eat. In general the two teams tried to keep apart, but there were bound to be moments when we were all thrown together, regardless of how difficult those moments turned out to be. In the event, they were very difficult. DJ the elder was made uncomfortable by his younger brother's friends. The night before he had refused to shake Robert's hand when introduced to him and, arriving last for lunch, discovered that he had no choice but to sit between Robert and Jim. DJ the elder asked Robert, the smaller of the two men, if he would move his chair as far away as possible. This was not a gracious request and it was not made in a gracious manner.

Hey, you, what is your name, again? DJ the elder asked.

Robert.

Roger? DJ the elder said, confused. I'm sorry, what was that you said?

Robert.

Oh, yes, Robert. I'm sorry. I've been in America so long I have trouble understanding your accent. Robert. I see. Tell me: how long did you say you've known my brother?

I didn't.

Oh. Well, how long has it been then?

Five years.

Five years. Really? You've known my brother for five years? Isn't that interesting? Anyway. Listen – I'm so sorry. Tell me your name again?

Robert.

That's right. Really, I'm very sorry. It must be the jet lag. I travel so much but I'll never get used to it. Listen, Robert, would you mind moving your chair away from me. It's the air. I need air and you're in the way.

Robert got up and found another place to sit.

DJ the Elder turned to me and said: You know, Bill, it's the strangest thing but since moving to America, I have met a greater variety of English people than I ever would have met had I stayed in Britain. It really is very interesting. I've meet people from East Acton, from Hackney, even from Romford.

Later, when ordering, neither Jim nor Robert understood the menu, and it was left to DJ the elder to explain moussaka and calamari to them. This was painful to listen to, and, in the end, I'm sure that neither Jim nor Robert understood a thing about moussaka or calamari. Jim and Robert decided that they were not hungry (actually Jim decided that he was not hungry; Robert realized that he was not hungry, after all), and they both ordered diet Cokes: that is, Jim ordered a diet Coke, and Robert thought that he would have one, too. DJ the elder spoke to Robert one more time before the afternoon was finished. He continued to have trouble understanding the accent and had to ask him to repeat his name.

Mrs DJ, meanwhile, had become very distressed that Jim, and therefore Robert, were having nothing more than a diet Coke. She remonstrated heavily with them both, but it made little difference. Her pledge to pay for the meal – and the drinks – didn't help.

The best food on the island, Mrs DJ said, turning to me for no reason that I understood, was at Alexis's. Mrs DJ had mentioned Alexis's several times before and she reassured me that if I stayed through to Friday night she would add my name to their reservation.

Jim, she said suddenly, do you like lobster?

I have never had lobster, Jim said.

Oh, it doesn't matter, she said. I'll get Alexis to fix you something special. I'll get him to put fish in batter and then fry it. Like fish and chips. You like fish and chips, Jim, don't you?

Jim had to admit that he liked fish and chips.

DJ was freed; both he and Martin Roche were let go with a £2,000 fine and an eighteen-month suspended sentence, nine months of which had already been served: they were, thus, found to be not wholly guilty, nor wholly innocent. Their companion Andrew Cross had done the decent thing and changed his story. He had, he said, never seen either DJ or Martin Roche before, although he was inclined to agree with the judge that it was a coincidence, here on the island of Rhodes, to meet up with Martin Roche, a stranger, from Romford. Andrew Cross was also from Romford. And, yes, he was also inclined to agree with the judge that it was also a coincidence that DJ, another stranger, lived only a mile or two from Romford as well. Cross apologized to the court for wrongfully accusing his newly-met companions, these strangers from the Romford area; he had panicked. He was, he said, the only one involved in the counterfeiting racket.

And the wallet that was found on the ground outside the hotel room of DJ and Martin Roche?

Cross had no idea where it came from.

Cross was found guilty and sentenced to three years. Everybody agreed that he was a strange, lonely, evil man.

When DJ was freed, he chose to retire to Michelle's room in the Grand Hotel Astir, along with her father, Robert and me, but the effect was to estrange one team of his followers, and several attempts were made to invite DJ up to his mother's suite. At one point DJ the elder, with DJ the sister-in-law in hand, came down to pay a personal visit, but the discomfort, made manifest on his face the moment he stepped in the room, was insupportable, and he and DJ the sister-in-law beat a rapid retreat. Later, a porter appeared with a request from Mrs DJ herself. A porter was required because the telephone was always engaged: DJ, out of prison for thirty minutes, was on the line to London. He was already making deals; he was back in business.

I suddenly did not like being there. The feeling emerged like a rash or an allergy; something in me was protesting vigorously: this isn't my world, and I have seen too much of it. DJ was sharing confidences with me that I didn't want to hear. He was telling me stories that I didn't want to know. I had always regarded DJ as problematic – I liked him too much to write about him – and now, with Jim sitting outside on the balcony staring at his hands, and Robert nearby doing the same, I was listening to my clippings file come alive again. What was I meant to do with what he was telling me? Why didn't he stop? I wanted out. I had reached some kind of limit.

I excused myself – I said I had to make some phone calls – and went to my room.

And I sat there. I wanted to leave but my flight was scheduled for the next day. Tonight was the celebration dinner at Alexis's.

Surely I wouldn't want to miss that? I asked myself.

Surely I would, I answered.

I phoned the airport. The last flight left in an hour, and I managed to get on it.

DJ wasn't a bad case. He didn't bite out people's eyes; hadn't stabbed anyone, as far as I knew; wasn't interested in killing. That kind of violence wasn't his thing. There was nothing about him that compelled me to leave. I had simply had enough. I knew that it was right to get off the island, that I didn't want to be there for another minute, even if I was not entirely sure why. There is a tendency, in any analysis of violence, to look upon it in one of two ways: as a deviation from the past *or* as a continuation from it. *Either* the violence of 'today' is symptomatic of the rot of our times (our urban blight, the loss of our faith, the disintegration of our families, the want of discipline in our homes) *or* the violence of 'today' is fundamentally no different from what it was yesterday: there is always violence in one form or another. The first view, the more obviously sentimental one – with its implicit nostalgia for a golden age – seems to be especially prevalent in Britain if only because the self-image of the British as civilized and law-abiding is still, remarkably, so deeply rooted in the culture. It is the modern *and* modernist view that sees violence as a continuation: that it is a manifestation of inherently unchanging patterns – sociological, biological, psychological – something, in any event, beyond our controlling. The modern, modernist view notes that England has always been violent, that its working class has been especially so and that there has been trouble associated with the game of football since it began.

The truth, I feel, is not to be found in any thinking so obviously exclusive and categorizing. It is not the case that the violence is either a deviation or a continuation, but that it is both deviation and continuation. It is not: either . . . or . . . But: both . . . and . . . and . . . and . . .

I believe in the modern behavioural models of our conduct, and much of this book has set out to prove their validity: that the crowd is in all of us. It isn't an instinct or a need – being in a crowd isn't necessary to our being complete human beings – but, for most of us, the crowd holds out certain essential attractions. It is, like an appetite, something in which dark satisfactions can be found.

But it is also possible both to acknowledge the validity of certain universal determinist models and recognize difference as well: that society is shifting and rearranging itself in important political and economic ways as much as it is being governed by its own constants. Yes, there has always been working-class violence, especially associated with the game of football, but it is also true that the last generation – and possibly the last two generations – of young working-class supporters have appropriated the violence in a way that is distinct and distinguishable.

The generation is different, and I spent – I wasted? – three years confirming it. It wasn't only John Johnstone and his Millwall mates; or Tom Melody and the lads from Croydon. It was also the ones in Leeds, in north London, in west London, in Reading: I have withheld their stories if only because they repeat so many others. On my street, in the university town where I live, my neighbour is keeping a scrap-book of the violence: my *neighbour*. Another has a video collection. Two streets away is the lad who tipped over a chips van, causing a fire in the middle of a Leeds match. I had spent time, too much time, with all of them, wanting to discover something new. I wasn't finding it. And, finally, I could see that I wasn't going to find it in DJ either. I was ready to stop looking.

I got a flight to London the next morning and arrived around lunch time. It was an April Saturday afternoon, sunny and warm, the beginning of spring. Half-way home, I turned on the car radio and was reminded of the FA Cup semi-finals. The first one was between Liverpool and Nottingham Forest, and it would be a good game. I thought I could get home in time to see it on television.

I didn't make it. I was still on the road when the match began, and after two minutes the radio commentator said that something was wrong. There was trouble on the terraces behind the Liverpool goal. There was a sad, not-this-again feeling in his voice, a quality of resignation, that the supporters, especially those from Liverpool, were sacrificing a game of football to pursue their own violent entertainment: *again*. The play continued, but you could tell that the commentator was not watching it, that he was trying to figure out what was happening on the terraces. He couldn't definitely say that it was crowd trouble, but it was something serious, and the police were gathering near the spot. And then, in an instant, that was it: the game was over. The referee had been told by the police to stop play. That was about the time I arrived home. The stadium was about to become the most famous in the world.

I recently came by a copy of a video made by the West Midlands police, and it provides a useful way of examining what happened that day. The West Midlands force had been asked to carry out an investigation to decide whether criminal proceedings should be brought, and the video formed part of their evidence. It is a compilation drawn from at least seven different cameras. Since the deaths in Heysel Stadium, most grounds have closed circuit television, and video operators have been trained in filming crowd trouble.

The first video sequence, made a short time after the event, is background information; it shows the visitors' entrance on the west side of the stadium and the arrangements for the supporters inside. A voice points out the seated section upstairs and the terraces below, paying particular attention to 'pens' three and four. 'The pit' is the area at the bottom of the 'pens', just before the perimeter fence. The fence itself is a high one – taller than a tall man – and is made of chain-link steel and bent back towards the terraces to prevent people from going over the top. Each 'pen' has a small, locked gate. I have mentioned elsewhere that the experience of standing in the terraces is a herd experience, but I had not known, until watching this police video, that the accepted language used to describe the supporters' arrangements – *pen*, *pit* – is borrowed from livestock farming. I also hadn't known that the accepted term for the fencing is 'caging' or 'the cage'.

The second sequence comes from a video camera situated outside the entrance on the day of the match. The entrance consists of seven turnstiles housed in four small wooden huts. By 14.30 – the time appears in the upper right-hand corner of the frame – there is a terrible crush: there are no queues, only people, several thousand of them, packed as closely as possible, pressing forward. By 14.34 the surging starts, and the crowd tumbles in one direction and then, like water when it crashes against a wall, comes tumbling back the other way. It is impossible for anyone to stand still. I, like any other supporter, have been in a crush of this kind and would have known, even with thousands of people in front of me, that, somehow, I would eventually get in. I might miss the first minutes of the match; I would never miss the match itself. I would never hear these words: the game is sold out; go home. The police would want me inside – whether or not there was room. It is an accepted practice. It is also an accepted practice to fudge the figures. It follows that, if more are admitted than have been officially deemed safe, then the numbers have to be adjusted accordingly. Besides, it's a trade-off; the terraces are a cash business – no tickets, no receipts. You can't pay tax on revenue that doesn't exist.

By 14.39, the crowd, large to begin with, is considerably larger; in nine minutes, the crowd appears to have doubled, spilling out of the waiting area and into Leppings Lane behind it. There are now about six or seven thousand people, a thousand people for each turnstile. You can see panic on the faces of the policemen. They can't hear each other and can't be heard by any of the supporters. In the video you see one shouting ineffectually to one of his colleagues. A superintendent, grown agitated, suddenly starts pushing supporters out of the way for no reason other than an apparent need to have some room around him. Another policeman, on a horse, starts abusing people at random; he hits one in the face with his fist. There is spittle collecting on the corner of his lips, and his eyes dart from side to side. A policeman will later be thrown from his horse.

The start of the match is twenty minutes away.

On the other side of the turnstiles, facing the supporters as they emerge from them, are two more video cameras. By 14.41, they are recording a steady traffic of supporters entering the ground by going over the roof of the ticket huts. Every now and then a policeman apprehends one of the lads as he lands after jumping from the roof, but there are too many coming over to be stopped. I find the sight extraordinary – I count about a hundred supporters before I stop counting – and the little huts are dwarfed by the people swarming around them.

I also find myself studying the legitimate, paying supporters. Each one emerging from the turnstiles shows some sign of what he has just been through. His clothes are crushed or crunched up. If a supporter is wearing a sweat shirt, the sleeves have been pushed up his arms. His trousers are askew and need re-arranging; his shirt has been twisted round and has to be tucked in again. His hair is a mess and he runs his fingers through it. Several supporters pat their clothing to confirm that they haven't been pickpocketed; one emerges holding his ribs. Most of the supporters then go straight into the ground, but many – just less than half, it would appear – linger for a while. They have now been admitted, and, with the match a few minutes from starting, they can afford to wait for a short time. They stand around, catching their breath, having left one crush behind, about to enter another inside. It is as if they are delaying the next encounter, putting it off for a minute or two. In fact, from 14.30 until the stadium is cleared about an hour later, this interim waiting area, this no man's land, will be the only place where a supporter can claim that his body belongs to him – where he can govern its movements – and not to the crowd.

These two video cameras also record the supposed 'cause' – minutes before the start of the match – and much footage is given to it: a blue gate, normally used as an exit, is opened and it allows people to come rushing through, forcing their way into 'pens' three and four of the terraces, even though both are filled past capacity. But can this blue gate be the cause? I rewind the video; true: the gate *is* opened and a large number of people are admitted without tickets. But there is more. I slow down the video; I let it proceed frame by frame; I look at the faces. I know these people. I have seen them endlessly. Each one entering that gate is prepared for the experience he is about to undergo. He has been educated. He knows what he is. A lad knows what is expected of him, how he will be seen, what his value is. A history of Saturdays, a culture of Saturdays, has taught him that he is pocket money for the organization that will shortly pack him as closely together with the other lads as is humanly possible. He is an item of cash flow. He knows that he will be caged, locked up, held in by spikes and barbed wire. He knows, too, that the police know his face, that it is endlessly replicated in an endless vault of police videos, an always-accessible archive that could prove in an instant, if proof is ever needed, that he is a criminal. When he passes through this blue gate (*or* through the turnstile *or* over the roof of the ticket hut), he looks neither left nor right but straight ahead. In view is Tunnel A, the long dark passageway that, rising slightly, then slopes into the pit below, and he is already a member of a crowd. He has changed in this way so many times that he doesn't even think about it. There is little self-awareness; hardly a choice; no moment when he abandons volition or control or identity. He is gone, climbing slightly as the passageway rises, dropping slightly as it slopes, gaining speed, moving fast, pushing on the bloke in front, being pushed by the bloke behind, herd speed, unthinking speed. There is no room, but there is always no room – it doesn't call for a moment's thought – as he presses on, crushing and being crushed, doing as he is being done.

The match has just begun.

The crowd on this particular day is a large one – this is a Cup semi-final, after all – but, in most respects, the scenes both outside and inside the gate are not remarkable. This, as I have tried to show repeatedly, is how people attend football matches. This is normal. It is only the ending that is different and that is because ninety-six people died. I don't want to relive that ending, except to mention one last thing, the work of a particular camera. It is my last digression.

Its footage begins at 15.05 and lasts for eleven minutes. Unlike the other cameras, this one – the seventh in the evidence – is hand-held, and the operator, walking back and forth before the pen, is using it to find out what has happened: no one seems to know yet. The match has just been stopped, and the press photographers are starting to gather round. It would appear that a few police still believe that they have been called over to stop a pitch invasion. One youth, who has ventured too far on to the playing field, has had his arm twisted behind his back.

In the background, you can hear a chant: *It's a shitty ground*. It is weak and breathless; this is at 15.06. There will be no more chants.

A policeman – a big, round-shouldered man, with a large flat face – has seen something and steps up close to see what it is. The video camera follows. It appears to be the concerned expression on the policeman's face that has attracted the operator; he is using the camera unusually, like a pair of eyes, and it seems possible to follow his thoughts.

The policeman leads the operator to the front corner of the cage. This is the point where one 'pen' ends – 'pen' three in fact – and the next 'pen' begins. The next 'pen' is not crowded, and the people there are trying to rescue those caught in 'pen' three. You then hear someone shouting: 'Open that gate,' and the camera swings in the direction of the voice. It belongs to a lad in his early twenties, dressed in jeans and a black-and-white check jumper. He is standing in the uncrowded 'pen' and is upset by what is taking place in the neighbouring one. He is angry. 'It's my fucking little brother,' he says. 'Open your fucking gate . . .' His voice is squeaky and full of emotion. The camera swings to the right. There is no gate. It swings back to the lad in the jumper. He is now screaming at the policeman, pointing a finger at him. The camera swings back to the policeman: he is helpless; he is trying to tell the lad in the black-and-white check jumper that he can do nothing, that it is not his gate, that there is no gate, but the lad doesn't understand. The camera drifts to the right of the policeman, to 'pen' three, and there is a boy crushed into the corner, with his arms above his head. Someone tries to reach over to pull the boy up by his hands, and the boy seems to respond but then his arms slip down, limp, as though he is asleep and doesn't want to be wakened. His lower lip looks bloated, and his expression is one of drowsiness.

It is 15.07 and this is the first hard look at what has happened, and the camera becomes a little erratic. It swings back to the lad in the jumper. He is calling the policeman a scumbag, a fucking scumbag. The abuse seems so light and ineffectual against the power of the feeling that it is trying to express: 'It's my fucking little brother.' The camera swings back to the right, for the boy, but he is not there. The camera rocks from side to side. It swings back to the left – nothing – and then once again in the direction of the boy. He is not there. The camera is lowered and focuses on a small hand clinging to a piece of the fence. The operator then walks a few paces, to get another angle, but, having made his way past a policeman, still can't get an image. His equipment, meanwhile, is starting to pick up bits of background speech, which I notice only on my third viewing of the video.

'I don't believe it,' a voice says.

'Look at that,' another says.

'They're all collapsed in here.' This one is high pitched, uncomprehending.

A man steps in front of the camera. He is in his twenties – good looking, with dark hair, wearing a bright red shirt. He wants the attention of the policewoman crouching before the fence, and as he taps her on the shoulder, his gaze follows hers into the crowd. He then touches the sides of his head with the tips of his fingers – he does this very delicately – and his face crumples. 'Oh, my God,' he says. He turns in the direction of the

255

camera and then back to the crowd. 'Oh, my God,' he says again. The camera follows the line of the lad's vision and then it goes wild. The distress is manifest. The camera swings left, left again, and then right. The operator walks away, stops and turns for one more look – confirmation? duty? – and enlarges the image, but it is too much and the camera is rapidly thrust in the direction of the ground, at the operator's feet. It is brought up again, sharply, but avoids the scenes directly in front of it and focuses, instead, on someone escaping by going over the top of the fence. The camera dwells on his buttocks. It then swings back in the direction of the lad with the black-and-white check jumper – he is still there, with so much distress, so much unhappiness in his eyes – and whirls round again towards the corner: his little brother is gone. Left, right, and then out towards the pitch, up to the sky, and then back again, dwelling, accidentally, on the face of another young boy who falls at the operator's feet, but the boy is expressing terrible grief, and you can tell that the cameraman is unhappy to have come upon this, that it is wrong to be intruding on this grief, and the camera swings away again – up and then to the left – and finds a policeman. It is possible, I felt, to infer the operator's will, his determination not to move the camera. It focuses on the policeman; it stays with the policeman, although the policeman is engaged in a fruitless, desperate act: he is trying to pull down the fence. No one is helping him. He has not said a word to any of the police alongside him. He has no tools. He is trying to pull the fence down with his hands – his fingers are wrapped round the steel mesh of the chain link – but the fence will not come down. On the other side of the fence, someone is dying; someone is dead; but the fence will not come down. He pulls, but nothing happens. He pulls and pulls and pulls and pulls.

Hillsborough: the most famous stadium in the world. What happened there confirmed something in me. There was something inevitable about the ninety-six dead, relentlessly logical, even overdue. I found it eerily appropriate to have turned on the radio then. I had left DJ so precipitately because I had become surfeited by his company, by him, by his life, by his culture; I had decided that I had seen enough; and then to have discovered that I was turning on the radio just as the lads were starting down Tunnel A: I felt I had reached a resting place. My adventure had come full circle.

There is such a raw terrible power in the crowd. Fascists and revolutionaries understand its power. The National Front knows its potential and how rare it is to see that potential realized and how difficult it is ever to control it. A small discovery: I recently learned that Mussolini and Gustave LeBon, the father of crowd theory, were great correspondents, mutual admirers: Mussolini re-read LeBon's book every year; LeBon praised Mussolini's iron will, his traits as a leader, a commander of crowds. Mussolini understood the crowd and knew to respect its power. It was football – its administrators, its cowboy owners and operators and the lad culture that has built up around it – that didn't understand either the crowds it was creating or the terrible, killing power that was in them.

DJ RETURNED FROM Greece the next day, a Sunday. We spoke and agreed to meet up the following weekend. West Ham was at home to Millwall.

We met up at the Builders' Arms, the place already packed. DJ introduced me to the people there, although he was clearly uncomfortable. He had been in prison for nine months on a Mediterranean island. He had lost weight. He hadn't been in company. He was finding it difficult returning to London habits. He went out of his way to avoid trouble – there was some that day, inevitably. He was not in a hurry to return to prison.

DJ insisted that we watch the match from a seated section – it was not the done thing any longer to stand on the terraces.

Ninety-six people had died on the terraces only seven days before; I was happy to watch the match in the seated section. I like seats. To be able to sit down is a fine thing, a commendable way of watching a sporting event.

Before the match began, a minute's silence was called for to honour the ninety-six people who had died. The same minute's silence was held before every match in the country that day, and, as far as I know, there was only one place where the silence was not honoured.

A minute, it would seem, is a long time at Upton Park in East London.

The disturbance started softly, a handful of supporters embarking on the Millwall chant: 'Nobody likes us and we don't care.' And then, each time it was repeated, it was picked up by more people: 'Nobody likes us and we don't care.' It was going to be a long minute. About half-way through, the chant was being repeated by everyone in the Millwall end – probably about five thousand people. Five thousand people were saying: ninety-six people died and we don't care – we're thugs; fuck off. The chant made the West Ham supporters angry, and the people round me stood up and jeered at the Millwall supporters. They were waving their fists or jerking their hands up and down, calling them wankers and scum. There was probably another ten or fifteen seconds to go, when the Millwall supporters changed their chant from the traditional 'Nobody likes us and we don't care' to the more pithy: 'Fuck off, cunts.' This they repeated until the minute had elapsed.

The announcer expressed his thanks and gratitude to the crowd.

There was a party that night for DJ – an acid house party that began at midnight. A warehouse had been found somewhere in the nether regions of East London, and everyone there at the Builders' Arms was talking about it after the match. But I decided not to go. Later in the summer, DJ and Michelle would marry, but I decided that I wouldn't go to that either.

In George Orwell's *The Road to Wigan Pier* there is a passage describing life in the thirties, in the north. The passage is worth recalling. It is an evocation of a 'typical', although reasonably well-off, working-class home. Orwell invites us into the sitting-room on a winter evening just after tea. It is the time

> when the fire glows in the open range and dances mirrored in the steel fender, when Father, in shirt-sleeves, sits in the rocking chair at one side of the fire reading the racing finals, and Mother sits on the other with her sewing, and the children are happy with a penn'orth of mint humbugs, and the dog lolls roasting himself on the rag mat – it is a good place to be in, provided that you can be not only in it but sufficiently *of* it to be taken for granted.

We know the image: the unselfconscious working-class family ('not only in it but sufficiently *of* it'), happy and unaware, surrounded by the details – the steel fender, the rocking chair, the rag mat – of enduring Victoriana and the warm-bath comfort of the strongly structured family. We've seen variations of the image in films, and it is still possible to find an image of this sort in a pub or working-man's club or terraced house in isolated communities in the north of England.

The image is cosy, reassuring and, even in Orwell's time, intensely sentimental, which he implicitly seems to acknowledge, when he says later that although this fireside scene is duplicated in many English homes, there are fewer and fewer, and the very picture itself, 'of a working-class family sitting round the coal fire after kippers and strong tea, belongs only to our own moment of time and could not belong either to the future or the past.'

Orwell then predicts what working-class life will be like during the 'Utopian' socialist future, about two hundred years hence. It is this image that interests me:

> The scene is totally different. Hardly one of the things I have imagined will still be there. In that age, when there is no manual labour and everyone is 'educated', it is hardly likely that Father will still be a rough man with enlarged hands who likes to sit in shirt-sleeves and say 'Ah wur coomin' oop street'. And there won't be a coal fire in the grate, only some kind of invisible heater. The furniture will be made of rubber, glass and steel. If there are still such things as evening papers there will certainly be no racing news in them, for gambling will be meaningless in a world where there is no poverty and the horse will have vanished from the face of the earth. Dogs, too, will have been suppressed on grounds of hygiene. And there won't be so many children, either, if the birth-controllers have their way.

Orwell's prophecies were always unstable, and, although there is no socialist utopia, we don't have to look two hundred years hence to find an image that matches what he describes. The image exists now. The man with the rough hands has disappeared along with the heavy industry that required them: the mine workers and steel workers and automobile workers who have retired or been made redundant or anticipate redundancy in the future are not being replaced by their sons: they will not be found in a factory. They, like the majority of the employed population, are working in what we've learned to call the 'service' sector. If still engaged in a labour that requires their hands, they are self-employed, working as painters and decorators, plumbers or electricians. They might be couriers or drivers of delivery vans. But most will be found in offices – in businesses being run by bankers, accountants, stockbrokers, insurance salesmen and computer programmers or the 'private enterprise' equivalent of the civil service: the giant corporations of British Telecom or British Gas.

They do not live where their fathers lived. The coal fire grate has, as Orwell predicted, disappeared along with the kind of house that would have had one. The tight, dark working-man's terrace, with the corner shop and the local across the street and the lavatory in the back, has been replaced by a cheerful, sunny Brookside suburban home, with a driveway, a garage, a back garden for a summer barbecue and central 'invisible' heating. Inside there are stereos, colour televisions, CDs, tape cassettes, video players, computer games, portable telephones and electronic kitchens – simple box homes filled, as Orwell also predicted, with rubber, steel and glass, or some other comparably mass-produced, although usually synthetic, material purchased at one of the new modern super-stores located just outside the 'community', with easy access and plenty of parking. The racing news, it should be pointed out, has not disappeared entirely – Orwell did not get that quite right either – although its place has been effectively taken by another publication. It is not a socialist broadsheet – Orwell got that wrong, too: it is the *Sun*.

I am in a tricky area. I have lived in England since 1977, and one of the things I've learned is that you don't talk about the working class, at least in any detail, unless you are working class yourself. You don't criticize the working class or make generalizations about being a member of it. You would never point out its traits in someone. It is not done; even today, you leave it alone. It is understood that non-working-class people don't have the right to do so.

As a consequence, however, few people have come out and observed that the working class doesn't exist any more. In itself, this wouldn't be particularly significant – after all England is not the first technologically advanced country to see its working

class disappear; it could be argued that it is one of the last –
except that no one is admitting that the thing is no longer around.
The reverse seems to be the case, at least among the members of
the first non-working-class working-class generation, my 'mates':
working-class habits, like those manifested by Tom Melody's
East London lads, have simply become more exaggerated, ornate
versions of an ancient style, more extreme because now without
substance. But it is only a style. Nothing substantive is there;
there is nothing to belong to, although it is still possible, I
suppose, to belong to a phrase – the working class – a piece of
language that serves to reinforce certain social customs and a
way of talking and that obscures the fact that the only thing
hiding behind it is a highly mannered suburban society stripped
of culture and sophistication and living only for its affectations:
a bloated code of maleness, an exaggerated embarrassing
patriotism, a violent nationalism, an array of bankrupt antisocial
habits. This bored, empty, decadent generation consists of
nothing more than what it appears to be. It is a lad culture
without mystery, so deadened that it uses violence to wake itself
up. It pricks itself so that it has feeling, burns its flesh so that it
has smell.

SARDINIA

The need of human beings to transcend 'the personal' is no less profound than the need to be a person, an individual. But this society serves that need poorly.

Susan Sontag, 'The Pornographic Imagination' (1967)

I KNEW I would not be going to the 1990 World Cup. My story was finished. My characters were no longer around.

Sammy was no longer around. He had been arrested for arson, having gone through a bad phase of setting buildings alight. His sentence was commuted to treatment and he had been committed to institutional care. When I met him, it was evident that he had been through a great deal. He had grown heavy and bloated and appeared to be suffering from the effects of tranquillizing drugs. He was slow to recognize me; his speech was slurred.

Roy was no longer around. Roy had not been around for some time. He was said to be in Morocco. Someone else mentioned Algeria. Then Egypt, Turkey, locations further east. His business interests had shifted, and he was having to travel – some trips lasting several months. Then there was a new development: I heard that he had been arrested for drugs; that he got three years.

Robert was no longer around; he was claiming to have settled into a real job – 'complete with a business card' – and was thinking about paying his taxes, but he didn't know how. He had an apartment in New York, where he now lived; a green card (he was 'writing' a book, a lad's tour through the States); and love: Robert had at last found love. It had always been his complaint that no relationship ever lasted because no woman was prepared to be number two; Manchester United would always be number one. Things, evidently, had changed. My last communication was a postcard – the picture, taken at sunset, depicted a man with a cowboy hat, drinking a bottle of beer, sitting in a canvas chair on a Barbados beach. 'Sunbathing,' Robert wrote, 'good food and great sex is so much better than being a thug.' It was signed, 'One of the boys of the old brigade.'

Actually I did see the boys one last time – in May 1990: Manchester United was in the FA Cup Final, and on the Friday before the game just about everyone had come to London: Steve, Ricky, Micky, Robert from America, Sammy from wherever he had been. Gurney was there: he had bathed and – such were the times – had made a *number* of highly improving and, no doubt, very expensive visits to a dentist: his mouth looked normal. In fact, the only people not there – five pubs around Leicester Square were packed with members of the 'firm' – were those in prison. It was a family reunion, and no one had an excuse for missing it. For many, this would be the first match they had attended in some time. People had still been going to matches, of course – the 'family' was fundamentally intact – but not in the numbers of the past. You got the sense that being a thug was slowly being abandoned for being something else. People did not talk about violence. They talked about drugs, or acid house parties, or the Manchester music scene.

And so, in my heart of hearts, I knew that I wouldn't be going to the World Cup. There was no need. My weekends had been reclaimed. Even I, with my insatiable anxieties – that I didn't know enough, hadn't seen enough, hadn't understood enough – could see that there was nothing more to do.

I remained curious, of course, and it was natural that I would be. There was bound to be violence at the World Cup, and I was interested, in an intellectual sort of way, to see where the trouble might come from.

I had my first clue during the opening ceremony of Italia '90, many months before the first match: a highly Italian affair, done in a made-for-television Academy-Awards style. Luciano Pavarotti sang 'Nessun Dorma', and Sophia Loren drew the lots that determined the schedule of matches. The occasion was momentarily but visibly marred – you could see it on the faces of the officials from the International Football Federation – when, by the bad fortune of the draw, England was once again picked to play Holland in its second match: and *everyone* knew about the supporters from Holland.

Or everyone claimed to. But I wondered: did anyone know what the supporters from Holland were like – really? I didn't, although I had once tried to find out. I had tried to find a violent Dutchman during the interminably long evening that I spent with Grimsby. Grimsby was convinced that he would find a violent Dutchman and we entered every bar in Düsseldorf looking for him. We did not find him. The violent Dutchmen, Grimsby concluded, were in hiding.

There were no violent Dutchmen in London the year before. That was when I first became properly aware of the violent Dutchmen's existence. The occasion had been a friendly between England and Holland at Wembley, and in the days leading up to the match terrible street battles had been predicted. Journalists were dispatched to Amsterdam to accompany the violent Dutchmen on the ferry over. They were also sent to the main railway stations to follow the violent Dutchmen to the ground after they arrived. I, too, sallied out into a blustery, cold night, visiting the appropriate pubs, filling myself with lager, afraid that I might otherwise miss an incident that would reveal new things about violence and nationalism and the Dutch character. In the end, there *was* trouble, but it was between the English supporters who, having read the papers, had come out to meet the violent Dutchmen, and, failing to find any, fought among themselves.

In fact, I had seen nothing, *ever*, to suggest that once the Dutch and the English were put in the same place they would then want to beat each other up. Even so, evidence or not, it was accepted that this time would be different: this time there would be trouble.

It was reported on the television news that there would be trouble: that England had been picked to play Holland was the lead item that night and the front-page story in every English paper the next day. By the next evening – the story was still a news item – the match was no longer being described as the one between England and Holland; it had already become the 'feared' England-Holland match.

The match would be played in Cagliari on the island of Sardinia – as would all the matches played by England during the two-week first round. This was unusual, and I had heard that the venue had been fixed beforehand – that while the authorities couldn't do much about the schedule of matches, they could at least keep the England supporters in one spot, on an *island*, to make the policing easier. And to help out, the island was then visited by a succession of British law enforcement advisers: key members of the Metropolitan Police, of Scotland Yard's football unit and of the Transport Police. Finally the British sports minister himself appeared and, after some difficulty, persuaded a nation that drinks more wine per person than any other country in the world not to sell alcohol on match days. A considerable achievement, but many Sardinians were made anxious by the minister's appearance – not by the ban particularly but by the fact that he had come. It was without precedent; another country's cabinet minister does not visit a nation about to hold a sporting event, with this kind of message. If you invite a friend and his family over for lunch, and then, after accepting your invitation, he mentions in passing that his children will probably destroy parts of your house (they'll rip up your lawn, pull out your shrubs, urinate on your bathroom walls, get sick on your carpets, break most of your windows and then grind fish'n'chips into your new sofa . . .), you would be inclined to withdraw the invitation or, at the least, suggest that perhaps the kids could be left behind this time. The Sardinians were in a similar position: if they knew that it was likely that their city would be damaged by the English being in it – if a minister had then come over to confirm that their city would be damaged – why was the British government allowing the supporters to leave? Why were the Sardinians being so foolish as to accept them?

There was another important detail, although at first it was not mentioned in any news report, English or Italian: the World Cup would mark the first time that English supporters had set foot upon Italian soil since thirty-nine Italians had been killed at Heysel Stadium in Brussels five years before. In fact, the last time that the English supporters had been in Italy I had been with them: it had been Manchester United's Red Brigade.

I ended up following events in the *Guardian*: although every paper had reporters on the spot, the *Guardian* seemed to have the best coverage. It had a journalist based in Rome and two more in Sardinia, plus a photographer – all there to write about the supporters. Two weeks before the England-Holland match, the *Guardian* ran two stories – one about 'Operation Umpire', set up by Scotland Yard and the Transport Police to monitor the progress of the English fans on their way to the continent; and another one about alcohol: it had been banned on all British trains, again at the insistence of the sports minister.

On Monday, there was more news. The sports minister had, according to the *Guardian*, convinced the charter airlines to withhold alcohol on all Italian flights as well. The article also noted the first arrest in Sardinia: three English supporters had been jailed for stealing their hotel sheets. This seemed to me to be an insignificant event, but I was wrong. By Tuesday, the arrest was the big story: stealing sheets was a serious crime, and the culprits were fined £300 and sentenced to twenty days in prison – a punishment that would serve, according to the sports minister, as a 'warning to everyone going to Sardinia.' You can only wonder what would have happened had they taken the towels as well.

The *Guardian* had more to report that day: another victory for the sports minister. You had a sense that he was working his way through a list. Having got alcohol banned on match days, charter flights and British Rail trains, he had now persuaded the airport duty-free shops not to sell drink. This cut right to the heart of the tourist industry and was certain to discourage people from making the journey: buying duty-free drink is often the principal attraction of going abroad. I imagined hundreds of dismayed supporters who, not having heard about the ban, then emerged from the airport shops dismayed and confused, having impetuously bought vast quantities of tax-exempt perfume in a spirit of displaced compensation.

At the end of the week, I noticed a brief paragraph about Paul Scarrott – a supporter said to have forty convictions for disorderly conduct – who had been spotted in Rome, travelling on a false passport to slip through the security operations that had been set up to stop anyone with a criminal record from entering the country. The next day the fuller story duly appeared: Paul Scarrott had been arrested. He had no money, no change of clothing and was very drunk; after having driven a stolen motorbike into a food shop, entering by one aisle and leaving by another, picking up bottles of drink *en route*, he spent the rest of the afternoon racing up and down the railway platforms of the main station in Rome. He was not travelling inconspicuously; it could be argued that he wanted to be arrested – perhaps for the attention he knew he would receive from a media so ready to report trouble from the English supporters. And so it was. For two days, Paul Scarrott was a celebrity: the lead item on every news programme that evening, with a picture of his scrawny, skinny, pinched little face on the front page of every tabloid newspaper the next morning. The *Guardian* had four articles – being a quality newspaper it published Paul Scarrott's photograph on the back page – although it also made him the subject of its mid-week profile, 'Wednesday People', a column usually given over to politicians and businessmen.

Seven days before the feared England-Holland match, and the media's scrutiny of the English football supporters actually increased. This would have seemed impossible except that more journalists had arrived on the island and more stories followed. When the World Cup began – the first match was between England and Ireland – there were only two thousand England supporters in Sardinia; by the end of the first week, there were *more* than two thousand journalists: so many that the British Consulate had set up a press office, with briefings twice a day, to keep everyone abreast of what the supporters were up to. There was a regular television news report every evening in every country that had sent a team to the competition. To keep order, there was a combined force of seven thousand law enforcement officers: the police, the *carabinieri*, the national guard, the army and a special crack amphibious team that I had seen on the back page of my *Guardian* the week before: they were called the 'anti-yob mob', a division of the Italian anti-terrorism police who had been photographed, having just jumped out of a helicopter, in various positions of readiness; two of them, their legs apart, were aiming sub-machine guns at the photographer. All in all, for every one supporter there were at least three people interested in him – to write about his habits of drinking and dress and behaviour, to photograph these habits, to film them being enacted, and – most difficult of all – to contain their excesses.

With only a few days before the England-Holland match, the *Guardian* was now devoting its daily stories – two of them, plus photographs – to a new, uncovered subject: the living conditions. I would have thought that journalistic potential in the supporters' living conditions was limited, but, once again, I was proved wrong. There was a story about where the supporters spent the night when they arrived (with so much attention given to security, no one had thought about accommodation), and another about the campsites where they were then put: thirty miles from Cagliari – too far to get to after England's first match, when, it turned out, there were no buses anyway. There was then a story about the fact that there were no buses. Without buses, many supporters spent the night at the airport. There was a story about that: the airport story. Finally, the sports minister – an obvious *Guardian* reader – stepped in and asked the authorities to provide buses for the supporters at the end of England's next match. And there was a story about that: the-now-there-are-buses story.

The now-there-are-buses story was published on a Wednesday – the feared England-Holland match was on the following Saturday – and the *Guardian* was now running three stories a day. Everything was covered: getting a drink when alcohol was banned, the woman running the press conferences, the members of the press themselves, plus even more stories about the living conditions. Amid all these many stories, a pattern was emerging, and it was this: nothing was happening. Each day, I picked up my morning paper and straightaway turned to see what the *Guardian*'s correspondent had discovered, which was, invariably, a new way of writing about the fact there was nothing to discover. Two days before the England-Holland match, I had the impression that the *Guardian* correspondent was starting to tire. He was starting to get bored. And can you blame him? Every day was the same. Every afternoon he was back in his hot hotel room, phoning his editor in London, admitting that he had nothing to say; the editor then reminding him that he had been removed from the paper to sit in Cagliari and write about what he saw: space in the paper had been allocated; it was not possible that he would have nothing to say. In seven days, the *Guardian* ran 471 column inches devoted to football supporters – nearly forty feet of reports that said: there is nothing to report. The cost incurred by the *Guardian* – keeping a man on the island; plus a photographer; plus another journalist, by now roving the mainland, hoping to find something there; plus one based in Rome – is negligible compared to what the television companies were spending. It was an expensive business, reporting nothing, and you could see why journalists and the television presenters had to report it as interestingly as they possibly could: they had to report nothing as if it were something after all.

And then the thought occurred to me: if so much was being spent on what was happening in Sardinia, then despite the appearance that nothing was happening, it was possible that something might happen after all. By virtue of the investment, something was bound to come from nothing. Or so I concluded. Because on the day before the Holland match, I found that I had stopped reading the *Guardian*. I was in the seat of an airplane bound for the island of Sardinia. I was going to the World Cup: it was essential, I had decided; something was going to happen and I didn't want to miss it.

I GOT INTO Cagliari at about eight in the evening; had a drink at a bar; visited the main square to watch a small group of Chelsea supporters performing for a large group of reporters and television cameramen; noticed that they were surrounded by an even larger group of armed police and soldiers – many driving round the square in tanks; decided, after four minutes, that I had seen more than I needed to see; had a drink at a bar; cursed audibly for not being at home reading the *Guardian*; had a drink at another bar; asked a taxi-driver to take me to my hotel. The taxi-driver couldn't believe his luck; my hotel was fifty miles away.

The next day there was only one route into the city – all others had been closed by the police – and it was a long, out-of-the-way route that passed through three road-blocks, each manned by a law enforcement agency whose members were dressed in pretty white cotton safari suits and white colonial hard helmets – the kind made for the tropical heat. They were also wearing a matching belt, holster and gun – all white. I was driven into town by one of the hotel cars and we were stopped twice. I was frisked. I had three pens, and each one was taken apart. I have contact lenses, and each time my interrogator insisted on opening my plastic lens case. I was wearing shorts, trainers and a cotton shirt, and I looked, I would realize later, like any other England supporter.

We made our way to the city centre, and I was dropped off by the railway station.

It was four o'clock – five hours before the match – when I reached the Piazza Matteotti, the square by the railway station and the port, and they all were there. I had learned that two thousand tickets had been sold, but twice that number must have been at the Piazza – another two thousand, therefore, without tickets, although I soon discovered that the place was filled with touts having to sell off seats at below face value.

It was a memorable sight. So, I thought: *This* is what all the press coverage has been about.

The supporters had been at the square for several hours. Many had been in Sardinia for a week, stuck in a dusty campsite with little running water and no change of clothing. They were sunburnt and tired. They smelled. They were very quiet. There was no singing or shouting or chanting: the only sound was the noise of the traffic. Several hundred supporters were sitting, tightly packed, on a concrete platform by the taxi rank, where they had clearly been sitting, tightly packed, for many hours. They were bored. They weren't talking to each other; they weren't sleeping. They sat, arms wrapped around their knees. The day was muggy.

I went inside the railway station. The bar, like every bar, was not selling alcohol, and there were long queues for mineral water.

Hundreds of supporters were sitting on the concrete floor of the station – and along the train platforms. They, too, were staring straight ahead, dully, saying nothing. I don't think I had ever seen so many English males, between the ages of eighteen and thirty, so quiet and so still. And then the thought occurred to me: I had never seen so many English males sober. This was the largest gathering of sober English males I had seen in my life.

English football, I thought, has come to this.

In Britain, fifteen million people would watch the match on television – a quarter of the population, a staggeringly popular manifestation of popular culture. It was an important match; England's progress towards the World Cup depended on the performance tonight. Sardinia was only ninety minutes from London by plane; at any other time in the history of English football, thousands would have shown up on the day, but those thousands would not be appearing. Everybody knew what the supporters were going to be subjected to.

I wandered back out to the square, in time to see a procession of ambulances. They went by slowly and drove on down the Via Roma towards the football stadium. The ambulances were new – shiny, bright, no dents or chips in the paintwork – and there was an element of pride involved in the display of them. Two lines of armoured personnel carriers came up next. Like the ambulances, the armoured personnel carriers were formally arranged in pairs. It was only then that I realized that I was watching a parade. A number of khaki buses were next, filled with policemen in riot helmets, their visors pulled down over their faces: mean and nasty. The khaki buses passed, and behind them were more buses, windowless ones: in case the four thousand English supporters, currently senseless with boredom, suddenly had to be arrested *en masse*. It had been meticulously thought out – soldiers armed with machine-guns were next – but I wondered for whom this display was intended. It had no impact on the supporters. They hadn't moved and were staring at their feet. They were bored – unspeakably bored.

In front of the bus station was a gathering of about fifty police, huddled tightly in a circle, pressed together, hands on the shoulders of whomever was in front. It was a pep talk – the kind you see on the sidelines before an American football game. All this preparation and the big game was but moments away. The real match was not inside the stadium; it was here in the streets outside it. This was where you found the crowd; the press, the television cameras, the audience.

I returned to the railway station. I had spotted a supporter I recognized from the night before. He had long, woolly sideburns – the shape was distinctly lamb-chops – with a tiny door-knob chin poking through. He was not young. He was at least thirty-five, my age, but he looked older. Perhaps he was forty. He had a creased old-man's face with furrows across his forehead and wrinkles around the corners of his eyes.

I introduced myself, adding tentatively that I was writing about football supporters. Journalists were not popular figures in Cagliari.

'Six o'clock,' he said. It wasn't a reply or a greeting; I'm not sure what it was: a declaration perhaps. He then repeated it, looking straight at me. 'Six o'clock.' He said this slowly, as if I didn't speak English.

'Six o'clock,' I said.

'Six o'clock,' he said, dead pan, and waited as if I was expected to answer.

I tried to think of something to say. 'Six o'clock?' I asked, finally.

'That's right,' he said. 'Six o'clock. Pass it on.'

A group of supporters walked past; he stopped them. 'Six o'clock, mates. Got it?' He said this in an intense whisper. 'Pass it on.'

They nodded.

Others appeared and were stopped. Old Man Mutton-chops was in the middle of the railway station, in everyone's path. The exchange was repeated.

A group of eight or nine lads wanted confirmation.

'So it's six o'clock?' one of them asked.

'That's right,' he said. 'Six o'clock. Pass it on.'

They were animated by the idea of six o'clock – you could see it in their eyes. They did not have Mutton-chops's cool. I was growing interested by the prospect as well.

There was a lull and I was able to reclaim Mutton-chops's attention. I mentioned that he and I had been drinking at the same bar the night before. It was a way of re-introducing myself – my first attempt had had so little impact. It was always a slightly nervous moment introducing yourself to one of them. In the event, Mutton-chops had already sized me up. I was a journalist – that was what mattered. Mutton-chops, I would discover, took public relations very seriously.

I asked him about the significance of six o'clock.

'That's when we march,' he said casually – still very cool – and then theatrically grabbed someone else by the shoulder, urging the news upon him: 'Six o'clock.' And then, hissing: 'Pass it on.'

Others continued to cross and re-cross Mutton-chops's spot and were all brought up to date about the march. It seemed to me that in the short time I had been standing there, hundreds of people had probably learned about it: the march. That was the word that everyone was using: the march.

Mutton-chops explained what would happen. On the dot of six, the lads, all four thousand, would set out and head down the Via Roma, walking against the traffic, in such numbers that the city would come to a standstill. That would be the march. 'Then they'll know we're here,' he said. He repeated the sentence, with emphasis: 'Then they'll *really* know we're here.'

Stopping traffic was a familiar supporters' tactic – crossing the street *en masse* so that every vehicle comes to a halt – and this march sounded like it would be the same thing but on a grander scale. The supporters wanted, at last, to behave like a crowd, and a march offered itself as a way in which numbers can show off the power of numbers. Even so, I had never heard anyone describe this sort of thing as a march. This was new. A march sounded so purposeful. Protesters march. Demonstrators march. Armies march. But football supporters?

I asked Mutton-chops about the march; I was interested in the use of the word.

'It will be fuckin' brilliant,' he said. 'We will take over the fuckin' city,' he said. Then he added, as though for clarification: 'They won't be able to fuckin' stop us now.'

Mutton-chops was trying to prove something to me. He wanted me to understand that this was my lucky day. I was a journalist; I had now met Mutton-chops. I was privileged. I must admit that I did not feel particularly privileged. But he was not to be deterred.

What he wanted, I suddenly understood, was for me to pull out my notebook. He wanted to see me writing notes – particularly his name. It was his name in print that he was hoping for.

He pulled out a cutting from his back pocket. He did this carefully, looking over his shoulder. The clipping was from the *Daily Express*. It was today's edition, Saturday, 16 June, and between the headline ('GENERALS OF HATE') and the sub-heading ('SOCCER THUGS SHOW UP FOR BATTLE') was a photograph of Mutton-chops.

I was impressed – not by the story, which was like every other one I had been reading for the last two weeks – but by the existence of the picture itself. It had been taken the night before – it was the spectacle of the supporters surrounded by the reporters and television cameramen that I had witnessed on arriving – and yet, such were the efficiencies of the modern newspaper when it sets out to cover an event of (such obvious) importance, that it was here, the very next day, in the hands of its subject.

Mutton-chops told me why the article was meaningful. It was about the one hundred most wanted hooligans in Britain – the Football Intelligence Unit's danger list – and the authorities' inability to keep them out of Italy. He read aloud the crucial passage:

> The most dangerous soccer hooligans in Britain have slipped into Sardinia and are planning a showdown with their Dutch rivals. The hard-core hooligans, many with names on the British Football Intelligence Unit's top 100 list of convicted soccer thugs, have gone to extraordinary lengths to beat the tight security . . . Some have dyed their hair while others have even changed their names by deed poll to get new passports.

Mutton-chops was shocked at the incompetence, never more manifest than in this very photograph: Mutton-chops himself, he said, was on the list of one hundred.

This was offered as a revelation. A confidence had been extended to me, something private and dangerous. Mutton-chops regarded it as a matter of great prestige to be on the list of one hundred – and of even greater prestige then to slip into Italy. The operation to keep the 'one hundred' out of the country was extremely sophisticated. Undercover police, even spies, were said to be everywhere. You could never check into a hotel because, on giving up your passport, you would be detected and thrown out of the country within hours. You must be careful about what you said on the phone; it was bugged. Mutton-chops himself made a point of wearing dark glasses during the day and, despite the heat, a large woollen hat. You just couldn't take any chances.

Mid-way through his account, he stopped. 'Shouldn't you be taking notes?'

I said nothing. I stared. I couldn't believe that I was subjecting myself to this thing again, that I had once found it interesting.

But he wasn't to be stopped. He named the people on the list who had got into Italy. I wondered how he knew. Had the list been published? He carried on – it would seem that almost everyone had got through – each name a notorious troublemaker, I'm sure, except for the fact that, even though I was nodding knowingly, I did not recognize any of them. And the more trouble-makers he named, the more I had to fight back a profound and potentially devastating despair: perhaps I had not done enough research. My insatiable anxieties rose up in me like a sickness. Did I need to do more work? Should I spend the remaining days of the World Cup in the company of this short, fuzzy old man, drinking cans of his warm lager, sleeping at his filthy campsite, foregoing all those little luxuries – bathing, cooked food, flushing toilets – that I had now grown so accustomed to, while pretending to be interested in the same stories that I had heard over and over for the last eight years?

Weakly I commented that there did not seem to be many from Manchester.

'No, they're not big on the international matches,' he said, which was a consolation.

And, I said, there did not seem to be many from West Ham.

'No, there is crisis in the leadership at the moment,' he said, which was a further consolation, until finally, cheering me up considerably, he mentioned two people I had heard of: Stephen Hickmott ('Hicky!' I exclaimed, as if he were a long-lost friend) and Terry Last ('Not *the* Terry Last,' I cried, bubbling now with enthusiasm).

I hadn't known that they were out of prison, I declared, cheerfully.

Of course, of course, Mutton-chops said, almost dismissively.

Hickmott and Last, he said, had both got out early for good behaviour. He showed me Stephen Hickmott's card – he was in the roofing business with his brother in Tunbridge Wells – and said that Terry Last wouldn't be showing up until fifteen minutes before the match because of the undercover policing.

And then he added, sententiously: But they're not really important now, if you see what I mean.

I said I didn't, but before he could explain we were interrupted. A Canadian had appeared.

Mutton-chops had told me about the Canadian – it was evidence of the increasing international appeal of English crowd violence. Apparently, there were many foreigners – three Canadians, two Germans and a Swede.

Mutton-chops introduced us, but the Canadian wasn't interested in me. He was troubled by something.

First, he wanted to know, should he bring his guitar?

Mutton-chops did not understand. 'Your guitar?'

The Canadian wanted to know if there would be singing, and, if so, he would bring his guitar. 'Especially with all the television people here.'

Mutton-chops suggested that the Canadian should leave the guitar behind unless he wanted to use it as a weapon. He laughed knowingly and winked at me.

The Canadian did not appreciate the implications of the statement. No matter, he had other questions. There was dinner, for instance. When would they be eating dinner?

Mutton-chops again did not understand the question. Neither did I.

Dinner?

Yes. The Canadian was concerned. 'If the march starts at six, and the game is three hours later, it doesn't leave much time for dinner, does it?' The Canadian had assumed that, since Mutton-chops was organizing the march, he would know when they were scheduled to eat.

Mutton-chops smacked his forehead with the palm of his hand and looked at the Canadian in a way that suggested the Canadian's life was in danger. I had the distinct feeling that Mutton-chops's inclination was to suck the young Canadian's head off his neck and swallow it. I don't know why this particular image suggested itself, but it was very strong.

The Canadian, meanwhile, continued to express his anxieties about his meal: it was just inconceivable that the schedule did not leave any time to eat; it showed bad planning.

'It is,' Man Mutton-chops said in a low intense voice, 'not that kind of march.' He stared. And then he said: 'You stupid fuckin' cunt.'

And then something in me sagged. I watched the Canadian. He still hadn't got the point – he was taking out his guitar to show Mutton-chops what he could do – and I slapped the old man on the back and said that I was off: maybe I would see him later. I had had enough. In a few more moments Mutton-chops would be asking about how to get on television.

I wandered round.

Yes, I probably should have stayed in England, except I could see that something unusual was emerging. As it got closer to six o'clock, there was what the supporters described as an 'atmosphere'. In my notebook, I wrote: 'Five forty-five and the atmosphere is charged and surprisingly ominous. Something is going to happen.'

ONE OF THE reasons I have written this book as a series of narratives is because narrative is best suited to represent what I regard as the most important feature of a crowd – as it exists in time. It is also the most neglected. I have already discussed how a violent crowd is represented rarely by its members but by its victims – the witnesses who become fully aware of its existence only when they are threatened by it. These are snap-shot moments, invariably the very moments when a crowd is at its most frenzied, its 'leaders' at their most prominent, the conduct of both at their most ostensibly irrational. But so much of the nature of the crowd and its mechanisms of behaviour is, as I have also tried to show, determined before these snap-shot moments, before a crowd is dangerous or conspicuous enough for people outside it to take notice.

A crowd can never be formed against its will, and it is the great fallacy about the crowd that it can be: this is the leadership fallacy, the rabble-ready-to-be-roused theory. A crowd needs leading and uses leaders, but comes into existence by a series of essential choices made by its members. Mutton-chops may have proffered himself as a leader, but it would be for the crowd to decide. Or put another way: a crowd creates the leaders who create the crowd.

I was not overjoyed to be in Cagliari. It was a last-minute, expensive trip, and, in the most cynical spirit possible, I wanted something to happen quickly, so that I could watch it, write about it in my notebook and go home. I was there because I couldn't stand not to be. And that was all. I had little idea that I was about to see this motley assembly of four thousand vagrant football supporters pass rapidly through a sequence of identities: that it would become a crowd, then a violent crowd, then a very violent crowd at a speed that was far faster than anything I had witnessed before.

The first step in any crowd, the essential *a priori* choice by the potential members of it, is this: will we, as individuals, choose to cease being individuals and become a crowd? It sounds contrived, put so explicitly, but the choice is always an intensely conscious one.

This was how that moment was experienced in Cagliari.

Everyone was ready for something to happen, expected it. There wasn't a supporter among the four thousand who did not know about the six o'clock march. By five forty-five, most people had gathered in front of the railway station, which was crowded now and active with a low, steady buzz that seemed to come from the same concentrated whisper. There wasn't a single person among those who had been crushed together on the taxi rank who was now sitting. Everyone was up – and ready. I wandered round the square, and the people I met hissed: 'You know, don't you?' They had stopped using the word 'march' or mentioning the time, as if talking about what they wanted to do might prevent it from happening.

And then six o'clock came: nothing.

I heard distant church bells ringing the hour – it was that quiet – and when they were finished: nothing.

I looked for Mutton-chops, but couldn't find him. Everyone was looking at everyone else, waiting. A whole minute elapsed, slowly. A second minute: nothing. And then somebody – someone I didn't recognize and who didn't seem to be known by the others – stepped out into the main street. He stepped out conspicuously, in a manner that said: the march will now commence. He strutted bravely into the Via Roma and stopped. There was a problem: no one had joined him. He hesitated and turned round quickly – right, left, right – looking for the others: they weren't there. And then a choice was made: two others joined him, friends it seemed, who had been behind him but inhibited from taking the first step. They then stopped and looked round, panicky. No one had followed them. Their faces knotted up in sudden anxiety; their faces said: What have we just done? – as if they had done something exceptionally reckless or brave, although the only thing they had done was something exceptionally lucky: they had walked into the middle of a busy street and not been knocked down by a bus.

I thought: Perhaps the march at six o'clock will be three nervous friends standing in the middle of the Via Roma.

Everyone was watching, everyone except the police who did not – it was obvious by now – know what was going on. They hadn't noticed that three English supporters were standing in the middle of a busy street, unable to cross it. The police, gathered in clusters, were chatting, not bothered. The match was three hours away.

Then two others stepped out, equally deliberate. Like the three friends, they did not say a thing, which suddenly I found peculiar. No one was singing 'Here we go'. There were no chants for England. No one had shouted, Come on, lads – if only to urge the others to follow. It was quiet.

Three others stepped out. And then two more. And then five. And then suddenly: everybody. Spontaneous consent. Hundreds and hundreds at once. People crowded through the doors of the railway station – so many that they were having to squeeze through, with others pushing behind them – and people came down the little streets from up the hill, and others came rushing up from behind, from the port area. Everyone moved at once.

The threshold had been crossed – not by a leader but by the willed consent of everyone there.

The next stage was characterized by a powerful sense of achievement. A crowd had been made by the people who had stepped into the street, and everyone was aware of what they had done; it was a creative act. Obvious metaphors apply: the members of the crowd were both the crowd and its creators; they were clay and potter, stone and sculptor, voice and music. They had made something out of themselves.

This, too – this sense of crowd – was achieved at a remarkable speed, within *seconds* of the 'march' commencing.

The estimated number of English supporters that day was small, but now, with four thousand supporters packed into one street, the number seemed very large. It might have been more than four thousand. I knew only that, with most of the crowd behind me, I was unable to see the front: the street was too densely packed.

This crowd – this new entity, no longer 'they' but 'it' – filled the Via Roma and the pavement alongside it, trapping cars, buses and lorries in place, just as Mutton-chops had predicted. The crowd, sure of itself, was moving quickly. It walked past the international news kiosk, where Mutton-chops would have bought his *Daily Express*, past the arcades and one of the bars where I had been the night before. It entered the main intersection, where four or five policemen, the only ones in sight, were huddled defensively, standing behind a car, and then divided up, into several lines, each one moving between the narrow traffic corridors: you had to twist your hips to avoid knocking the car mirrors – or even cigarettes, held out of the windows; Italians were on motor bikes and mopeds, and you had to be mindful of their feet. Here were the *hooligans inglesi*, thousands of them, on the very day of the Holland match, marching through the streets, as everyone had said they would, as everyone had feared, but the actual people in the streets – exposed, vulnerable – were not even rolling up their car windows. Many were laughing.

Who was around me? In front was a lad and his girl-friend. He was stocky, flab flopping in his T-shirt, and she, also quite chunky, wore a loose-fitting pink blouse – possibly silk – and pink-framed spectacles that, as she was jostled around, kept falling down her nose which was wet with perspiration. He had his arm around her shoulder, shielding her. This was her first football match – the look was unmistakable – and he was manifestly pleased to be introducing her to an experience that was so intensely felt. They were smiling, foolishly, unnecessarily; they were experiencing joy.

Everyone was experiencing some kind of foolish joy. Next to me was a lad covered in tattoos. I had spoken to him earlier and stuck close by him now; I wanted to look as if I belonged. And then it occurred to me: no one belonged. No one knew anyone else. The others near me: they were from anywhere, everywhere. They were all strangers. This march was a march of strangers.

More to the point: this march *was* a march. It recalled not football crowds, but demonstrations or protest rallies. You could see the surprise in the faces of the people near me; they had created something big, but weren't sure how they had done it.

The march reached the end of the square, and it was only then that I saw the police, jogging behind three armoured personnel carriers. Each vehicle was being driven fast, so that people had to jump out of the way or be run over. The vehicles accelerated and stopped and then lurched forward again. I thought that the police would also be at the front by now – somebody must be calling back the bus-loads I had seen earlier – but no attempt had been made to direct the march or stop it.

This phase of the crowd – this happy, happy phase – lasted for about four minutes. During these minutes, everyone, myself included, felt the pleasure of belonging, not unlike the pleasure of being liked or loved. There was another pleasure at work as well, one derived from power, even though the power had not been exercised, even though it was only the potential of power: the power of a crowd that had taken over a city.

The next stage – the first lawless stage – also happened quickly, although not so cleanly. It was achieved in starts, stops, restarts. Again, a threshold had to be crossed, but it was one of a different kind.

A flat-bed lorry appeared, a television crew in the back filming. As it passed, photographers jumped on board. Photographers were everywhere, their heavy, brightly-coloured press tags swinging from their necks. Six or seven photographers had clustered on the steps of a hotel, shooting as the crowd approached. One, to get closer, walked down the steps, but the crowd hissed and chanted – the first chant; a crude *fuck-off-press* chant – and I thought that the photographer would be set upon. The anger surprised me – spontaneous and unanimous. The photographer scurried back, with two supporters chasing him half-way up the steps. I was grateful that I wasn't carrying proper press credentials. It was the only threatening behaviour I had seen.

Crowd barriers had been set across the street, but they were lifted up in a matter-of-fact way and pushed over to the side. The street was widening and I sprinted along the pavement, working my way closer to the front. I spotted three Dutch supporters getting out of a car, the first ones I had seen. They watched the crowd for a moment, realized what it was and ran. No one followed.

And then, the pace, brisk from the start, accelerated noticeably, and the acceleration sent a message – something was happening, something that mustn't be missed. There was a feeling of agitation, and I was watchful, curious to see how this message would be received. The crowd's future behaviour depended on how it now responded: I knew this; everyone knew this. The pace quickened, deliberately, self-consciously, and then quickened further and suddenly there was space around me and everyone was running. I also recognized this run; I had seen its kind endlessly; I had seen one only a few weeks before, the night before the Cup Final, when several hundred United supporters – not expecting trouble, not wanting it, police in pairs on every corner – suddenly saw *something*. It didn't matter what it was. Beer glasses were dropped, a terrible crash, and everyone was gone, even though no one knew what he was running after.

No one, here, knew what he was running after. If I had been lifted magically out of my cramped, crushed space and dropped near the front, I would have found nothing to have provoked this crowd of English lads, no matter how hot-blooded, into sprinting down the street as though in pursuit – no Dutch supporter or hostile Italian youth or belligerent policeman. They *were* in pursuit, but in pursuit of nothing. Within a span of seconds, four thousand strangers were overwhelmed by the urge to chase nothing – except, possibly, an intention. An alarm had been sounded, a call to urgency, the irresistible call to be a different kind of crowd. A march *walks*; a march does not run. The moment this crowd started running the march was finished.

But then, as abruptly, it stopped. I crashed into the person ahead of me; others crashed into me. So, there were police in the front after all. I lifted myself up off someone's shoulder to have a look. There were police, but not many. Two hundred, maybe more. They had riot helmets and rifles, and had formed a line to hold back the crowd, which although crushed up against it, was still pushing forward. If the police expected to maintain order they would have to contain the crowd now, diffuse the signal that had been conveyed by that sudden run.

People continued pushing, not the ones in front, pressed up against the rifle barrels held across the policemen's chests, but everyone else behind them. I was lifted – my feet left the ground – and carried forward, and there was a surge, everyone surging, and the police line broke apart. It came tumbling down. I fell, the people around me fell, the policemen fell. The march had disintegrated. I understood what had happened and, in my cynical self-interest, was grateful.

The next stage was, if not the most important, certainly the most daring. The crowd was about to become a violent one, but, unusually, its violence would be directed against the police. All violent crowds destroy the codes of civilized conduct; but, as was apparent with the United fans jogging up the High Road to Tottenham, few crowds go so far as to attack the institution that enforces those codes.

The police and supporters had got quickly to their feet and stood opposite each other, separated by a small intersection. Behind the police was the Hotel Mediterraneano, filled with journalists and photographers, many now gathered by the door, about to take some of the very pictures that I would see on the front pages of the papers on sale at the airport in the morning.

Behind the supporters was a building site and a dirt car park. And there they stood: despite the preparations, there were only two or three hundred police, and they were looking uneasy and bewildered. The police looked young and inexperienced, uncertain in their use of their rifles, which seemed to frighten them as much as they frightened me and which they appeared to be proposing to use as clubs, holding the barrel in one hand and the butt in the other. There were probably fewer supporters now – in the run, some must have fallen away – but still a large number: two thousand, possibly three. It was as if a line had been drawn in the dirt, and the supporters were urging the police to cross it. The supporters were shouting at the police – Come on, they were saying, come on – dropping their hands to their sides, dropping their guard, the familiar street-fighting gesture.

With the world's media bearing down on them, the supporters wanted to take on an island militia that had been preparing for this event for months. The lads wanted to fight the police. For a brief moment, I was able to stand back from what I was witnessing, remove myself from the threat and the adrenalin and the excitement of it all, and reflect: Are not adults a marvel to watch?

One of the lads – understanding, as everyone did, that this was a pivotal moment – decided to offer himself up as the leader that it appeared that the crowd needed. The outcome was interesting to witness.

He was a big lad – all shoulders and neck, with a jagged and crooked face like bad plumbing. He had cropped hair, cut so brutally close that it was nothing more than a fuzzy shadow across the rough, bulging contours of his skull. I would not want to be blocking his path, which, surely to their regret, the Italian policemen ended up having to do.

His intention, with everyone facing each other, was to burst through the police line, leading the supporters behind him. He put down his head, and, shouting, 'Come on, England,' ran straight ahead. He was much bigger than the Italians and came crashing past them. He knocked one policeman down with his forearm, swinging it straight into his face, and pushed over several others. A policeman grabbed at him from behind, but the lad turned and threw him to the ground. It was an impressive physical effort – there was a lot of deep grunting – and then he broke through the line, stumbled slightly, recovered his balance and threw his hands up in the air like an athlete. He looked behind him as though expecting applause. There was no applause. Nor were there any people nearby. The big lad had thought that the other supporters would follow. He was wrong. His face collapsed in a look of bewilderment and betrayal and then he was pulled to the ground by the police – fifteen, possibly twenty – who immediately surrounded him. He disappeared under their blows, squirming at their feet.

So: it didn't happen. But the moment wasn't far off. There was more to-ing and fro-ing and a lot of dust. And then I saw the most extraordinary thing: it was a hand-gun being held in the air by one of the officers (the natty little cap, the elegantly cut jacket). It was fired – there was one shot, a second and a third – and moments later there was the sweet, sharp smell of gunpowder.

It was six twenty-three. Within twenty minutes, there had been a peaceful march of several thousand people, followed by a disturbance that almost became a riot but never quite managed to be one, and now the firing of a gun.

I had never been in a crowd in which people were firing guns. I didn't like it. The supporters didn't like it either. The one near me responded by lifting a large stone over his head and dropping it through the windscreen of a car, and the sound of the glass collapsing was loud and surprising. I swung round on hearing it – incredulous that the reply to a gun's being fired was to destroy property, when I saw that the others were doing the same. As everyone was pushed back into the dirt car park, they availed themselves of the material at hand – the stones on the ground and the windscreens of the cars parked there – until someone decided that throwing stones at the policemen would be more gratifying: why destroy property when you can hurt a real person instead? It was an inspired moment, until some other, even more inspired youth, started throwing tear-gas canisters as well.

He had found the canisters on the ground. Shortly after the hand-gun was fired, tear-gas followed. The police had been prepared to put up with a march, if only because they were not in the position to stop it, but no one, including the police, was under any illusions about this crowd now. It was on its way to confirming everyone's fears of what it would be. And so canisters of tear-gas were fired to disperse its members. And, on the whole, the desired effect was achieved, with most supporters immediately fleeing upwind.

But not all.

One inspired little scientist discovered that, with such a strong Mediterranean breeze coming off the port, he had only to step to one side of the brown cloud issuing from the canister on the pavement, grab it from behind – as if picking up a lobster – and throw it back at the very people who had fired it at him. It was like a revelation inverted: in an instant, the canister lost its mystery and power. It also lost all significance, except one: it became a new thing to throw at the police. The inspired lad then set himself the task of picking up one canister after the other and audaciously lobbing them back into the police ranks, confident that the police would not dare respond in the way that I thought, and feared, was the most obvious: by shooting him dead. It wasn't until his fourth canister that he paused, a brown cloud issuing out of his fist, and turned to the other supporters – they were about a hundred yards up the hill, out of harm's way, clustered closely together, a nervous flock – and urged them to join him. Actually it wasn't the other supporters he addressed exactly; it was the entire nation. What he said was this: Come on, England. There was the familiar hesitation – first one supporter, and then another, and then several more – and then everyone came running back down the street.

I had never seen trouble escalate so quickly. The firing of the hand-gun now seemed ludicrous; it had served only to inflame. The crowd that was now running back down the street was a different crowd from the one that had fled in panic from the tear-gas. It had become different the moment it started destroying property – the familiar border. It was liberated now, and dangerous, and had evolved to that giddy point where it was perfectly happy to run amok with a comprehensive sense of abandon and an uninhibited disregard for the law. It was running hard, the people in it angry and wild. They were screaming something. I couldn't make it out – it was some kind of aggressive howl – but its object was clear enough: it was the police.

I watched one policeman. He was young – nineteen, twenty years old – with a narrow face and tousled, thick hair: his helmet had been knocked off earlier and was dangling by the strap round his neck. He was standing in advance of the police line, which had retreated behind him – twenty or thirty feet. Why hadn't he joined the others? It wasn't reckless bravery; he was too fidgety; there was no bravado in his stance. More likely, he hadn't noticed that his colleagues had retreated – things were now happening very fast. He swung his head right and left and saw two other policemen on the ground – they were the only ones nearby – and he urged them to get up. He screamed at them and lifted one by the arm. I was standing off to the side, between the police and the supporters, who were close now, coming down the hill at full speed, stones in both hands. The supporters were not going to stop. They looked very frightening.

One of the three policemen in the front went down, hit full in the face by a stone, and the young policeman noticed – with a flick of the head – that his partner had been felled. Now there were two. I was fascinated by this young policemen. He was shouting at the others – he still didn't know how far behind him they were – calling for support. But there was no support. It seemed to take an eternity for the supporters to reach him. Tear-gas canisters were being shot into the crowd, but were having no effect. I watched the young policeman's eyes. He was frightened. His face was soft and brown, and every muscle – the way he was standing, or holding his head, or keeping his rifle in place before his chest – was expressing that he was afraid but that he was resolved, that he wasn't going to back down, that he wasn't going to run, that he was proud and determined, and then the first supporter ran straight into him and the policeman tried to smack him across the head with his rifle butt but the blow went askew, and then another supporter ran into him and a third and then the young policeman was hit with something, and he went down, falling underneath the feet of the English supporters, many, many English supporters. I saw him on the ground being kicked – I had a brief glimpse of him covering his head – and then I didn't see him again.

Stones were coming from several directions and everywhere the brown fog of the tear-gas. I heard a sharp, crisp sound – hard, loud, like concrete being dropped from a height – and I turned and saw that the supporter inches from me had been hit in the side of the head. I had seen nothing – not so much as a blur, but I heard it: it wasn't the soft sound of a blow; it was the hard, hard sound of the skull. I was convinced that his head had been cracked; the blow was too sure. He didn't understand what had happened to him or who I was or why I was interested in him. I led him off to the side of the street and propped him against a wall. He was talking to himself and had lost the colour in his face.

The crowd was in its final stage: complete lawlessness. I had been in crowds of this kind before, but several features made this one unique. One was the object of its violence – the Italian police.

The Italian police were different from Italian football supporters, or supporters from any country for that matter. You could not get away with beating them up like so many frightened fans from Reading or Southampton and hope that they would then scurry on home nursing their injuries. They might, to labour an old metaphor, lose the odd battle, but they were assured of winning the war: having now attacked the police, the England supporters were going to have to pay a penalty at some point.

This was certain to be true because of the context – the other unique feature. There had been so much publicity predicting exactly what had now occurred, and there were so many people here to report its occurrence, that the Italian police were on the spot. In a way, they were on trial – or at least would have felt themselves to be – and had to show that they could contain this thing. No, there was no question but that the police would win the war.

There was one last feature that made the violence unique. And that was its duration. It seemed like it would never end. You would have thought that, with all the pressure on the police, and with the vast reinforcements that would shortly come to their aid, they would have been able to squash this thing straightaway.

I was standing by myself half-way up one of the hills, about a hundred yards in advance of the crowd. It had stoned a petrol station – the large plate-glass of its shop front had collapsed with a spectacular crash – and a policeman's motor cycle had lost control and slid into the petrol pumps. I feared an explosion. A policeman had fired his hand-gun again, and it appeared that the police were regrouping below us.

And then: nothing. We were left alone. There were no police charges or tear-gas.

After a time, several people turned and started up the hill in the direction of the ground. The others followed. It was the natural thing to do, although, after so much violence; it was also a little strange. We walked over the top of the hill, the police behind us, somewhere on the other side. No one was running; there was no need. The police appeared not to be following.

We walked on. I saw the Sardinian ruins, caves carved out of the brown Italian stone at the island's high point. Further along I saw the cathedral – D.H. Lawrence had mentioned it. Lawrence had been at this very spot; he had written about the view. The Mediterranean was below. The day was still hot, and I was sweating.

Then the police must have charged, although I didn't see it. I was in the middle and knew only that everyone around me was running again – not the impulse run I had seen earlier, not a crowd run, but a run of fear, a sprint. I saw two people ahead of us in the street, elderly women, dressed in black, who were rushing quickly to the pavement, indignant but afraid. I saw little else. I noticed a wedding, the bride and groom and their friends rushing for cover. We must have been running through the cathedral square.

The supporters around me were slightly hysterical, pushing people out of the way, recklessly trying to get up to the front. I couldn't see the police behind us, but knew that they had to be close, and I didn't like that. They must have decided to charge once everyone was out of view, to take the group by surprise. I kept thinking that the police had guns, and I didn't want to get caught at the back of the crowd.

I was running hard – everyone was running hard – and, once past the cathedral, we turned down a residential street. I didn't know who was in front, but the crowd was clearly being led and this street was in the direction of the stadium. I smelled oleander and sage, and there were leafy trees along the pavement. Everything conveyed comfort and security and solidity. There were iron fences, gardens, balconies, ornate lamp-posts.

The *hooligans inglesi* who appeared at the top of this elegant avenue, filling its width, running hard, must have been an incomprehensible sight. It was suddenly quiet; no one was singing or chanting or shouting. In fact there was only one sound, the regular, systematic noise of things breaking. The automobiles were new and expensive – BMWs, Mercedes, sports cars – but each one, by the time I came upon it, had already been damaged: the windscreen was cracked or had been blown out entirely; the side mirrors were gone; the door was kicked in. An older woman, large, matronly, confident, was shouting from her balcony, gesticulating, enraged, and then a stone was thrown and it missed her, and another stone, and a bottle, and a clay flower pot near her fell apart, and her window broke, and then more stones, many stones, one after another, until all of her windows – the sliding balcony window, the kitchen, the small one, which must have been the bathroom – were gone. I heard burglar alarms ringing.

Then I collided with the people near me. Someone had brought the crowd to a stop. I didn't understand why: the police were behind us; they would appear at any moment. Someone then shouted that we were all English. Why were we running? The English don't run.

I felt I had been doing nothing but running, but this was all it took: there was the roar, and everyone turned and headed straight for the police. It was the first time I had seen them since they gave chase after the stoning of the petrol station. There were now many more police than before, dressed in proper riot gear – shields and helmets and heavy jackets. And they all had guns. The English supporters seemed not to think much of the Italian guns. I could think of little else.

I wanted no part of this. I stood back, while everyone rushed forward, stones and bottles in hand. I was getting a feel for the rhythm of this thing, and I suspected that – after an incident characterized by large quantities of dust, flying objects, tear-gas and a gunshot – everyone would come running back in my direction. Which, in due course, they did. And thus, once again, I found myself running.

And so it went on. Having fled in panic, some of the supporters would then remember that they were English and that this was important, and they would remind the others that they too were English, and that this was also important, and, with a renewed sense of national identity, they would come abruptly to a halt, turn round and charge the Italian police. Stones would be thrown, people would be felled, until the police contrived to regroup and again give chase. This went on for a long time. This went on for an interminably long time. It went on for the entire length of this long street. I didn't see much of the actual fighting because I didn't want to be close enough to be able to. I was in the middle of the crowd and the only reason I was in the middle was because I never got to the very front. I wanted to get to the front – that was where I would be safest – but I was having trouble keeping up. This chase was being conducted at a sprint, and I was running out of breath. I felt heavy and fat. Sweat was pouring down my forehead and into my eyes. I was running with my shoulders hunched up, as if to protect my neck, because I was afraid of getting shot or hit or hurt from behind in some way. All around me injuries were appearing, and I didn't know why. It was the strangest thing: one moment I was looking at the fellow ahead of me, watchful of his feet, not wanting to trip him or trip over him; the next moment, the back of his head was wet and red and glistening in the sun. Blood was pouring down the sides of his neck and being soaked up by his shirt. He kept reaching back with his hand, touching the liquid. When had this happened?

I spotted the flabby boy and his girl-friend with the pink spectacles. They were running with great determination. What were they doing here? I spotted other people I recognized, but only briefly, because I was having to concentrate very hard on my feet, not wanting to fall over, but not having the room for the speed at which we were running. I could feel someone touching my back, for balance or to ensure that he wouldn't trip over me, just as I was touching the back of the person in front. And then suddenly the pavement opened up – a sewer had been dug out – and a deep well appeared before me. The person in front dived to the side, and I twisted and somehow managed to jump over him. I heard sounds behind me – glass breaking, stones, scuffling – I don't know what it was, because when I looked I saw only glimpses of things: dust, and the sun brown and hazy, and the glint of the riot shields. I was going to get caught – I was going to feel some terrible hot pain across the back of my neck or my head, I just knew it – and then finally this long, never-ending eternity of a residential street ended and gave way to a square.

There was openness and an expanse of sky, and poor simple shops and unadorned concrete buildings. I ran to the far side and leaned against a wall, hunched over, hands on my knees, heaving from the effort to catch my breath. I watched as the supporters on the other side turned and once more did battle with the police as they came running into the square in pursuit. I was wet and red and hot and couldn't get a full breath.

I don't know how long I was there – time enough to regain my composure and slowly take in the people around me. The square was filling with supporters. I watched one. He was on his own, laboriously pushing a large rubbish skip out into the middle of the square. The skip was full and one of its wheels was broken. He pushed and the skip swung off sideways and he pulled it back and pushed a little more and then finally got it to the position he wanted. He then walked round, lifted himself up by the big metal lip of the bin and pulled it over. It slammed on to the pavement and the rubbish – glass, bricks, bits of food, tins, papers – tumbled out. He picked up a wine bottle by the neck, adjusted his grip and threw it, end over end, against one of the flat, concrete houses. He picked up another and threw it. He must have thrown five bottles before one finally slammed into a bedroom window, which then exploded, the glass falling on to the pavement below. He picked up something else – something heavy, solid – turned and threw that at another house. He was in the middle of the open square and able to turn in any direction and blow out someone's window, pick up another bottle, brick, piece of plumbing or any other object yielded by his skip full of treasures, turn and break something else. He was becoming increasingly autistic. You could see the world receding from him; his mates, in combat on the other side of the square, were disappearing. Nothing disturbed him.

I felt heavy. I was exhausted, but it was more than physical tiredness: the fear was gone and the animal excitement and the nerves, and I was left with nothing more than the act of observing this little shit. Why was he of interest? What was there to say but: I have now watched a little shit.

I was next to a shop and the man who ran it appeared. He had dashed out to collect his children – when the crowd came running into the square, his daughters had been playing in the middle – and he was now hustling them back. His wife and two of his children were already inside, and he was left behind pushing a baby stroller that kept getting caught on the step. The child in the stroller must have been about two. He lifted up the stroller – his wife had already pulled down the shop's metal shutter half-way – but he was in a rush and couldn't get the stroller over that last step. Glass was breaking all round him; the autistic maniac in the centre of the square was still at it. The shopkeeper tried three times. His wife, crouched on the other side of the shutter, was shouting at him.

I was appalled by the sight; I was appalled at myself – at my crude voyeurism. The scene disturbed me. But it also disturbed me that other scenes had not. This had become my thing: to be a witness, yet again, to the ugly arrogance of the little shits who had driven this man to hide behind metal shutters, waiting for the sounds of the violence to end. These images were not modern. This square – simple, poor, unsophisticated, undisturbed by tourists or foreigners – was at odds with the poison that had come pouring into it. I tried to imagine this man's fear, looking up to see his family surrounded by men who had appeared as if by some terrible magic, filthy, bleeding men, breaking windows, hurling benches into the small shops run by his neighbours, throwing stones, bottles. I haven't known a fear like the fear this man must have felt, when, screaming for his wife and the members of his family, he bolted out of his shop. What social mutation has resulted in these bored ugly boys of the Union Jack believing they are entitled to inflict this pain, this fright?

I then looked up and was surprised by what I saw: it was the Italian police, on the far side of the square, retreating. They had turned and run. You could see them jogging down a side-street in formation, the backs of their riot shields bobbing up and down, refracting the light from the setting sun.

This was inconceivable. What did this mean? That the supporters had won?

No one realized what had occurred – the police had left so rapidly – but once it became apparent, the supporters started chasing down the street after them. They threw bricks and bottles at their backs. But none of them hit their target. The police were gone; they had retreated; they had disappeared.

Silence. It was over.

I looked around, trying to catch an expression that would help me to interpret what I had just seen, but everyone was as mystified as I was.

A chant broke out – the first that afternoon – and it grew louder as more supporters appeared, entering the square from the various side-streets that fed it.

England.
England.
England.
England.

There were more people.

England.
England.
England.
England.

Now that I could take it in, the crowd was larger than I had expected, not the four thousand who had begun the march, but still one of considerable size – more than a thousand. They were appearing from all directions; they had all taken up this chant. They were celebrating: the national side had won.

I remained leaning against the wall, and remember saying aloud: My, my, my.

Many things fell in place. This chant: it was the only one I had heard in a day otherwise characterized by its enforced, sullen silence. And now: this declaration for England. It was such a simple but enormous thought: these fools, despised at home, ridiculed in the press, incapable of being contained by any act of impulsive legislation that the government had devised, wanted an England to defend. They didn't want Europe; they didn't understand Europe and didn't want to. They wanted a war. They wanted a nation to belong to and fight for, even if the fight was this absurd piece of street theatre with the local Italian police.

I was feeling a little concerned, however. While I found these nationalist celebrations interesting to observe, I did not believe that the Italian police had disappeared. They may have pretended to disappear, but they would be back – with reinforcements. I was convinced of it and worried by it. Where would they come from? And how? I looked round but there was not a policeman in sight.

None of the supporters was worried. They had adjusted to their victory and were taking it in: they had beaten up the Italian police; the police had run away. Having had their day, the

302

supporters now headed for the match. And so they turned and started walking up the hill that led to the ground.

Did they really think that they would now be able to stroll casually to the game? They were relaxed, chatty and, I felt, incomprehensibly stupid.

We walked through an intersection. I looked in both directions: no police. I looked up: no helicopters. There wasn't even any press. Why? Were they being held back behind some police line, out of sight? Was something about to happen that the press would not be allowed to see? It was eerie. Why was I the only one who appeared to be worried? There was no traffic and no one else in the streets, although I could see people looking out through their windows. I was starting to feel agitated. Where should I go? Should I flee? I wasn't about to walk in the direction in which the police had retreated; they would be waiting. Everyone was climbing up the hill, hundreds and hundreds of supporters, filling another street from side to side.

I made a point, this time, of getting up to the front. Something was going to happen, and I didn't want to get caught in the middle. I didn't want to get hit from behind.

About half-way up the hill, it happened.

It started with tear-gas, and, strangely, I was relieved to see it: there was something to respond to. The quantity of tear-gas, however, was enormous – greater than anything that had been used so far – and I couldn't tell where it was coming from. The canisters, shot high into the air, followed a long, slow arc and came crashing down in the middle of the crowd. They seemed to come out of nowhere, one after another. It was as if they had been fired by a high-powered cannon or were being shot from the balconies of the nearby flats, as though tear-gas snipers had been planted there hours before. There were so many canisters that I covered my head. Several landed near me – close enough to be dangerous as missiles in their own right.

This was the retaliation I had feared. The smoke was

everywhere, and I was afraid of what I might see emerging out of the brown clouds. I started running. I was up at the front of the crowd and made a point of remaining at the front. I ran hard. In this afternoon of continuous running, I never ran as fast as I ran then. I wanted to be as far away as possible. The police would be out for revenge and I didn't want to be the object of it.

I sprinted to the top of the hill. I was the first one to reach it, with most of the supporters about twenty yards behind me, and as I arrived at the crest I saw them: the police. They were waiting down at the bottom of the hill, as if behind the starting line of a race – all primed, alert, leaning forward slightly, waiting for the signal, truncheons in hand. Behind them was another line: it consisted of more police with truncheons. Behind them was another line: more police with truncheons. There was a fourth line: the police with guns. And behind them was some kind of arrangement of vehicles: cars, vans and armoured personnel carriers. I would notice later that three large military helicopters circled above. Since arriving in Sardinia, I had seen a lot of police, but never as many police as I saw now.

I said: Shit, shit, shit.

I had run into a trap. The pretence of a police 'retreat', the tear-gas, the hill hiding what was on the other side: it had all been a trap.

I looked round, admiring the details. The street was very narrow, and the houses were built alongside each other, without alleys or passageways. Nice touch. There were no side-streets. It was a corridor of punishment. If I carried on, I would run straight into the police waiting at the bottom; I would be killed. They would not intend to kill me – it would be an accident – but they would do so all the same. If I turned round and went the other way, I would, once I emerged out of the tear-gas, run straight into the other mob of police. I did not think they would kill me – for some reason, I was equally confident about that – but I was certain that they would injure me badly. I did not want to be injured badly. I concluded, therefore, that there was no way out. I was trapped. I was impressed, but trapped nevertheless.

Shit, shit, shit.

I looked back down at the policemen. They were still waiting, leaning forward. I recognized one, an older one, with a round face and woolly eyebrows. He was one of the uniformed superintendents, and I had watched him trying to contain the crowd as it surged down the Via Roma. His face had been memorable – it was humane, sympathetic, expressive, warm. It was a different face now; it was hard and full of hate.

The other supporters had now charged over the crest of the hill and saw what lay ahead. Seeing that they, too, were trapped, they did the thing that anyone else would do in the same situation: they panicked. There was a petrol station a little further down the hill, a self-service Esso station, and behind it was a narrow passageway. It was the only escape. Why hadn't I seen it? Immediately, this passageway to safety, however, took on the appearance of a passageway to death, as all the supporters rushed towards it at once. The passageway, not more than two feet across, was barred by a shoulder-high gate. It looked dangerous, and somebody started screaming 'Hillsborough', afraid of being crushed.

Just I was wondering if it would be worth the risk of joining them, I looked back down at the police and saw that they were charging up the hill: each of the great lines, one after the other, everyone sprinting, his head tilted slightly down, his truncheon swinging back and forth. Each one had this same look of powerful and uncompromising hatred. It was the intensity that impressed me; it was wild and exciting and savage. They had probably been waiting at the bottom of the hill for a long time, listening to reports from other parts of the city, counting up the injuries done to their colleagues, the damage to their homes, their property. They had been insulted and were now indignant and, in all likelihood, also afraid – tense, expectant, waiting for the first supporter to appear at the crest of the hill. And then it occurred to me: that was me. I thought about my clothes: a cotton shirt, shorts, dirty trainers. I looked like one of *them*. The police, I suddenly realized, had identified me as one of the leaders: I was about to be punished by the leadership fallacy.

I found myself regretting so many things.

My arrogant attitude towards those heavy, yellow plastic press badges, for instance. I wanted one. One would be useful now. In my wallet somewhere I had some tattered press credentials but there wasn't enough time. I imagined digging around for them and then displaying the limp, filthy things – one press pass was in Turkish – while running backwards in the face of several hundred truncheon wielding policemen and *then* being beaten to the ground.

I looked back down the hill. Time, in that punishing, familiar way, was starting to slow down, and I felt I was watching every step each policeman took, and, although I knew they were running with great determination, they didn't seem to be running very fast. They seemed to be running in water. Their faces were vivid and distinct. Most of those faces were looking at me. I found myself reviewing my prospects again: go forward, get killed; go backwards, get injured. Fly? Can't fly. Damn, I wish I could fly.

What would you do?

What I did was this: I crossed the street. I wanted to get as far away as possible from the Esso station and the thousand or so supporters crushed into its corner. That was where the police would end up; I could see that. So I crossed the street and got between two parked cars. I took one last look at the police – very close – and got down on all fours (bits of gravel pressed against the skin of my knees), covered my head and curled up into a ball on the ground. I surrendered.

I thought: I fooled them.

I thought: I've deprived them of the chance to beat me up. You can't beat up someone who has surrendered and is lying on the ground.

And then I thought: Maybe they'll truncheon me once *en route* to the other supporters. I had been truncheoned before; it stings, but the sting soon goes away.

I noticed three things the first time I was hit. One was the effort to ensure that I was hit powerfully. My head was down but I could tell that the policeman, rather than smacking me once on his way to the other supporters, had come to a complete stop: I could see his boots. He then pulled back his truncheon and paused, aiming his blow. I thought: he won't do it.

And then I thought: OK, OK, so I was wrong.

Second, the target. It was my kidney. The policeman, I infer, had sized up the situation – fat man on the ground, curled into a ball, head covered with hands, cotton T-shirt rising up the back slightly – and concluded that the kidney, thus exposed, was the most obvious target: that was where he could do the greatest damage.

Third, I noticed that the blow did not sting. It hurt. It sent a sharp impulse of energy – like an electric thread – from the point of impact straight to my stomach.

There was a fourth thing. The policeman did not leave. He hit me again. This, I admit, surprised me. I thought I had fooled them. Then he hit me again. This, inevitably, surprised me less. Then he hit me again. This was no surprise at all. By the time he had hit me five times, I realized that he was not going to leave. He was going to stand over me, taking his time, lifting his truncheon, aiming it and then smashing my kidney. Each blow went to the same spot, the kidney. And each one, I found, hurt just as much as the one that came before it.

There was a fifth thing. Not only was this policeman not going to leave, but he was to be joined by a colleague. This did not make sense – why waste another policeman on me, when there were so many people still to beat up? – but the temptation must have been too great: here, on the ground, showing little resistance, was a perfectly adequate specimen, even if a bit fat. He couldn't pass it up. The second policeman went for my head. My head was covered by my hands, and I remember thinking: although it hurts having my hands smashed up, I am grateful that I thought to cover my head with my hands because I would not want to see my head smashed up. The second policeman really wanted to see my head smashed up. I infer this from the damage he inflicted upon my hands – each knuckle was colourfully bruised, except for one, which was both bruised and broken. I believe his intention was to smash up my fingers so badly that finally I would pull my hands away – thus exposing an expanse of skull – so that he could then smash up my head. After a while, he gave up on the smashing-the-fingers tactic and took to pulling them away, grabbing my fingers with one hand, while pummelling the intermittently exposed bit of skull with his other.

The two policemen were soon joined by a colleague. It was getting pretty crowded, but there were still my shoulders. They became the concern of the third policeman. His real concern, I concluded after examining the bruising, was not the shoulders as such; he was trying to get to the collar-bone. He, too, was trying to move me around with his free hand, so he could get a clear view of his target; it was the snap-crackle-pop sound that he was after, the one the collar-bone makes when it breaks in half.

All of this was exceptionally painful, as would be expected, but my experience of it was different from that of the others who were being beaten up. Their experience was one of simple pain. For me, it was more complicated, because I knew that I would be writing about it. While being beaten up, I was thinking about what it was like being beaten up. I was trying to retain the details, knowing that I would need them later. I thought for instance that this experience was not so different from the one I had witnessed in Turin several years before when a Juventus fan, who had also surrendered, was beaten up by a number of Manchester United supporters. I thought of the fact that I could even think of this coincidence and marvelled at the human mind's capacity to accommodate so many different things at once. And I thought about that, the fact that, while being beaten up, I could think about the human mind's capacity to accommodate so many different things at once. I thought about the expenses I had incurred and was grateful that I was going to get something out of this trip after all. But mainly I was thinking about the pain. It was unlike anything I had known and I wanted to remember it.

The beatings went on so long that I was convinced the police would have to stop from exhaustion. But they didn't let up, and after a while the blows blurred together and became one terribly loud crashing noise. I felt explosions of energy and, up and down my body, a long, protracted sensation of heat. It burned the way a fire burns – hot, hot, hot. I want to say it was a white heat, but only because I was seeing white. My vision was intermittently lost and I saw white flashes. These flashes seemed to emanate from the points where I was hit, as if some network of nerves had become overcharged and was carrying too much sensation.

As the beatings continued, I grew a little worried. I did not think that my kidney could sustain this much punishment and I was resigned to spending the night in an Italian hospital. I noticed that I was breathing very heavily. I was gasping for air but unable to get any. Why did I need more oxygen – what body function, in an experience so inherently passive, was requiring it? The need for air increased; it was imperative; I had to have it. Suddenly I felt that I was going to suffocate, and this made me angry and I stood up and wanted to fight back, but the moment I raised myself up I was hit across the forehead and I blocked one truncheon with my arm but was hit across the forehead again and then on my chin. I was astonished by the intensity of feeling that I saw on the faces of the policemen. It would have been impossible for me to communicate with them, to convey something powerful enough to counter the strength of their hatred. I was not a human being. I was some kind of object, some thing. Strangely, I thought of myself as a fact, one that they wanted to hurt, and I dropped back to the ground and curled up and covered my head, and one policeman went for my kidney, and another went for my head, and another went for my shoulders. I had lost interest in wanting to describe this experience, except that I briefly recall noting that I had lost interest in wanting to describe it. The experience then became something I wanted to end. But it didn't end. I don't know how much longer it went on. I don't know what happened next. I had ceased to be a person writing about it. My next memory is that finally it ended. It was over. It had stopped because there was no one left to beat up.

Afterwards, I noticed little except my pain. I ran round in circles and went from one side of the street to the other. I couldn't stand still. My body was full of a sharp electric stinging, and I was trying to shake it out but it wouldn't go away. Slowly I started to take in what had happened.

Everyone was very still, except for the people who were writhing from injuries. There were many people on the ground. It was very quiet. The sense was of the old cliché made real, that the life had been beaten out of the people there. Near me were several lads who had got caught standing up – too proud to curl up and fall to the ground. One was bleeding badly, and all around him were great globs of his blood, balled up and animate, seeming to breathe. A deep gash ran from his ankle up the side of his leg and past his knee, and two flaps of skin fell off heavily to the side. Next to him was a fellow leaning against the side of a car. He was wheezing and throwing his head from side to side and his eyes were glassy. When I approached him, he started screaming and swinging his arms to protect his head and then he collapsed, clutching his leg. He was in shock, and his leg was broken: he had been beaten until his thigh-bone cracked into several parts. I thought it must be difficult to beat up someone with such force that it breaks the thigh-bone into several parts.

Most people had been beaten round the head, and their shirts were covered with blood. One was hunched up and retching from the pain, and on seeing that the supporter was vomiting, a policeman kicked him in the ribs. I remember the face of this policeman. I saw him on the television two days later at a press conference.

There were in fact several supporters vomiting. It wasn't from drink. They were vomiting from pain.

Supporters were arriving from the other side of hill – some had got caught there as well – and they appeared, in two and threes, many holding their heads, wrapped up in T-shirts and bits of clothing. The number of head injuries surprised me; they included the girl with the silky pink blouse. She had lost her spectacles and had been clubbed across the forehead. She was bleeding badly – there appeared to be a cut just below the hairline – and the blood poured down her face and neck and across her blouse. Her boy-friend had not been hurt and, although holding and comforting her, he was very upset. They were both upset. They were trying to persuade the Italian police to get a doctor or an ambulance, but couldn't get the attention of the officer in charge.

The area was slowly filling up with members of the press.

When the ambulances finally showed up, they did not include any of the attractive modern models that I had seen on parade. Those, along with most of the men and the arms and the machine-guns and the high-tech bazookas that I would see later, were reserved for the ground. I wasn't sure if that was because more trouble was expected there – we still hadn't seen a Dutch supporter, after all – or because that was where the television crews were waiting. The ambulances that were arriving now were not ambulances in fact, although the people inside wore white coats. They looked like family holiday campers, mom and pop nursing services, and three or four supporters would be packed inside each. I saw five supporters put into one.

As I watched, still out of breath, leaning against a car, a journalist from Finland came up to me. He was very angry. With great indignation he told me that *'That'* was unbelievably stupid.

I was intrigued by his indignation, although I didn't understand why he had picked me out to express it to. I thought perhaps he had seen me beaten up, but he hadn't.

I agreed with him, though. It had all been very stupid.

But he wasn't about to let it rest. He wasn't satisfied that I had understood him. The *whole* thing, he said as though for clarification, the *whole* thing was unbelievably stupid. He swung his arm through the air, so as to take in everything: *Everything* was very stupid.

You don't mean only the England supporters? I asked.

No, everything, he said, still very angry, and becoming impatient. *Everything, everything, everything.*

And then I realized that he might well have seen the whole thing – that he might have been one of the few journalists who had not been kept back. You mean everything? I asked.

Everything, he said.

You mean *everything*? I repeated the word for emphasis. You mean the police and the supporters and that silly march at the beginning?

Everything, he said. It disgusts me.

And the press, I continued, realizing that he really had taken in the whole thing. You mean the waste and injuries and the pain – I was excited by having discovered an ally. The nationalism and the machismo. You really mean, everything: that this very stupid thing should never have happened.

I have never, he said, seen something so stupid in my life.

I looked at him and liked him very much. No, I said. Nor have I.

I got to the airport at five the next morning – determined to wait in every queue to get on a flight, even though I had been told that there were so many journalists in Cagliari that every flight off the island was booked up for the next three days. Photographers – their equipment strapped to their bodies – were asleep on the floors. There were several journalists on the luggage conveyor belt. There was no place to sit. But, somehow, I got a flight and got home and followed the progress of the England team on television.

Despite a disappointing start, the team played well and, with each new match, seemed to improve. There was trouble – 247 supporters were rounded up outside a bar in the resort town of Rimini – but many supporters claimed that the trouble had been provoked by the Italian police. There were more fights later, some violent. An English fan was killed when he was hit by a car after running away from two Italians who had been chasing him. There was a stabbing. And then the inconceivable suggested itself: the England team had reached the quarter-finals against Cameroon. If England won, it would go on to the semi-finals, which, in all likelihood, would be against Germany, the country whose supporters were as violent as England's. And worse: the game would be played in Turin.

Attention given to the *hooligans inglesi* increased. More reporters were sent to Italy – more television crews, more photographers. Was it possible to send more? I spoke to a friend, a journalist, who was already in Turin. It was impossible, he said, to get a room. It was like a presidential campaign or a war or an international disaster: everyone was there.

In the morning, I bought all the papers – ten, fifteen, more – in all the European languages. I was doing it again; I could see that I was doing it again. I read that the mayor of Turin had appealed to the World Cup authorities to play this semi-final in another city – anywhere but Turin. 'Please save us from these fans,' she was quoted as saying. There was another article: the businessmen of Turin had joined the mayor in her plea: 'Please save us from these fans.' There was another article: the flags of Cameroon had been displayed in Turin; nobody wanted England to win.

England won. The England supporters would be returning to Turin.

I booked myself a ticket to Turin. But then, the day before I was meant to leave, I was depressed – a heavy, heavy depression. It was the prospect of the drink and the crudeness and the bellies and the tattoos. It was the idea of making conversation with all those little shits. It was the look that I anticipated seeing in the eyes of the Italian shopkeepers and of the fathers and of the women dressed in black. It was the thought that every member of that city will have watched that one video, over and over again, the European Cup, Juventus and Liverpool, and thirty-nine Italians dead – dead because of a country of little shits.

My flight was at six in the morning. I stared at myself in the mirror. I was perspiring. My flesh was grey and had the texture of cardboard, with beads of sweat across my forehead. I looked at myself – it was mid-summer and the bathroom was already filled with light. I continued staring for ten or fifteen minutes. The sweat started building up along my eyebrows and then poured down into my eyes. My shirt was drenched. I felt sick.

I missed my flight.

There was another one in two hours. I phoned my friend in Turin. I woke him up – there had been violence until three in the morning the night before.

Yes, he said, there had been trouble. There was a lot of tension.

No, he said, it was not the Germans. It was the Italians.

Yes, he said, there would be trouble that night. Why didn't I come out?

No, I decided, finally. No, I wouldn't come out. I couldn't. It was not possible.

That night there wasn't much trouble. Some fights at the railway station and some later at the square. The real violence was in England, when, after the national team lost, lads across the country spilled out of the pubs, angry and full of feeling – the crude feeling of their miserable nationalism. They were drunk. Eleven o'clock at night and England had lost: lad culture on the loose. There were fights in Harlow Town and Stevenage and Norwich. There were fights in the Midlands. There were fights in the suburbs of London – Croydon and Finchley and Acton. There were fights three blocks from where I live in Cambridge. The familiar litany: the shop windows were broken; property destroyed. Arson. German cars were vandalized – the windscreens, the mirrors, the doors. A German boy was stabbed and killed.

ACKNOWLEDGEMENTS

Two citations, one describing the violence at Hampden Park in 1909 and the other describing the Stretford End in 1974, are from *The Roots of Football Hooliganism: An Historical and Sociological Study* (1988) by Eric Dunning, Patrick Murphy and John Williams. The discussion of the relationship between LeBon and Mussolini is to be found in R.A. Nye's *The Origins of Crowd Psychology* (1975). In addition to the obvious texts, two books proved especially useful, and I am grateful to their authors: Geoffrey Pearson's *Hooligan: A History of Respectable Fears* (1983) and George Rudé's *The Crowd in History*, 1730-1848 (revised edition, 1981). I would like to thank those who have read part or all of the manuscript: Tim Adams, David Hooper, Eric Jacobs, Derek Johns, Brian MacArthur of the *Sunday Times*, Richard Rayner, Salman Rushdie, Bob Tashman and John Williams. Good editors – rare, undervalued, wonderful creatures – are so hard to come by that I feel, especially privileged to have had three: Edwin Barber at W.W. Norton in New York, Ursula Doyle at Granta and the patient, inspiring, steadfastly encouraging Dan Franklin at Secker & Warburg.